Learn
Publisher 97

How to Order:

For information on quantity discounts contact the publisher: Prima Publishing, P.O. Box 1260BK, Rocklin, CA 95677-1260; (916) 632-4400. On your letterhead include information concerning the intended use of the books and the number of books you wish to purchase. For individual orders, turn to the back of this book for more information.

Learn Publisher 97

In a Weekend

NANCY STEVENSON

PRIMA PUBLISHING

PRIMA is a registered trademark of Prima Publishing, a division of Prima Communications, Inc. In a Weekend is a trademark of Prima Publishing, a division of Prima Communications, Inc. Prima Publishing is a registered trademark of Prima Communications, Inc. Prima Publishing, Rocklin, California 95677.

Publisher: Matthew H. Carleson

Managing Editor: Dan J. Foster

Acquisitions Editor: Deborah F. Abshier

Development Editor: Barb Terry

Project Editor: Kelli Crump

Editorial Assistant: Kevin W. Ferns

Copy Editor: Hilary Powers

Technical Reviewer: Paul Marchessault

Interior Design and Layout: Danielle Foster

Cover Design: Prima Design Team

Indexer: Sherry Massey

Microsoft and Windows are either registered trademarks or trademarks of Microsoft Corporation.

IMPORTANT: If you have problems installing or running Microsoft Publisher 97, notify Microsoft Corporation at (206) 635-7056 or on the Web at www.microsoft.com. Prima Publishing cannot provide software support.

Prima Publishing and the author have attempted throughout this book to distinguish proprietary trademarks from descriptive terms by following the capitalization style used by the manufacturer.

Information contained in this book has been obtained by Prima Publishing from sources believed to be reliable. However, because of the possibility of human or mechanical error by our sources, Prima Publishing, or others, the Publisher does not guarantee the accuracy, adequacy, or completeness of any information and is not responsible for any errors or omissions or the results obtained from use of such information. Readers should be particularly aware of the fact that the Internet is an ever-changing entity. Some facts may have changed since this book went to press.

ISBN: 0-7615-1217-9

Library of Congress Catalog Card Number: 97-69043

Printed in the United States of America

97 98 99 DD 10 9 8 7 6 5 4 3 2 1

This book is for all those folks who have helped me in my writing life, including my fellow authors and editors.

CONTENTS AT A GLANCE

CONTENTS

SUNDAY MORNING

SUNDAY AFTERNOON

Appendix E
Other Resources

ACKNOWLEDGMENTS

I'd like to thank the team at Prima for allowing me to write a book in this creative series—it was great fun. Thanks to Debbie Abshier for being not only a great acquisitions editor, but one of my dearest friends. Debbie is the definition of professionalism in the publishing business, and she has accumulated a legion of loyal authors to prove it (including yours truly).

Barb Terry contributed her usual thoughtful and enlightened comments in her development of the manuscript, and I appreciate all her help. I was blessed with an alert and tactful technical editor, Paul Marchessault, and an enthusiastic copy editor, Hilary Powers. Last but never least, Kelli Crump, my very able project editor, brought it all together, as usual.

A fond goodbye to my dear friends in Indianapolis who I'm soon leaving to move to San Francisco—you guys know who you are. Thanks for everything!

ABOUT THE AUTHOR

Nancy Stevenson has authored more than a dozen computer books about online topics and word processor, spreadsheet, and presentation software. A self-proclaimed creative soul, she has a particular fondness for any kind of desktop publishing-oriented software, including Microsoft Publisher. Prior to becoming an author, Nancy worked for Macmillan Publishing and Symantec Corporation. Nancy's other books for Prima Publishing include *The Essential Word 97 Book* and both the *Word 97* and *Excel 97 Visual Learning Guides*.

INTRODUCTION

Maybe Rome wasn't built in a day, but the basics of desktop publishing with Microsoft Publisher 97 really can be mastered in a weekend. You have too much to do to spend weeks poring over a weighty book covering keystrokes and software features. What you need is to quickly learn about the tools Publisher offers, and use them in real-world desktop publishing projects. If you are familiar with Windows software and have an interest in designing exciting, professional publications, you'll conclude this weekend with the skills you need to accomplish your goals.

Is This Book for You?

Do you need to have a degree in art from a fancy college and the creativity of a Michelangelo to master desktop publishing? Absolutely not! All you need is an understanding of the simple-to-use features of Publisher, including many predesigned elements that unleash your creativity.

I'm assuming that you have a publishing project in mind: maybe a newsletter for your PTA, maybe a wedding invitation, or perhaps you need to create a business card for your small business or a brochure for your civic organization. No matter what your need, you want to be able to produce such a publication quickly, not three weeks from today.

The good news is that this book will not only help you with your immediate needs, but will also teach you what you have to know when the next publishing project comes up, and the next, and the one after that. Whether you just want to use Publisher on a project-by-project basis, or want to begin to explore all the possibilities of desktop design, this book is the perfect place to start.

How Is This Book Organized?

I've organized this book around a typical weekend so that you can learn all you need in that defined period of time. Each section presented here, from Friday Evening to Sunday Afternoon, is designed to be completed within about three hours.

Do you have to follow the weekend model? Not at all. You can dedicate five evenings in a typical week, one to each section, and accomplish the same thing. Or use some evening time and some weekend time. The design of the book is flexible, but if you really want to get through it all quickly, start Friday and by Sunday night you'll have finished it all. It's entirely up to you.

I've also built in a couple of breaks in each section so if you'd rather take this material in smaller chunks, you can stop at a break, at which point you'll have worked through about an hour of material. If you do go straight through the weekend, however, you should still take heed of the breaks. They're there so you can stand up, move around, and get your gray cells in gear again.

This book focuses on projects because you're likely to use Publisher when a specific project comes up, such as a newsletter or flyer. Go through all the projects here the first time to learn Publisher's features. Later on, if you find yourself challenged with one of these types of projects, you can always go back and work through that section again to refresh your memory.

Finally, I've included several useful appendixes that will stimulate your creativity, provide ideas for publications, and give you samples of Publisher design elements you can page through for inspiration.

What Do You Need to Begin?

All you need to get going is Microsoft Publisher 97 installed on your computer (check the software packaging for system requirements). It might

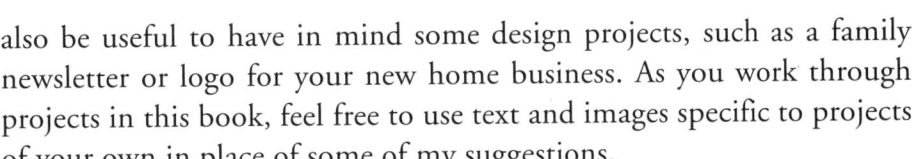

also be useful to have in mind some design projects, such as a family newsletter or logo for your new home business. As you work through projects in this book, feel free to use text and images specific to projects of your own in place of some of my suggestions.

It would also be very useful to have a printer available so you can print out your publications and see how they look on the page. Don't worry, you don't have to have a fancy color printer, any printer will do.

Otherwise, I suggest finding a private spot for you and your computer where you won't be disturbed for three hours at a time, a comfortable desk chair, and a stash of soda and munchies to get you through the weekend.

What's Covered in This Book?

Here's a quick tour of what you'll learn as you move through your weekend.

Friday Evening: Design Basics provides some basic rules of good design for you to keep in mind as you learn Publisher. Your First Glimpse of Publisher gives you a first look at Publisher itself and lets you begin to learn how to use its tools and menus. It also gives you an overview of the help available to you in Publisher, including Wizards that give you the foundation to produce publications fast.

Saturday Morning: Creating a Flyer is where you'll start adding text and organizing text in columns. You'll work with pictures—inserting them, moving and resizing them, and setting up how text wraps around them. You'll use some tools to check your final document and then save and print it.

Saturday Afternoon: Making a Newsletter gets into topics like adding headlines to publications, using special text effects like reverse type and shadows, and rotating objects on the page. You'll add a table to your newsletter and format it, and work with colors, patterns, and borders.

Sunday Morning: Designing Invitations finds you creating your own drawings using Publisher drawing tools, as well as working with predesigned elements from the Design Gallery. What's an invitation unless someone reads it? Learn how to get your publications in the right hands by working through Publisher's personalized mailing feature, Mail Merge.

Sunday Afternoon: Creating Logos, Letterhead, and Business Cards is something of a combination of all the things you've learned up to now. You'll use your drawing skills to build a company logo, insert graphics, and fine-tune your use of fonts. You'll also get some experience with a couple of Publisher's wizards.

Special Elements to Help You Learn

There are three special elements you'll see throughout the book that offer additional information or advice you'll find useful.

NOTE Notes give you additional information or background on a topic under discussion.

CAUTION Take heed of Cautions! They are warnings about potentially disastrous moments when you could lose your file or take some irrevocable step. A caution might save you from disaster, or at least tell you how to backtrack and do it right the next time.

TIP A tip is a hint or piece of advice about the best way to accomplish something or how to get the best results.

Have Fun!

The most important thing for a productive weekend is to have fun. Publisher is truly easy to use and can really start your artistic juices flowing, so enjoy!

Design Basics

- ✿ Understanding the rules of good design
- ✿ Using graphics effectively
- ✿ Learning what Publisher can do for you
- ✿ Taking a look at the Publisher environment
- ✿ Working with tools and menus

It's the end of a long workweek. You're committed to learning Publisher 97, but you're probably saying to yourself right about now, "Can I really become a competent desktop publisher in a single weekend? Sure, I might learn how to get around Publisher and use some menus and tools, but don't I need talent (and maybe a beret) to design fancy newsletters and flyers?"

The answer is yes and no. Yes, you need a dose of creativity to use the tools Publisher gives you to best effect, but everyone is creative in his or her own way, so that's no excuse. And no, you don't need to be a professional designer to get professional-looking designs out of Publisher.

That's because Publisher gives you a whole slew of ready-made elements that you can use to add instant design appeal. It also provides sophisticated tools so that you can add to the mix as many or as few of your own design ideas as you like.

Let's ease into this weekend with a little background on the basic principles of good design. I'll reemphasize these principles throughout the book (but not nag you to death), so you'll easily have them memorized by Sunday night. Then I'll provide an overview of how Publisher helps you to be your most creative and you'll get to look at all those tools, menus, and Wizards close up.

The Rules of Good Design

If you're on schedule, you've probably just finished a nice Friday evening dinner, and are settling down to digest your meal along with your first serving of Microsoft Publisher 97. I bet you never thought that your dinner has a lot in common with good design, but it does.

Like a good meal, a well-designed document takes some forethought and planning. Anyone can use standard recipes, but truly great cooks embellish them and add their own touches to the tried-and-true dishes. Publisher's document templates, called *Wizards*, are like boxed cake mixes; they give you instant documents with standard elements. However, to truly enjoy the power of Publisher, you should also learn how to make documents from scratch.

Also, balance is key to making both documents and a meal succeed. A little starch (rice or potatoes), some veggies or a salad, some meat or other protein, and of course a sweet dessert make a balanced meal; three servings of meatloaf and a piece of parsley do not. In the same way, a pleasing combination of words and images, color, and white space make a document shine.

Too much food can make you feel uncomfortable, and that's true in design too. A page that's cluttered up with a whole pantryful of design tricks may seem clever, but in the end, it's not nearly as satisfying as a more simple, straightforward approach. This evening you'll take a closer look at how a few basic design principles can offer you tasty document solutions.

Less Is More

One of the most important principles of placing words and images on a page effectively is to avoid clutter and keep things simple. The concept of *white space* is key to this. What is white space? Well, in a word-processed document it would include the margins around the text and the space in between paragraphs. In a more graphically-oriented document, white space could include space between words and graphics, between headings and body text, and even blank space on the inside of objects. But white space is more than just space: it becomes a design element on its own—negative space balancing the objects you place on a page.

Figure 1.1

Simply adding every bell and whistle you can think of doesn't always make for exciting design.

Look at these examples of good and bad design to help make the point. Figure 1.1 is an invitation that uses everything but the kitchen sink to get attention. Figure 1.2 provides the same information, but with simpler devices and great use of white space.

You should strive in your documents for a clean, clear look. Never get carried away with graphics and don't go crazy with colors—especially if you don't even have a color printer! Remember: what you have fun tossing around the page might be making your document difficult to read.

Most documents you create, from flyers and brochures to your own résumé, are there to get a message across. Don't make that message hard to find among the clutter.

Provide a Flow for Your Reader

Try an experiment. Take another look at Figures 1.1 and 1.2. Where does your eye move when you look at each of them? The odds are that with the

Figure 1.2

A little restraint makes a busy page clean and attractive.

first document your eye moves around the page quite a bit, trying to figure out which of the many objects is being presented as the most important. Consider the way your eye takes in this document. Do the ideas emerge in a logical fashion? Does the design keep your eye too busy for comfort? Is there any confusion about what you should look at first?

Now look at the second version of the invitation. Your eye probably starts at the top right corner, on the Happy Halloween banner. It then travels lightly over the pumpkin, which acts as more of a background element because of its size and lack of border, and then down to the invitation text.

Consider the flow of the reader's eye when you design documents. Step away from the document after you've completed it, and then come back to it as a reader, alert to how the flow of the design is affecting the delivery of the message.

Now take a look at Figures 1.3 and 1.4. Which makes you want to buy this product more? Why? Here's what's going on, designwise. Figure 1.4 places

Figure 1.3

Create balance on your page by placing elements so they stand out and deliver the message you want to deliver.

Figure 1.4

Putting too many messages near each other on the page creates clutter and distracts the reader.

the text elements too close together: they fight for your attention and you're not sure which to read first. In Figure 1.3, on the other hand, there is a flow from the top to the bottom of the page, leading you from the product name to the free offering. In addition, in Figure 1.3 the product name is placed next to the graphic that identifies what the product is, helping the reader to understand the nature of what's being offered right away.

 TIP   It's said that the one word that gets the most attention in any publication is "free." Put that word somewhere to grab a reader's interest, especially if you're selling something: free sample, free consultation, or free evaluation, for example.

Text Can Make the Difference

Up to now you've been focused on the arrangement of objects and text on a page. Now it's time to look more closely at that text and how it can play a key role in design.

Text consists of the letters, numbers, and symbols that appear in a document. Text is displayed on the page in a variety of *fonts*. A font is simply a design style applied to text. Think of a font as a wardrobe for the individual characters of your text. Just like styles of clothing, each font has a unique look and feel, and therefore each can convey different things to readers of your document.

Fonts Convey Feelings

Look at the fonts displayed in Figure 1.5. Which would you choose for a formal invitation? Which for an informal flyer for a garage sale? What one do you think would make the best impression in a business letter?

Because you are a reader of documents, you already infer things from different fonts. Being a good designer means paying attention to the way you react to fonts and other design elements and using those reactions to your advantage in documents. Notice in Figure 1.6 and 1.7 how text can make a difference in the feel of a final document.

Time for a Change!

Time for a Change!

TIME FOR A CHANGE!

TIME FOR A CHANGE!

Time for a Change!

Figure 1.5

Fonts come in a wide variety, each making a unique impression on your reader.

TIME FOR A CHANGE!

Due to rising costs of coffee beans worldwide, the Freemont Coffee Club is forced to up its membership fees. The cost for a year's membership, with weekly coffee meetings included, is now $25.00.

Figure 1.6

This heading typeface conveys a light, friendly, modern feeling.

TIME FOR A CHANGE!

Due to rising costs of coffee beans world-wide, the Freemont Coffee Club is forced to up its membership fees. The cost for a year's membership, with weekly coffee meetings included, is now $25.00.

Figure 1.7

This heading is a little more formal, but its old-fashioned look still suggests a casual tone.

NOTE A good design rule of thumb is to never use more than three different fonts on a page. Keeping to a certain number of fonts and using them consistently throughout a publication keeps your page looking neat and makes your message coherent.

Serif vs. Sans Serif

One other thing to note about fonts: they are traditionally divided into two kinds, serif and sans serif. A serif is a little flag-like element that comes off the tops or bottoms of letters or numbers. Letters such as *l, k, d,* and *p* will have those flags in some fonts and not in others. Serif fonts have them; sans serif (literally from the French, without the line) fonts don't. Figure 1.8 shows a serif font first and then a sans serif font.

What do these two categories of fonts mean to you as a designer? Well, the thinking is that serif fonts (those with the little flags coming off the

Figure 1.8

Sans serif sports a cleaner look; serif is a little less modern—you'll find most books use a serif font.

letters) help move the eye along from one letter to another. They are best used in the body text of a document to help the reader move through lengthier bits of text.

Sans serif fonts, on the other hand, stop the eye after each letter. For that reason, they are often used in headlines to hold the reader's attention on shorter, more emphatic text.

Using Graphics Effectively

Graphic is a term that applies to a variety of visual elements you can include in a publication. A graphic may be a line drawing, a colorful illustration, or even a photograph. A graphic can even be a simple border or design element that is just for show. Each element in Figure 1.9 is a graphic.

The first thing to remember about graphics harkens back to the first point I made in this chapter: avoid clutter on the page. Graphics are fun to use and can add flair to a document, but they are also easy to overdo.

Second, use graphics that forward your document's purpose. Don't throw in a picture of a cat because you like cats. If your document's message is about the environment or cutting costs, use a graphic that fits that message. Remember, graphics will catch your reader's eye and even draw his or her attention away from the text; you want every bit of the reader's attention in delivering your message.

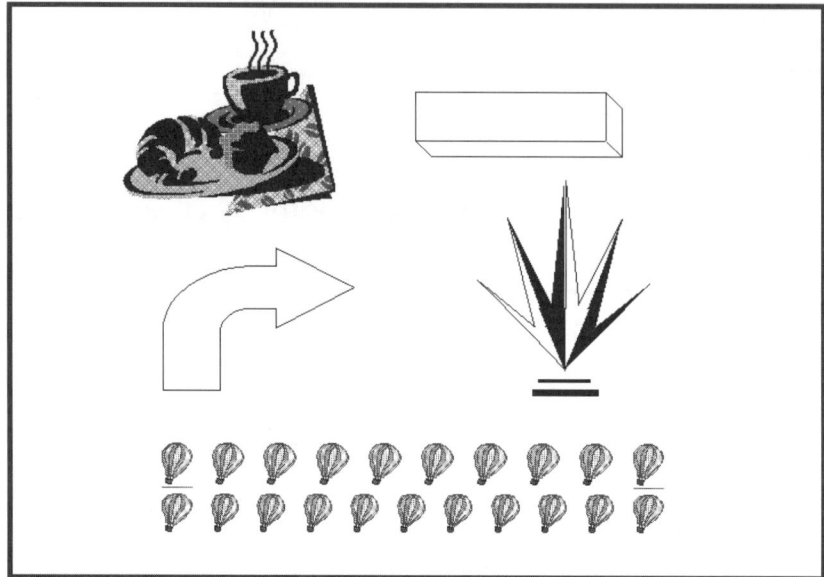

Figure 1.9

Graphics come in all shapes, sizes, colors, and styles.

Finally, if you're using a lot of graphics in a publication, try to use graphics with a similar look for consistency. There are several styles of clip art, for example. *Clip art* is the generic term for illustrations, whether in printed collection or electronically, that you can use without having to pay the artist. A great many software programs, including Publisher, make large collections of electronic clip art available, allowing you to use graphics in your work without drawing them yourself or scanning them from paper sources. If you're using several pieces of this art, try to choose clip art of a similar style. In Figure 1.10, for example, the top row of images is in one style, while the bottom row conveys a very different feel.

What Publisher Can Do for You

Now that you've had the nickel tour of design basics, you're probably wondering what Publisher can do to help you implement these rules and make dazzling publications.

Figure 1.10

In most cases, mixing and matching these styles of graphic is less effective than creating a single look for your document.

What's a Wizard?

Publisher is chock-full of Wizards (18 to be exact). Wizards consist of interactive dialogs with Publisher. You select a Wizard for a particular type of document, such as the Newsletter or Brochure Wizard, and then Publisher walks you through a series of choices. When you've responded to those choices and entered some simple information, Publisher creates the document for you, adding graphic elements and text blocks. You'll use several Wizards during the course of this book, beginning in Saturday Afternoon: Making a Newsletter.

However, Wizards will only take you so far. To design your own publications or even to modify the publication that a Wizard presents you with, you need to learn about Publisher's other tools.

Get Creative on Your Own!

Everything you've seen so far in this session is available in Publisher: all the images, typefaces, and options for arranging them on a page. Here's a list of the features of Publisher that will help you design your own great documents:

- A clip art collection containing hundreds of graphics in many different styles; you can use these images as often and in any way that you wish.

- A collection of fonts (over 100) including several symbol fonts that allow you to insert things like trademarks, smiling faces, and astrological signs.

NOTE Your font library may vary: Publisher provides some fonts, but most are part of Windows. If you've loaded fonts from separate font collections into Windows, those will also be available to you through Publisher. Throughout this book, if you don't have the same font that I call for, don't worry, just try to select a font that has a similar feel from those that are available to you.

- A design gallery of elements such as pull quotes, titles, sidebars, and ornaments that you can place in your document. You can even add text to many of them with predefined text blocks.

- A set of tools for drawing lines, circles, and squares as well as a Custom Shape tool that lets you easily create shapes like starbursts, arrows, and cubes.

- A mail merge feature that allows you to personalize documents such as form letters, invitations, and envelopes, and easily handle larger mailings.

- Tools for working with tables, columns, and borders to divide, organize, and set off your text.

You'll discover all these features and more as you move through your weekend. You can also use the Wizard Gallery (Appendix A) and Design Gallery (Appendix B) for ideas on how to use all Publisher has to offer for exciting documents.

Take a Break

Now that you've eased into the topic of desktop publishing and document design, it's time to get a first glimpse of the Publisher environment. In the next section you'll open Publisher, look at some of the menus and tools you use to get things done, and begin to understand exactly how Publisher builds documents and lets you view those documents in various ways. But first, you've earned it: go take a break, grab a soda, cup of tea, or whatever and take five.

Your First Glimpse of Publisher

Half the battle of learning to use Publisher is to learn your way around its interface: the tool buttons, menus, and various methods of organizing and placing objects on the page.

In this section, you'll explore the Publisher environment. You'll meet some old friends that you've probably used in other programs and a few new ones that unleash the true power of Publisher.

Publisher uses menus and tools as its main methods of performing actions, just as other Windows programs do. Publisher also sports a special toolbar on the left of its desktop that allows you to access drawing and design features easily. Figure 1.11 shows the Publisher desktop when you first open a blank document. With no text or drawings in the document yet, several of the tools on the Standard toolbar are unavailable.

In the figure, you see one page of a document. It sits on the Publisher desktop, the gray area surrounding the page. You can use this area to place objects you want to copy from one page to another or objects you just want to put to the side for the moment. There are a few other features of the Publisher window of which to take note:

- Horizontal and vertical rulers provide a means of placing objects precisely on your page.

- Page navigation and zoom features are located at the bottom left of the Publisher window. These allow you to move among pages in a multipage document and to see a larger or smaller display of each page, respectively.

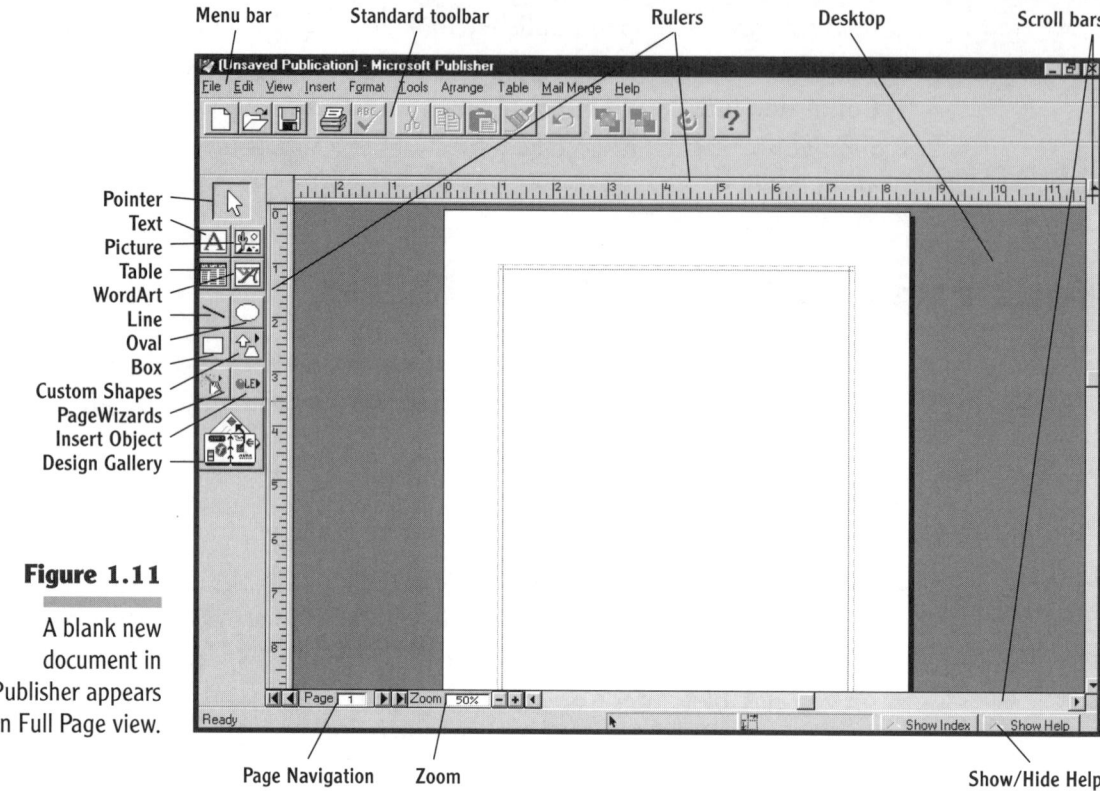

Menu bar   Standard toolbar   Rulers   Desktop   Scroll bars

[Unsaved Publication] - Microsoft Publisher

File Edit View Insert Format Tools Arrange Table Mail Merge Help

Pointer
Text
Picture
Table
WordArt
Line
Oval
Box
Custom Shapes
PageWizards
Insert Object
Design Gallery

Figure 1.11

A blank new
document in
Publisher appears
in Full Page view.

Page Navigation   Zoom   Show/Hide Help

Ready

Show Index   Show Help

⚙ The Status bar at the bottom of the window offers two buttons to
display Publisher Help topics and a Help index as you work.

⚙ Vertical and horizontal scroll bars allow you to move up and down
and across your page. This is especially helpful when you have zoomed
in on your document, so that you have to move around a page to see
everything on it.

Opening a Publisher Document

It's time to get to work, and the first step is to open your first Publisher
document. When you first open Publisher you're greeted by an online

introduction that takes you through several windows describing various features of Publisher. When you complete that (or click on Cancel to bypass it), you'll see a dialog box with three tabs; one gives you the option of opening a document Wizard for a wide variety of document types, such as newsletters and business cards. The Existing Publication tab offers you the option of opening a document you already have. The third tab opens a blank page; that's the choice you'll make now to open a new document:

1. Open the Windows Start menu and select Programs.

2. From the Programs cascading menu, select Microsoft Publisher. Publisher opens and the dialog box in Figure 1.12 appears.

3. Click on the Blank Page tab. The tab shown in Figure 1.13 appears.

4. The Full Page type is already selected for you, so just click on OK. A blank document opens.

Figure 1.12

This dialog box sports three tabs giving you a lot of flexibility in choosing the type of document to open.

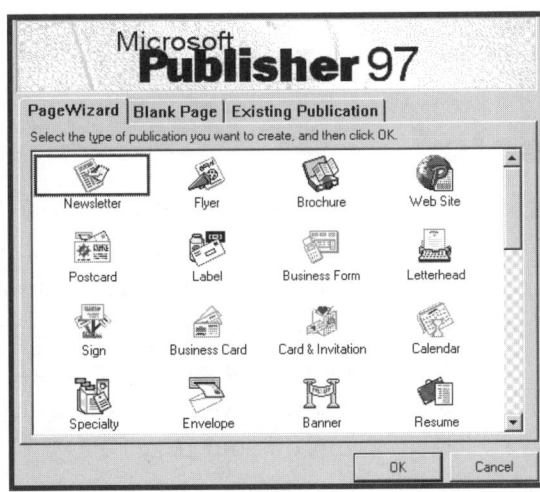

NOTE The various types of documents available on the Blank Page tab offer you preset page setups, including odd-sized pages like business cards and index cards as well as document folds, like the two-page setup of a book or pamphlet or a double-folded greeting card. This predefined page setup takes care of details like setting margins and lining up facing pages for you.

Working with Tools

Tools are appropriately named: they're what you use to get work done in software. Tools often provide quicker access to functions that can also be performed through menus. Click on a tool and Publisher will either perform an action immediately, such as cutting or pasting an object, or open a dialog box so you can make more detailed settings and choices to complete an action. When you activate a tool, its action will usually affect whatever object you have selected, if any, on your page.

TIP A very handy tool to get to know is the Undo tool on the Standard toolbar. If you do something you decide you didn't really want to do, you can use it to undo the last action performed. Consider it a computer user's safety net.

You can find tools grouped together by function in toolbars, such as the Standard and Publisher toolbars you saw earlier in this chapter. However, there are several other toolbars that appear depending on what type of work you're doing in Publisher. The text formatting toolbar and the graphics formatting toolbar are the two you'll see most often.

These toolbars appear when you're working on the corresponding type of object. To see these toolbars, you're going to have to create two simple objects for your Publisher page. Before you do so, however, you should understand how Publisher builds documents.

Using Boxes to Build Documents

Take a look at the document shown in Figure 1.14. This page shows some interesting things about the way Publisher builds a document. There are actually five objects on this page: three text boxes, one picture box, and a Design Gallery object (the Design Gallery is a built-in set of borders, pull quotes, and other decorative shapes you'll get a better look at tomorrow). Just about everything you do in Publisher involves a box.

In Figure 1.14 one of the text boxes is selected. It has black nubs around it called *handles*. These handles indicate that the object is currently selected. They also let you resize the box, which you'll learn more about in the next work session. Unlike word processors, which flow text freely across the page, text in Publisher is always contained in a box like one of these. To move all the text in a box you don't cut and paste it, you simply move the box.

To design Publisher documents you use boxes like these, moving them around the page and placing them next to or even on top of each other in various positions. You can even link text boxes so that text flows from one

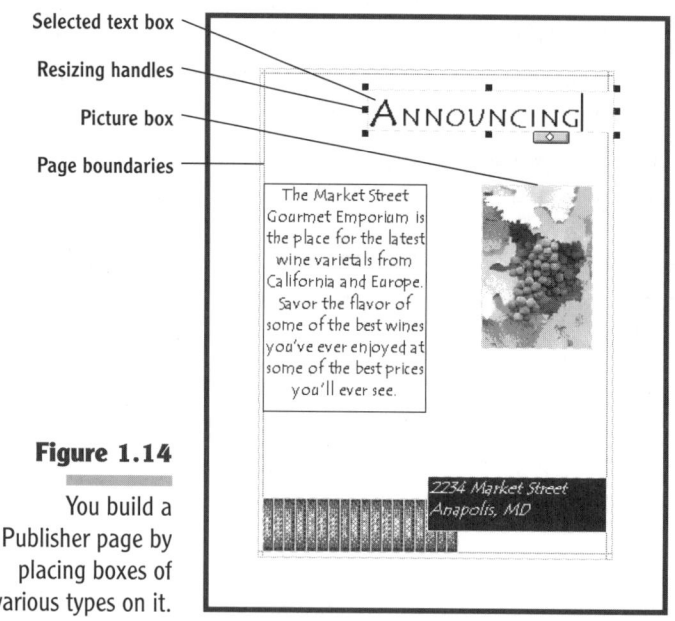

Selected text box

Resizing handles

Picture box

Page boundaries

Figure 1.14

You build a Publisher page by placing boxes of various types on it.

to the other; this is useful in publications such as newsletters where a story on page 1 might continue on page 3, for example.

Publisher displays the margins within which you can place these objects as a pale dotted line called a *boundary.* This use of boxes is a grid-based method of designing that is a foundation of desktop publishing. The geometric organization of these boxes helps you keep things organized on the page. You create these various boxes using the tools on the Publisher toolbar.

Using Tools to Draw Boxes

The first thing to try is creating a simple text box. You do that using the Text tool on the Publisher toolbar.

1. Click on the Text tool (the one with a large A on it) to activate it.

2. Click anywhere on the document page, keeping the mouse button pressed, and dragging down and to the right to draw a box.

3. Release the mouse when you have a box about one-third the size of the page. A box appears with handles around it to show that it's selected. It also has a blinking insertion point in it to show it's ready for you to enter text. A small button at the bottom, called the Connect Frame button, allows you to flow text from one frame to another, which you'll hear more about in later sessions.

4. Type this text in the box: **My Publisher Document**.

Your page should now look like the one shown in Figure 1.15. To show you the whole page, Publisher had to make the text so small that you can't read

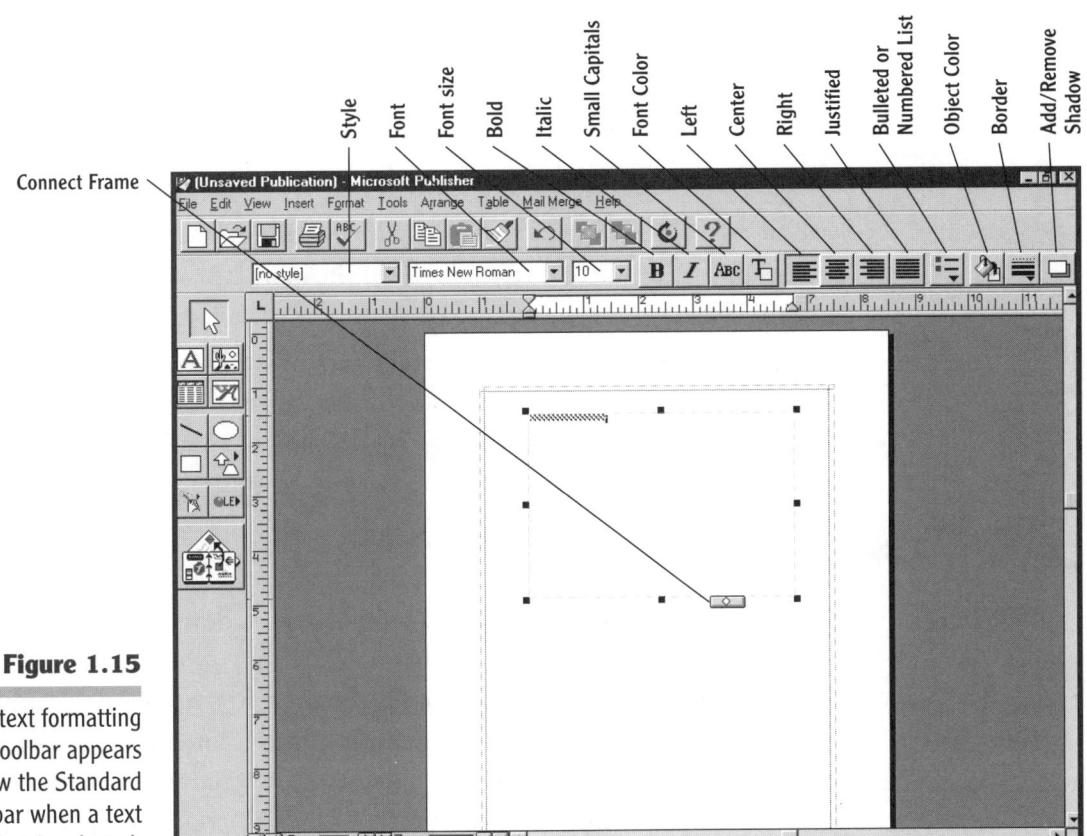

Figure 1.15

The text formatting toolbar appears below the Standard toolbar when a text object is selected.

the words. The text is there, though—you can tell by the line of checkerboard in the upper left corner! Notice that with a text box on the page and selected, a new toolbar, called the text formatting toolbar, has appeared.

You've probably seen many of these tools before in other programs: they're used to format text with different fonts, font sizes, and styles such as bold or italic. There are also text alignment tools that align text relative to the sides of its text box. Finally, there are some tools that allow you to use effects like color and shadows on the text on your page.

Now try creating one more object on the page. This time, you'll use the Box tool on the Publisher toolbar to draw a square. When you do, a graphic formatting toolbar will display.

1. Click on the Box tool on the Publisher toolbar.

2. Click anywhere on the page, hold down your mouse button, and drag to the right and down to draw a square.

3. Release your mouse button and the square appears.

Because the square is the currently selected object, a graphic formatting toolbar appears below and to the right of the Standard toolbar, as shown in Figure 1.16.

You'll use these tools to manipulate all kinds of graphics, from simple geometric forms like lines and circles to colorful illustrations. With them you can rearrange the object on the page by flipping or rotating it, and format the color, border, and shadow applied to the object.

Using Menus

You can grab a tool like a spatula and cook your own dinner, or you can go to a restaurant and get the same food by ordering from a menu. That's not too different from the way tools and menus function in software. In Publisher, menus are simply another way of getting at many of the functions tools provide—and a few more. However a menu offers a more text-oriented way of doing things. Instead of clicking on a little tool icon, you open a menu and select the name of the action or feature you want to use.

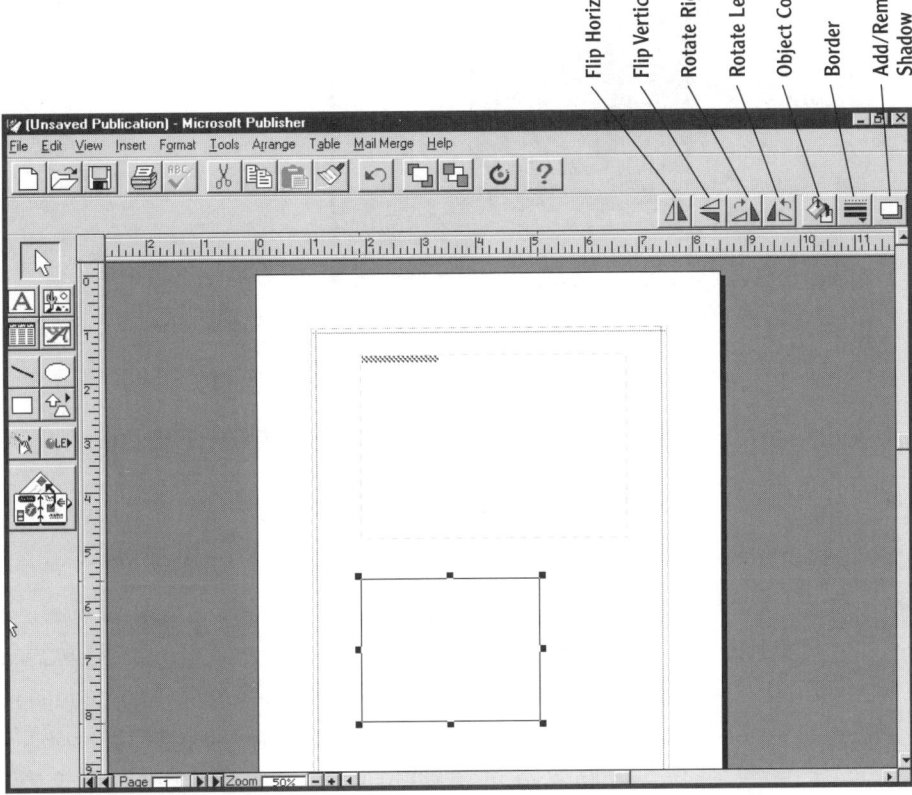

Figure 1.16

With a drawing object selected, Publisher displays the graphic formatting toolbar.

NOTE

For those of you who are more comfortable doing things with your keyboard, you can select a menu command by typing the underlined letter in the command. This is called a *hotkey*, and typing it achieves the same thing that placing your mouse pointer on the command and clicking on the item does.

Menus also contain nested submenus—also called *cascading menus* or *side menus*—which narrow down your choices. Figure 1.17 shows one of these.

Besides the actual menu commands, two other elements appear in Figure 1.17. First, any time you see a black arrow pointing to the right of a

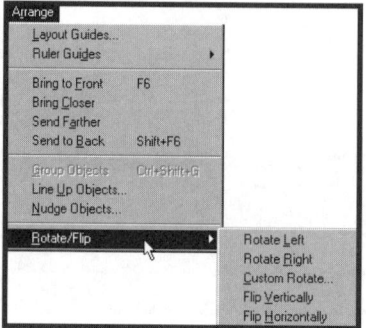

Figure 1.17

The Arrange menu
has a couple of
cascading menus
that give you
detailed choices.

command, there is a cascading menu of choices connected to that command. In the Arrange menu shown in Figure 1.17, for example, placing your mouse pointer on the Rotate/Flip item reveals choices of different directions in which the rotation could take place.

NOTE If you don't have much experience with menus, here's the lowdown on how to use them. Click with your mouse pointer on the menu name in the menu bar at the top of the Publisher window. When the menu appears, move your mouse pointer (without clicking it!) up and down the menu until the command you want to use is highlighted. When you've highlighted the one you want, just click. If a cascading menu appears when you highlight the first command, just slide your mouse over to the cascading menu, move to the item you want, and click on it. That's it!

The second item you'll notice on most menus is keyboard shortcuts for performing some of the functions. In Figure 1.17 you can see two keyboard shortcuts: to bring an object to the front you can simply press F6; to send an object to the back you press the Shift key along with the F6 key. To save screen space, the combination shows up as *Shift+F6*.

Table 1.1 gives you a general description of the types of commands you'll find on each of Publisher's menus. You'll use all the menus throughout the

TABLE 1.1   MICROSOFT PUBLISHER MENUS

Menu	Types of Commands
File	Open new and existing files, save and close files, create a Web page from the current file, set up your page, and print.
Edit	Edit, cut, copy, and delete objects and text, find and replace things in your document, and work with links between Publisher documents.
View	Manipulate the on-screen view to display the page in various sizes, show rulers and boundaries, view different toolbars, and display special characters.
Insert	Place a variety of items on your page, such as pictures, tables, files, symbols, or a new page. Also insert the current date and time or page number in a document.
Format	Apply formatting styles to text, work with fill colors and shadows, and add borders.
Tools	Access the Design Gallery, check spelling and design, snap objects to align more precisely, and access general Publisher options for how things work in the software.
Arrange	Move objects around the page, or rotate or layer objects one on top of the other.
Table	Use AutoFormat features, insert rows and columns, and fill data across several cells.
Mail Merge	Access the customized mass mailing feature of Publisher and create Publisher address lists.
Help	View quick demos of key features, get an introduction to Publisher, look up keyboard shortcuts, get help from a Print Troubleshooter, and access the Microsoft Publisher Web site.

course of the weekend, so their commands will become as familiar as old friends by Sunday night.

TIP Check out Microsoft's Web site through the Help menu to get updates on software, tips about using Publisher features, and free products like graphics collections to enrich your publications.

NOTE In this book when you're told to use a tool, you'll see the term click on. If I'm directing you to a menu, I'll ask you to select the menu to open it and then choose a command.

Exploring the Publisher Desktop

Now that you know a thing or two about how tools and menus work in Publisher, it's time to get more comfortable with moving around a bit and getting some perspective on your Publisher pages. In this section you'll learn how to move from page to page, change from a one-page to a two-page display, and how to zoom the page view in and out.

Inserting a New Page

When you open a new, blank document, depending on the type of document you open you will have a single page or multiple pages already in place. For example, the Full Page choice creates a single page, and the Side Fold Card creates two pages, both the front of the card and the inside page. To insert a new page into a publication, you use a few different methods:

- Go to the last page of the publication and click on the Next page arrow on the Page Navigation tool. Publisher will display a dialog box asking if you want to insert a new page. Click on OK.

- Select Insert, Page. Click on OK in the Insert Page dialog box that appears and a new page is added to your document. By default, a single, blank page is inserted after the currently displayed page. There are some modifications you can make to the default choices in this dialog box, which are discussed in the Saturday Morning session.

TIP The keyboard shortcut for inserting a new page in your document is Ctrl+Shift+N.

Whichever method you use, the new blank page will appear. Note that the Page number in the Page Navigation tool will reflect the new page (for example, if you have 5 pages and insert a new page, the new page appears and the navigation area will display a 6).

Changing Your View

Publisher can show you one page at a time or two pages placed next to each other, as shown in Figure 1.18. This two-page display is especially useful for book-style publications where pages face each other; in that case, you

Figure 1.18

Check the balance of two pages that might appear opposite each other with this view.

Figure 1.19

You can place a
new page or pages
before or after the
page currently
displayed using
these settings.

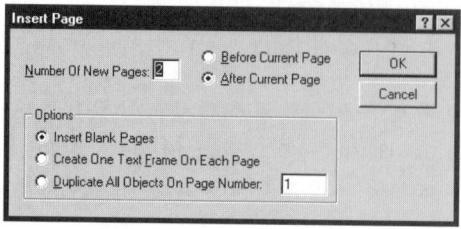

want the overall design of the two pages as a unit to be pleasing. This view helps you achieve that.

Create an additional page in the document and practice displaying the single and two-page views.

1. Select Insert, Page. The dialog box in Figure 1.19 appears.

2. Leave the default setting of 1 new page and click on OK to insert the pages.

3. Select View, Two-Page Spread. Two pages will appear side by side.

4. Select View, Single Page to return to the single-page format.

NOTE If you have only a single page in your document, or if you are displaying the first page of the document, the two-page view will show a page on the right side only. That's because, typically, the first page of any publication is on the right side and the facing page is empty. Look at the first page of this chapter if you don't believe me!

Zooming In and Out

When you're working on a Publisher document, you'll want to shift your view of the pages frequently. When you're working on the details of modifying text or a graphic object, you'll probably want to zoom in so you can see the details clearly. When you want to get a feel for how the overall design is working on the page, you'll want to zoom out. That's where the Zoom tool comes in (see Figure 1.20).

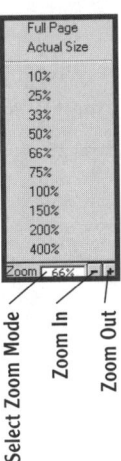

Figure 1.20

The Zoom tool is the quickest way to shift the perspective on your pages.

When you start a new document your page will appear at one-third (33 percent) of its full size, which is the full page view for a standard 8½ × 11 document. To zoom in and out, follow these steps:

1. Click on the Zoom In button. The zoom setting moves to the next highest preset zoom factor of 50 percent.

2. Click on the Zoom In button one more time. The page image magnifies, this time to a factor of 66 percent of the actual page size.

3. Click on the Select Zoom Mode area. The pop-up list shown in Figure 1.20 appears. This displays all the preset increments, as well as the Actual Size and Full Page choices.

4. Select 150 percent from the list. If you can see either the text box or square that you drew earlier in this magnified view, they're probably too big to work with.

5. Click on the Zoom Out button twice, so that the zoom factor now reads 75 percent.

6. Return to the Full Page display by selecting <u>V</u>iew, <u>F</u>ull Page.

TIP   You can display the Full Page or Actual Size setting by selecting them from the View menu, or by using the keyboard shortcuts Ctrl+Shift+L and F9, respectively.

Working with Layout Guides

Perhaps you've notice two thin lines—one pink and one blue—forming a box on each of your pages. These two lines are called *Layout Guides*. These guides don't print; what they do is help you place objects on your page and organize things. In addition to Layout Guides, you can place gridlines to indicate the columns, rows, and margins on your page and provide a structure for designing your documents.

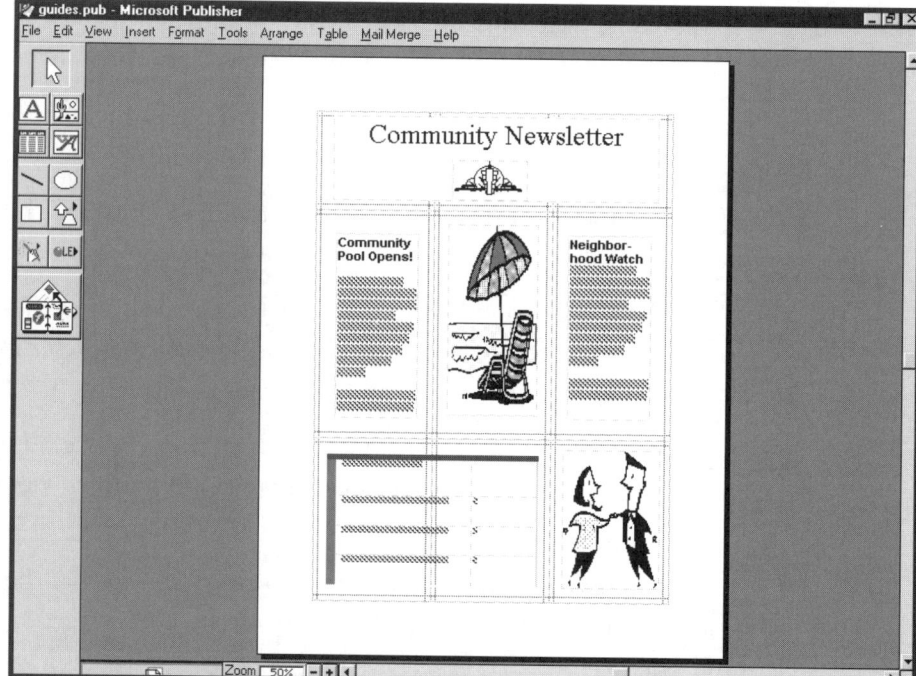

Figure 1.21

The various objects on this page are fitted onto the grid formed by Layout Guides, creating an organized feeling to the design.

You can add gridlines to your layout and move them around your page. Figure 1.21 shows a document that makes use of Layout Guides and gridlines to organize its content.

NOTE You can hide the guides to see how your design looks without them: select View, Hide Boundaries and Guides to do so (or use the keyboard shortcut Ctrl+Shift+O). Hiding these guides is the way Publisher lets you see a preview of how your document will look when it prints.

If you move an object near a Layout Guide, it will snap to it, causing the objects placed on your page to line up consistently. You can easily add and adjust Layout Guides using the Arrange menu, which you'll learn about during the Saturday Morning session.

Using Rulers

In addition to Layout Guides, you can use Publisher's rulers to help you align objects on a page. There are two rulers, the horizontal ruler and vertical ruler, which always appear together. When you move your mouse pointer around the page, a pale gray line on each ruler provides an exact measurement for the vertical and horizontal position of your pointer on the page. That measurement also appears on the Status bar as a two-part numerical measurement (horizontal followed by vertical), as shown in Figure 1.22.

Rulers can be displayed or hidden by following these steps:

1. Select View, Toolbars and Rulers. The dialog box in Figure 1.23 appears.

2. Click in the Ruler check box to remove the check mark and click on OK to hide the rulers. You can reverse this procedure to display the rulers once again.

You can use these rulers to help you place an object on a specific spot on the page, or to help you draw an object to an exact size. For example, to draw a box exactly three inches square, follow these steps:

Vertical measurement   Horizontal measurement

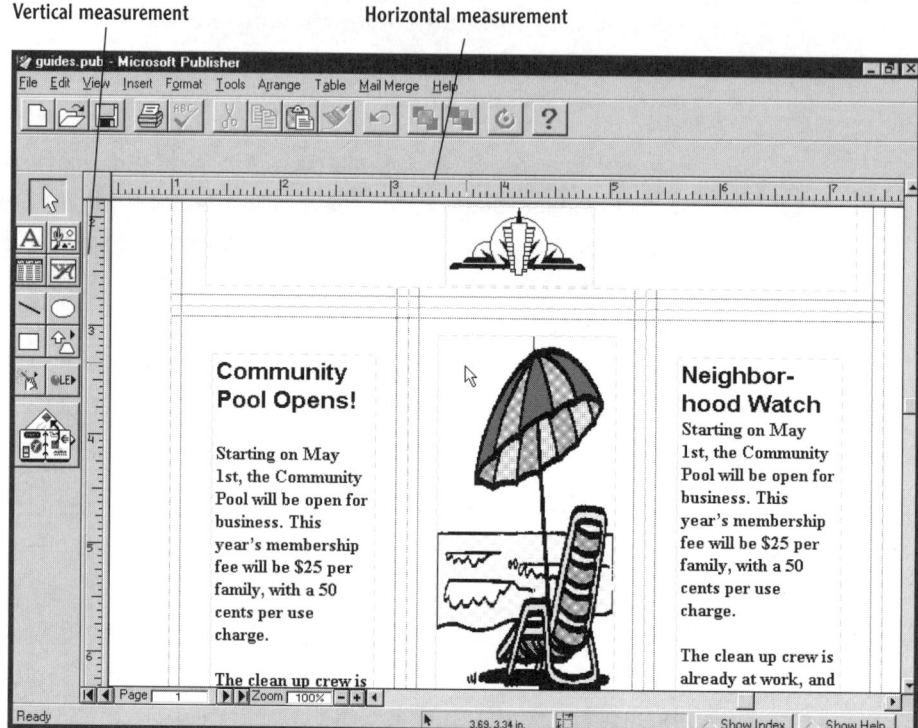

Figure 1.22

It's easiest to make out the pale gray lines that appear on each ruler onscreen; their precise measurement is given in the Status bar.

Measurement readout

Figure 1.23

You can choose to display or hide both toolbars and rulers with the Toolbars and Rulers dialog box.

1. Click on the Box tool on the Publisher toolbar.

2. Place your pointer so the measurement readout shows exactly 2.00 inches by 2.00 inches (you'll be near the upper left corner).

3. Click and drag until the markers on the rulers are both set on the number 5.

4. Release the mouse button and you have a perfectly square three-inch by three-inch box.

TIP When you want to see more of your document page onscreen, it's sometimes handy to hide both rulers and toolbars from your view by using the Toolbars and Rulers dialog box.

Navigating in Publisher

Another important skill you'll need for getting things done in Publisher is the ability to move around the page you're working on and move from page to page using scroll bars and the page navigation tools.

You've probably come across scroll bars in other Windows-based programs. In Publisher, you have both vertical and horizontal scroll bars, allowing you to move from the top to the bottom of a page or from side to side. There are three ways to use scroll bars:

✿ Click on the arrows at either end to move one line or column at a time in the arrow's direction.

✿ Click within the scroll bar right next to the scroll box—the square then moves along the bar to show your location—to move up or down (in the vertical scroll bar) or left or right (in the horizontal scroll bar) by a half-page increment, depending on which side of which scroll box you click.

✿ Click on the scroll box itself and drag it in any direction you choose to move as far in that direction as you wish.

Where the scroll bars allow you to move around a page (or around two pages if you have the two page view showing) the navigation tools at the bottom of the Publisher screen move you from one page to the next. If you have two pages displayed, using these tools will move you from one two-page spread (for example, pages 2 and 3) to the next two pages (say, pages 4 and 5). You can also use the navigation tools shown in Figure 1.24 to jump to the first or last page of your document. If you click on the Change Pages area, a Go To dialog box opens, allowing you to enter any page number you wish.

When you inserted a new page earlier, you moved to that page automatically. Here are two ways to move back to the first page of your document:

Figure 1.24

Use these tools to easily move to the adjacent page— or to any page you wish.

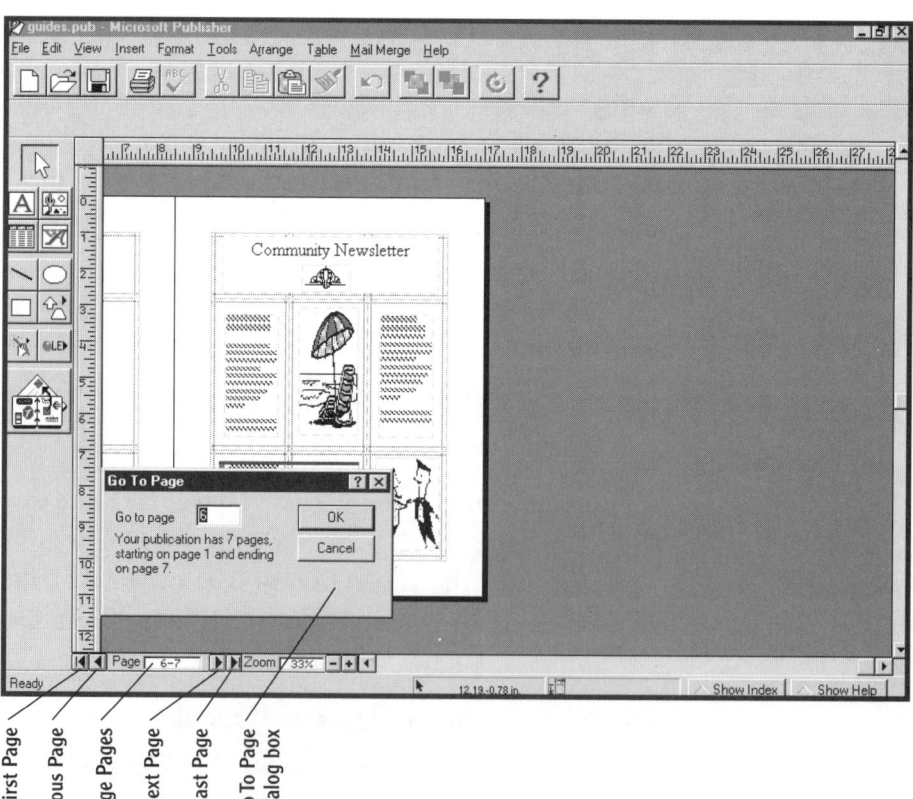

First Page | Previous Page | Change Pages | Next Page | Last Page | Go To Page dialog box

- Click on the Previous Page arrow.

- Click on the Change Page area, type **1** in the Go to page text box, and click on OK.

Take Another Break!

You are moving through this like a pro. If you hurry and finish the next section, you'll be done in time for the late night Star Trek reruns. But first, take a short break to recoup, touch base with the family, or refresh that glass of soda. You're almost done with the first evening of your weekend.

Getting Help

Hopefully, you're saying to yourself, this Publisher thing is pretty easy: I can see how to use tools and menus and I understand the basic structure of the page grid that Publisher uses to make design easy. Well, you're right, Publisher is pretty easy to use. But as with any software, once you're on your own trying to remember all these features, you'll occasionally need some help.

Using the Help Menu

When you need help, that's where the Help menu, shown in Figure 1.25 comes in. There are so many kinds of help here I could write a book just about using them. However, for now I'll give you an overview of what each command on this menu does and how to use Publisher Help.

Figure 1.25

Some of these items, like Microsoft Office Compatible and About Microsoft Publisher, simply display Microsoft product information.

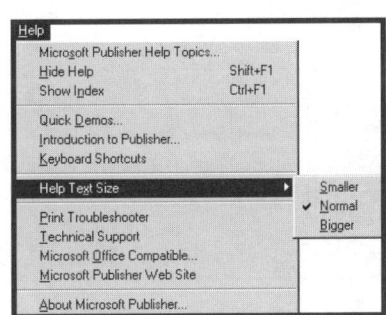

NOTE The Hide Help command on the Help menu changes depending on whether you have a Help screen displayed at the moment or not. If you don't, this command changes to Last Help Topic. The Help Text Size choice simply allows you to display Help text in a larger or smaller font.

Using the Help Index

The first few items on the Help menu are used to display on-screen help and an Index of Help topics. The Index is a search mechanism for locating the topic you need help with; the help is a window displaying subtopics or Help information. Notice that there are also buttons on the far right of the Status bar to do the same thing, called Show/Hide Index and Show/Hide Help. You can display the Help window without the Index, but not

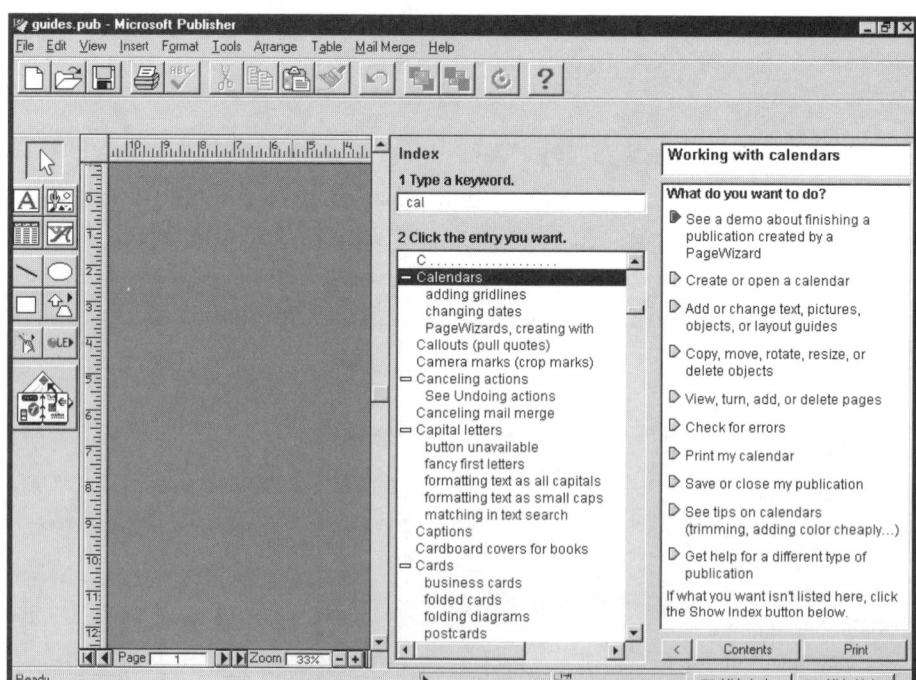

Figure 1.26

When you choose an item in the Index, the Help topics for it are displayed on the right.

the Index without the Help window. When you choose both of these you'll see a display like the one in Figure 1.26.

Follow these steps to get Help topics for creating cards in Publisher:

1. Select <u>H</u>elp, Show <u>I</u>ndex, or click on the Show Index button on the Status bar.

2. In the text box titled Type a keyword, type **c**. Notice that the list narrows down to the topics that begin with a "c."

3. Type **ards**. Your cursor now resets on the first topic beginning with the letters you typed—in this case, the word "Cards."

TIP You can also find a topic from the Index using the scroll bar to its right; select any topic visible in the Index display by clicking on it.

You can now choose a Help topic from the list on the right. Often, you'll see a demo of the topic available at the top of this list. Click on any of the arrows next to a topic or demo to display it.

Often several sets of subtopics may appear before you get to an informational Help window like the one in Figure 1.27. When you do get to this level of detail, Publisher often tells you the specific steps you need to do something. Notice also that there are two tabs now displayed above the topic: How To and More Info. How To provides steps, while More Info deals with troubleshooting or definitions of terms.

To clear the keyword text box and begin a new topic search, click the Contents button that appears under the Help topics list. To print a Help topic, click on the Print button in the same location.

TIP These Help windows take up space on your desktop and obscure your page. You can hide the Index or Help topics at any time by selecting their Hide commands from the Help menu, or by clicking on the Hide Index and Hide Help buttons on the Status bar.

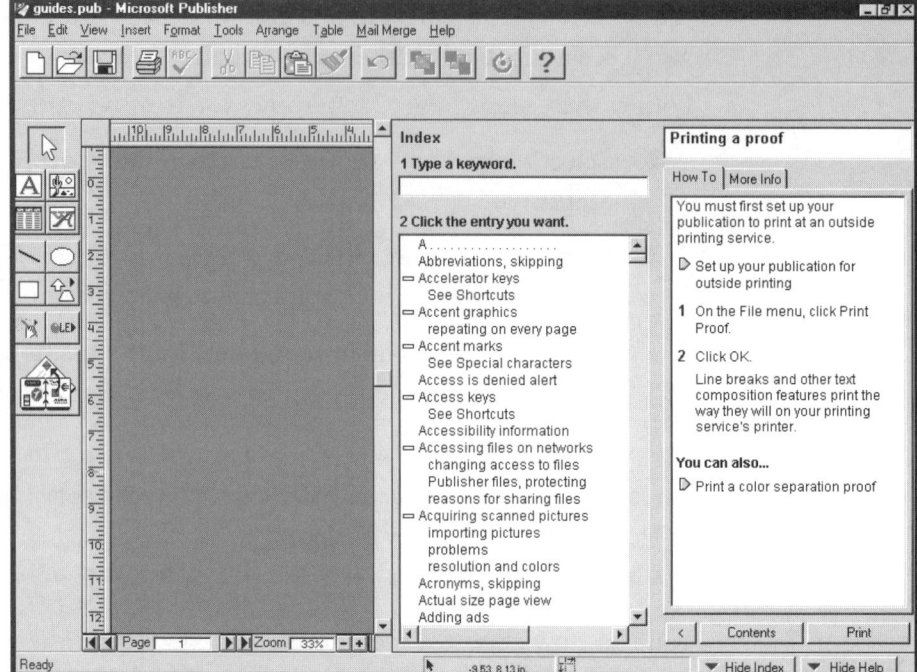

Figure 1.27

Publisher may take you through three or four layers of Help before you get to specific steps like the ones shown in this window.

Three items on the Help menu—Keyboard Shortcuts, Technical Support, and Print Trouble-shooter—simply take you directly to those topics in the Help panel. They're useful shortcuts for frequently requested Help topics.

Running Demos

If you come across a Help topic that offers a demo, you can run it by simply clicking on the arrow in the Help window. Or you can choose from a list of available demos in the Publisher Demos dialog box, shown in Figure 1.28. Demos aren't really demonstrations in the true sense: you don't see a process demonstrated. Rather you get several screens of information about a process with pictures of tool buttons and screens to help you visualize it. However, Publisher's demos can be very helpful in providing an overview of unfamiliar topics.

Figure 1.28

Many of Publisher's
features are
overviewed in
on-screen
demonstrations,
accessed in the
Publisher Demos
dialog box.

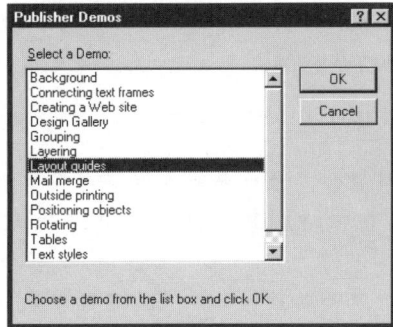

To run a demo, follow these steps:

1. Select <u>H</u>elp, Quick <u>D</u>emos.

2. From the Publisher Demos dialog box, select a demo by clicking on it in the list and clicking on OK. An initial demo screen, like the one shown in Figure 1.29 for the Layout Guides demo, appears.

3. The initial demo screen usually gives you an overview of the topic. To move to the next screen, click on Next.

4. When you move past the first screen two arrow tools become available. Click on the button with a single arrow to move back one

Figure 1.29

A small box in the
lower left corner
indicates how
many steps this
demo contains.

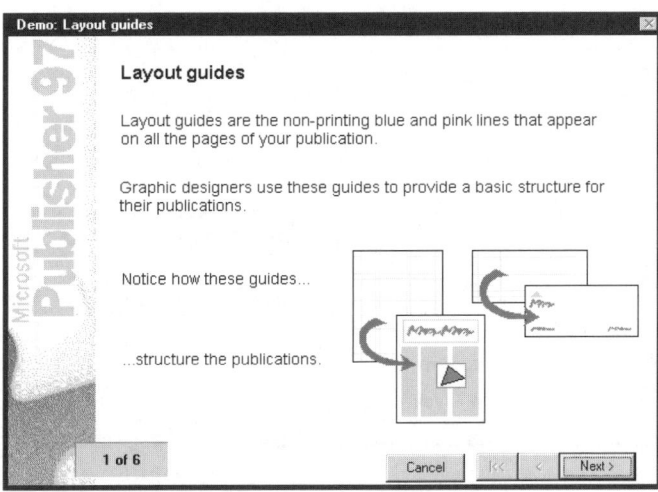

screen (the button with the double arrow jumps you to the first dialog box in the sequence).

5. Click on Next again to move forward.

TIP You can cancel a demo at any time by clicking on the Cancel button or pressing the Esc key on your keyboard.

6. When you reach the end of a demo, the Next button becomes unavailable (see Figure 1.30) and the Cancel button changes to a Close button. Click on Close to end the demo.

NOTE Two very useful demos, Introduction to Publisher and What's New in Publisher, are accessible through the Introduction to Publisher command on the Help menu. They're a good place to start to get a general picture of Publisher's capabilities.

Figure 1.30

You can go back to the beginning of the demo from the final screen by clicking on the button with the double arrow.

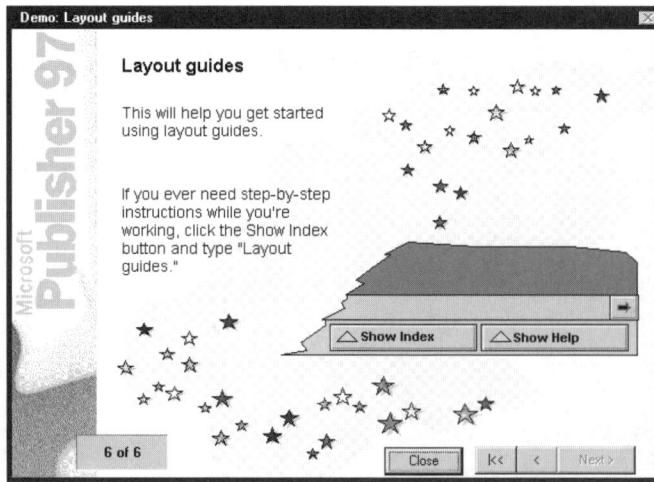

Figure 1.31

Quick Overview
takes you to a
demo; Step-by-step
instructions takes
you directly to a
topic in the
Help window.

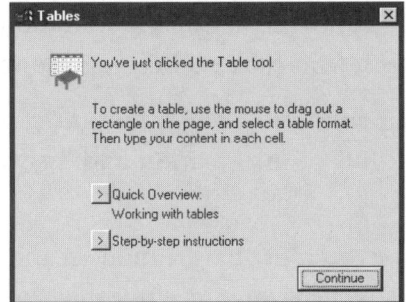

Getting Step-by-Step Help

When you choose to perform certain actions for the first time, Publisher offers you a dialog box like the one in Figure 1.31. This dialog offers you a demo or Step-by-step instructions on the topic. If you click on the Step-by-step instructions option, the Help panel opens directly to the appropriate Help topic.

Step-by-step instructions are offered automatically by Publisher at logical times when you're creating something or using a feature for the first time. You can make a step-by-step instruction appear by locating it among the regular Help topics.

Getting Help Online

Publisher 97 comes with a direct connection to the Microsoft Web site. From there you can get information about:

- ⚙ **The Publisher software.** The site describes upgrades, updates, and bug fixes.

- ⚙ **Product add-ons.** These are products created by third-party companies to work with Microsoft products. They may add features or enhancements to the way Publisher works.

- ⚙ **Free stuff.** You'll often find free clip art, sound bites, or photo collections on this Web site that are downloadable for use with Publisher.

- ⚙ **Online technical support.** You can send questions about Publisher and get answers from Microsoft technical personnel.

- ⚙ **Other Microsoft products.** Each Microsoft product has its own home page, chock-full of information and assistance for products like Word and Excel.

To access this online help, you must have a modem and be set up with an Internet Service Provider. When you are, Publisher will use Internet Explorer, a Microsoft Web browser that comes with Windows 95, to take you to its home page. If you've somehow deleted Internet Explorer from Windows, run Windows setup to reinstall it.

NOTE If you have replaced Internet Explorer with another browser as your default, Publisher should open that browser instead.

Select <u>H</u>elp, <u>M</u>icrosoft Publisher Web Site; Internet Explorer opens. Once you've connected to the Internet, the Microsoft Publisher page will appear, as shown in Figure 1.32.

A Quick Look at Wizards

I mentioned earlier that Publisher comes with 18 Wizards that can provide designs for your publications. Now it's time to take a look at how these work. Wizards can produce very nice-looking documents, but they often require fine tuning and they don't always fit every design need. However, they're a great jumping-off point, especially when you need a polished-looking document in a hurry.

A Wizard consists of a series of dialog boxes asking you questions or requesting that you enter certain information such as the publication title or your name. When you've finished working through these dialog boxes, Publisher will create the publication for you, using graphics and text blocks appropriate to your responses. Try working through this process with the Card & Invitation Wizard to create a simple Valentine's Day card.

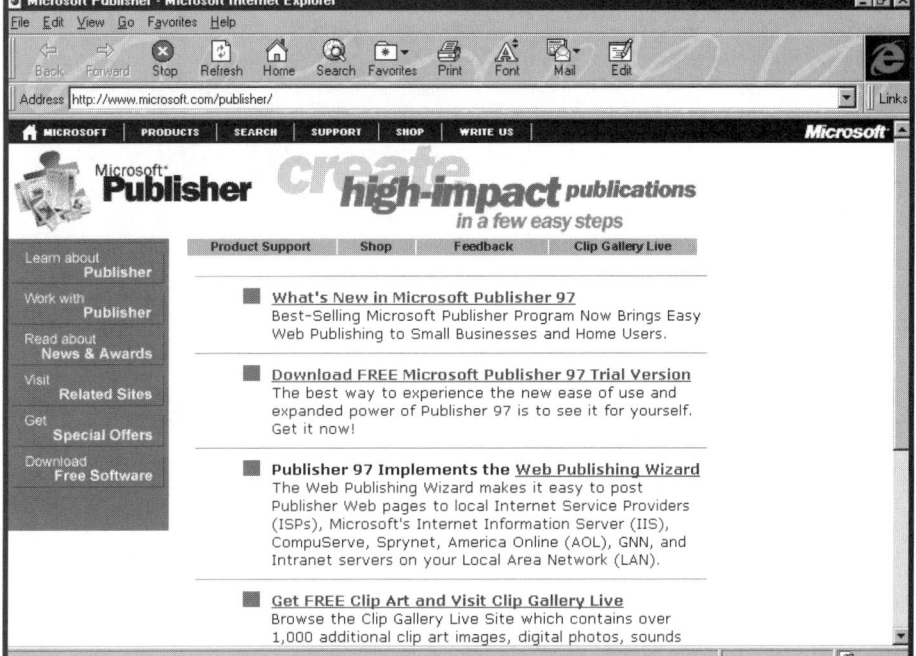

Figure 1.32

This site provides useful information about the Publisher product, as well as access to Microsoft technical support.

Using the Card & Invitation Wizard

You can start a Wizard from the Welcome screen that greets you when you first open Publisher (see Figure 1.33). Simply select the PageWizard tab, if it's not already displayed, select the Wizard you'd like to use, and click on OK.

If you're already working in Publisher when you decide to start a Wizard, follow these steps:

1. Close any document you may have open. Select File, Create New Publication.

2. Click on the PageWizard tab to make it active (see Figure 1.33).

3. Click on the Card & Invitation icon.

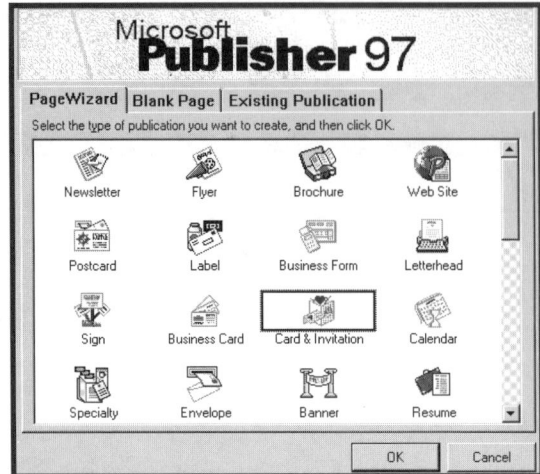

Figure 1.33

You can use the scroll bar to see more Wizards that are available to you.

4. Click on OK to begin the Wizard. The Greeting Card PageWizard Design Assistant, shown in Figure 1.34, appears.

5. Since Valentine's Day is a holiday, be sure that the Holiday option button is selected (it should be selected by default). If you wanted another choice here, you would simply click in its option button to select it (you can select only one).

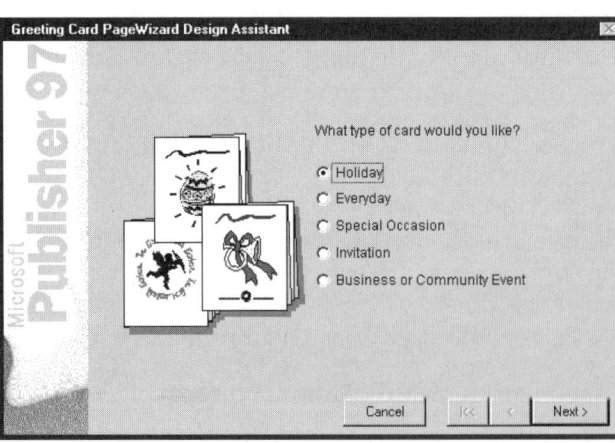

Figure 1.34

The first dialog box of this Wizard presents you with a decision about the way your card will be used.

NOTE If you wanted to produce a thank you or get well card, you would choose Everyday. The Special Occasion selection allows you to create a birthday, congratulations, new baby, or new home card. The Invitation option offers you invitations to wedding showers, baby showers, a birthday party, or a general party invitation. Finally, the Business or Community Event option takes you to designs for grand openings, promotions, and valued customer cards.

6. Click on the Next button to display the second screen, shown in Figure 1.35.

7. Click on the More button to see more choices. Select the first of two Valentine's Day card choices (in the second row from the top); a preview of it appears to the left and a description appears in the lower left corner.

8. Click on Next to proceed.

Figure 1.35

Use the button labeled More to display more holiday card choices.

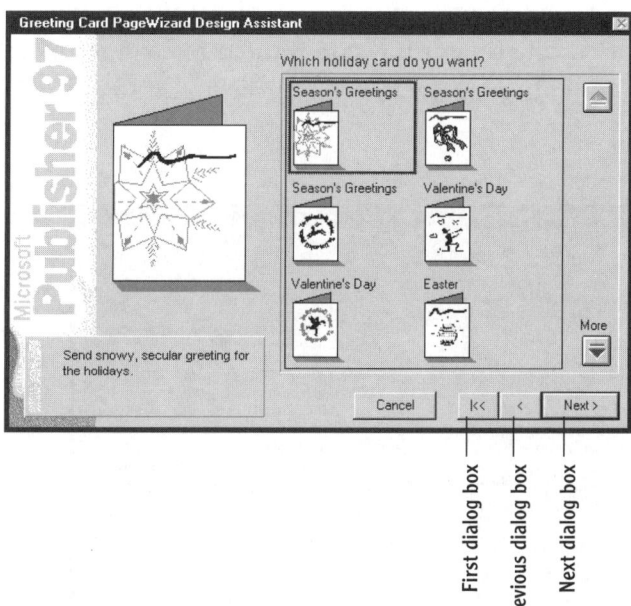

■ ■

TIP Remember, you can use the backward arrow key buttons to move back one step (the single arrow) or to the first step (the double arrow) in a Wizard. You can also cancel at any time by clicking on the Cancel button.

■ ■

9. The next dialog box allows you to make the choice to enter your own greeting, or choose from a list of suggestions. Leave the Yes, please! option checked to let Publisher suggest text, and then click on Next to proceed. You'll see the dialog box shown in Figure 1.36.

10. Click on any of the greetings in the list. Notice that the front of card text and inside text for your selection are displayed to the left.

11. Click on the greeting beginning, "Lean in cause I've got a secret," and then on Next to proceed.

12. The next dialog box (not shown here) offers you the option of putting text on the back of the card. You don't need anything on the back of this card, so click in the check box for No text on the back, thanks.

13. Click on Next to proceed. The final Wizard dialog box appears, ready to create the card. If you wanted to change any of your settings you could use the backward buttons to do so at this point.

Figure 1.36

These phrases provide clever greeting card messages if your creative well has run dry.

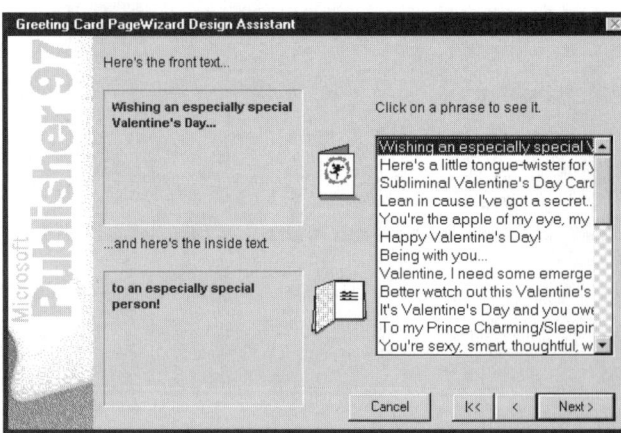

Figure 1.37

Here's your card with the Layout guides hidden.

14. Click on Create It! to create the card.

Publisher takes a moment to build the card and you'll see a little dialog box reporting its progress. When the card is done, Publisher displays one more screen, on which you can choose whether to get step-by-step help with modifying the card or to work on it on your own. Decline the step-by-step help, and your card should appear onscreen, as shown in Figure 1.37.

Display the different pages of the card using the page navigation tools at the bottom of your screen. Notice the first page has text, the inside left side page is blank, and the third page holds the inside greeting. That's all there is to creating a card using a Wizard.

Building on Wizards

So what can you do with a Wizard-generated publication once it's created? Anything you like. You can add or delete elements, replace the current text with your own text, and resize graphics or move them around the page. In fact, you can think of Wizard output either as a complete document or as a starting place for your own design.

Some Wizards for more text-intensive publications such as newsletters or brochures will appear with placeholders for text. It's up to you to replace the placeholder text with your own stories or information. In addition, you might want to take a graphic placed by Publisher and replace it with one more appropriate to your topic. You can do that by simply double-clicking on the graphic and selecting another from the Clip Gallery.

Why Aren't Wizards Enough?

At this point you might be asking yourself: why don't I just use Wizards for everything I want to do and go play hooky for the rest of the weekend? You could, but don't. At some point, you're bound to come across a kind of publication you need that doesn't have a Wizard in Publisher. Also, you'd be confining yourself to using Wizard-generated publications exactly as Publisher creates them, not knowing how to replace text and graphics with more appropriate content. Finally, you'd be denying yourself the power to understand how to use Publisher's simple-to-learn tools to build your own documents from scratch, adding your own flair and creativity to the mix.

TIP One other thing to keep in mind: if you're using Publisher Wizards, so is everyone else! There are only so many Wizard looks you can achieve, and you will begin to see the same graphics and look coming from every Tom, Dick, and Sally. To really produce unique and exciting publications, you need to learn Publisher inside and out.

The bottom line is that Publisher Wizards are great and give you more or less of a head start depending on which type of document you're producing. But stick with me through the rest of this weekend to really become a confident Publisher user, one who can take an everyday document and make it really unique.

To close Publisher, select File, Exit Publisher. When prompted, choose not to save the file.

What's Next

You've done a great job. You've learned about some design rules, picked up what's available in the way of tools and menus in Publisher, explored Publisher Help, and produced a snazzy greeting card (just don't forget to mail it by February 10!). Here's what you have to look forward to tomorrow morning:

- You'll create your first document—a flyer—from scratch, adding, formatting, and editing text.

- You'll learn about using columns and text wrapping to build well-thought-out documents.

- You'll insert pictures and resize them to fit with your text.

- Finally, you'll learn to save and print a Publisher document.

Creating a Flyer

- ✪ Opening a document
- ✪ Formatting text
- ✪ Working with columns and borders
- ✪ Modifying pictures
- ✪ Printing it yourself

Hopefully, you've had your morning coffee and are ready to begin working one-on-one with Publisher. The first project you'll tackle is the creation of a flyer to sell your 1958 Chevy (your spouse wants a new Toyota). In composing this flyer, you'll acquire skills in adding, editing, and formatting text, using columns to organize text, and working with borders to make text stand out. You'll also add a picture or two and print out your document.

As a desktop publisher, it's important that you keep in mind your purpose (in this case, to sell something), recognize your audience (old car buffs looking for a bargain), and then design a publication that will do the job.

Opening a Document

The first step in using Publisher is to open a publication. You went quickly through this process in the previous lesson; take a moment to look at your options a little more closely.

When you first enter Publisher, you are given a choice of creating a new publication using the PageWizard, creating a new publication with a blank page, or opening an existing document.

Opening an Existing Document

Whether you've just opened Publisher or you've already worked with Publisher files, the process to open a previously saved document is similar.

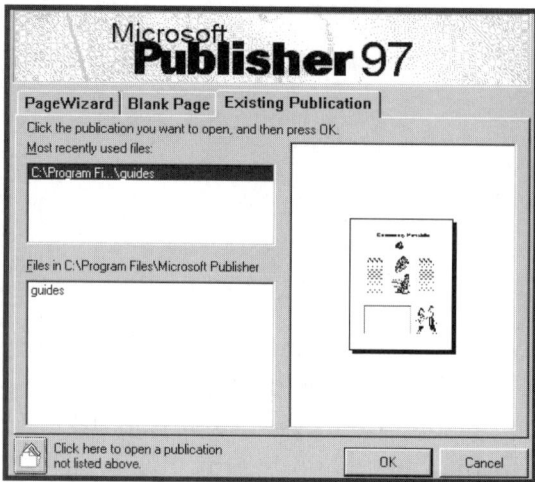

Figure 2.1

When you first open Publisher, this is the dialog box that greets you. Here, the Existing Publication tab is selected.

1. If you already have Publisher open, start by selecting File, Create New Publication; the dialog box that appears is also displayed when you first start Publisher.

2. Click on the Existing Publication tab to select it (see Figure 2.1).

3. If you worked on the document recently, click on it in the list of recently used files. Click on the icon in the lower left corner of the dialog box to open a document that you haven't used recently. The dialog box in Figure 2.2 appears.

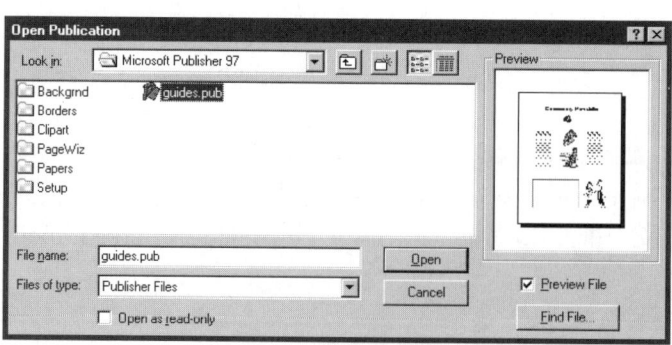

Figure 2.2

The extension for a Publisher file is .pub, and Publisher Files should appear in the Files of type list box.

The Publisher folder will appear by default; you can locate the file you want in a different directory or drive by using the Look in list box and double-clicking on folders to display their contents.

 **NOTE**   You can use the Up One Level button to the right of the Look in list box to move up one level in your computer's hierarchy quickly, or open the Look in list box by clicking on the arrow to its right and selecting a directory or drive from there.

> **4.** Click on Open to open the document.

Closing a Document

Unlike word processors that allow you to have multiple documents open, Publisher can only open one file at a time. If you try to open a second document and haven't saved the changes in the document currently onscreen, you'll get a message asking you to do so. When you respond to the message, the first document will close and the Publisher desktop is ready for a new publication to be opened. To close the first Publisher document you opened without saving it (you'll learn about saving files later), follow these steps:

> **1.** Select File, Close Publication. A dialog box appears asking if you want to save the current document.
>
> **2.** Click on No to close the file without saving changes.

Opening a Blank Document

The first few steps to opening a blank document are the same as when you open an existing document. Follow these steps to open a new document, which you'll use to build the flyer for this session:

> **1.** Start up Publisher, or if Publisher is already open, select File, Create New Publication to get to the New Publication dialog box.
>
> **2.** Click on the Blank Page tab to select it (see Figure 2.3).

Figure 2.3

Not just one blank page style but 10 possibilities greet you on this tab.

Take a moment to look at the different blank page styles shown in Figure 2.3. The Full Page is the standard $8\frac{1}{2} \times 11$ page used for letters and publications such as flyers and newsletters. Some styles, such as the Business Card, differ from the Full Page style in size. Others, such as the Tent Card or Book Fold, assume a fold in the page, but the overall page size is based on the Full Page size. For example, if you were to select Book Fold, you'd be producing a set of four pages: the front page, the inside two pages, and the back page of a folded piece of $8\frac{1}{2} \times 11$ paper.

 **NOTE** If you select a folded blank page style, you'll see a message that the publication layout includes more than one page. This message asks you if Publisher should automatically insert those extra pages. You can reply Yes to this to receive a multipage document, or No for a single page of appropriate dimensions for the folded page.

3. Select the Full Page style by clicking on it.

4. Click on OK to display the blank page.

One other option to note is the Custom Page. You can create your own page layout by clicking on this button; the Page Setup dialog box shown in

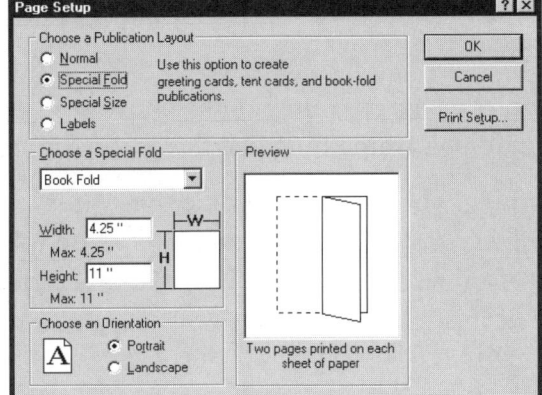

Figure 2.4

Labels is a shortcut to selecting a preset Avery label style from a list provided.

Figure 2.4 appears. Here, you can use the selections and drop-down lists to modify the size and fold used on a publication, and change the orientation between Portrait and Landscape. Portrait is the vertical orientation used in business letters; landscape is oriented with the longer side of the paper along the top. You can also reach this same Page Setup dialog box after you've opened a document by selecting File, Page Setup.

Working with Text

You should now have a blank page open. Are you ready to get creative? The first thing to explore is the use of text in your document. Most documents you create will include text to convey information, persuade your reader, or deliver a message. That text will often be reinforced by visual elements such as pictures or borders. But the text itself is a design element, and you should take as much care in its placement on the page as in your word choice within a sentence.

Entering Text

As you saw in the Friday Evening session, Publisher documents are made up of boxes that contain text, pictures, and so on. To enter text you must first create a container for the text, which is known in Publisher as a *text frame*.

1. Click on the Text Frame tool on the Publisher toolbar.

2. Move your mouse pointer over the blank page; the cursor becomes a crosshair.

3. Click on the page and drag down and to the right to draw a text frame that looks something like the one in Figure 2.5.

Notice a few things about this text frame. First, it is surrounded by small black boxes called *selection handles.* You can click on these and drag in any direction to make the box larger or smaller. For example, if you enter more text than will fit in a text frame, you simply expand it to accommodate all the text.

Also notice that there is a gray box along the bottom of the text frame with a white diamond in it. This is called the *Connect Frame button.* It's used to flow text from one text frame to another. It is very useful in multipage documents such as newsletters, in which a story that begins on one page

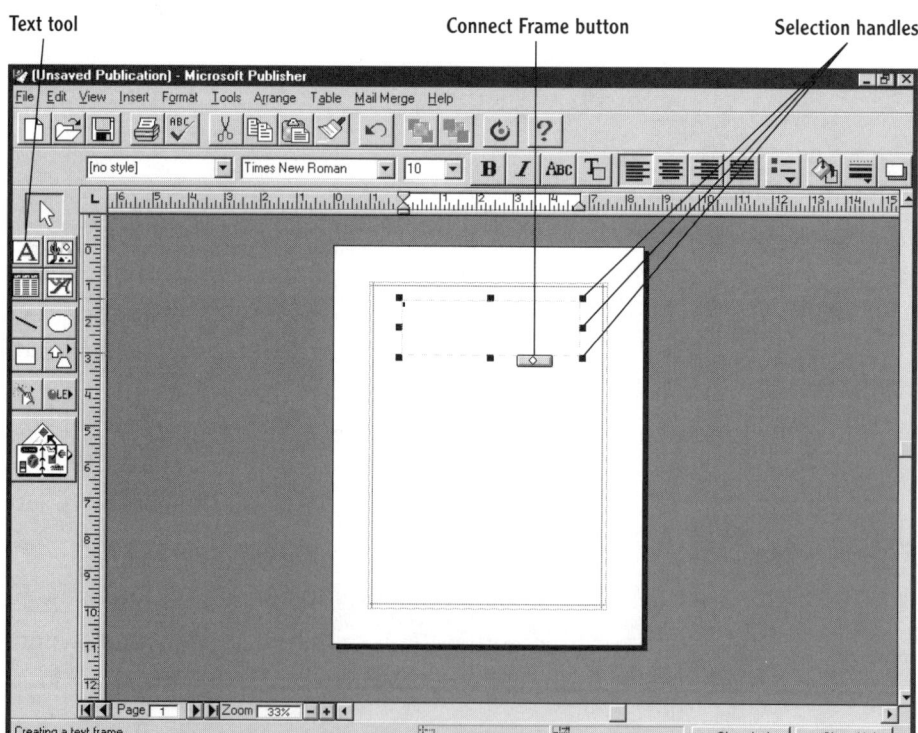

Figure 2.5

Don't worry about the size of the box; you can always resize it later.

may continue on another. You'll learn more about flowing text in the Saturday Afternoon session.

Finally, notice that a blinking insertion point is located in the upper left corner of the text frame. To enter text, you simply begin typing.

1. Start your flyer now by typing **FOR SALE!** (use the Caps Lock key on your keyboard or hold down the Shift key as you type to get full capitals). The insertion point moves along to the right of text as you type.

2. To see your text more clearly, press F9, which zooms your document to 100% of its size. Your document should now look like the one in Figure 2.6.

After you have created a text frame, you can enter text as you would in your favorite word processor. If you make a mistake while typing, you can use

Figure 2.6

The insertion point moves along to the right of text as you type.

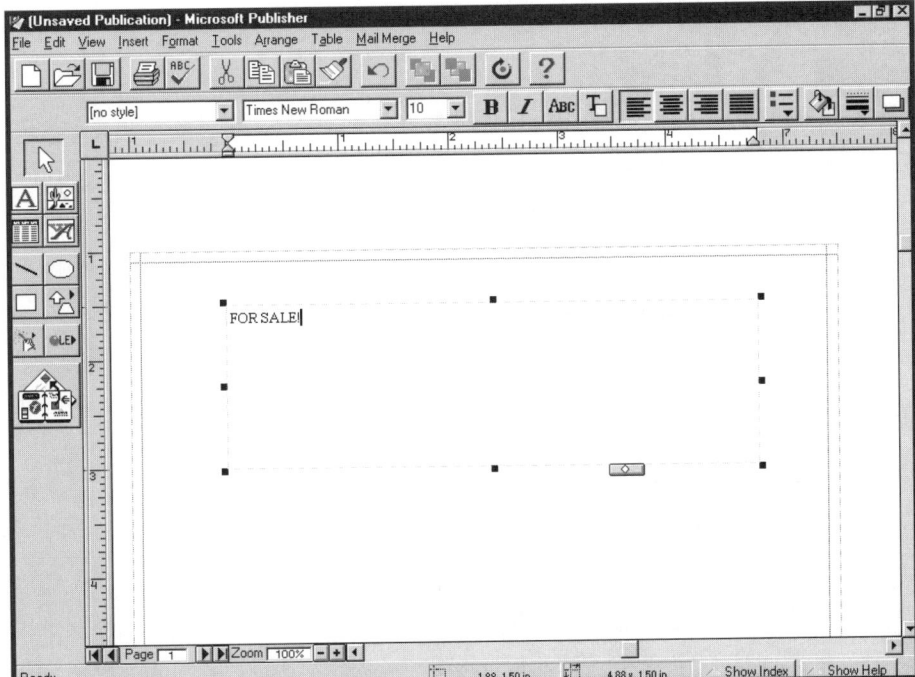

your Backspace key to delete text to the left of the insertion point, and your Delete key to delete text to the right.

TIP Publisher also has an Undo feature, but it undoes only the very last thing you did. Use the Undo tool on the Standard toolbar, or select Edit, Undo, to go back one step.

NOTE Although entering text is simple in Publisher, you may have already saved the text for your publication in a file created in another program. You can skip the chore of retyping all that information by importing a text file. After you've created a text frame, just choose Insert, Text File. The Insert Text File dialog box shown in Figure 2.7 opens. Locate the file you want to insert and click on OK to insert the file in your document. If the text you're importing is more than the selected text frame can hold, you may see a message asking whether Publisher should create additional text frames to place it in. Depending on how much text you're importing, Publisher may even create additional pages in your publication to fit everything.

Resizing, Deleting, and Moving Text Frames

If you're like me, you don't always do it right the first time. That's OK—you can easily resize text frames, delete them, or move them around on

Figure 2.7

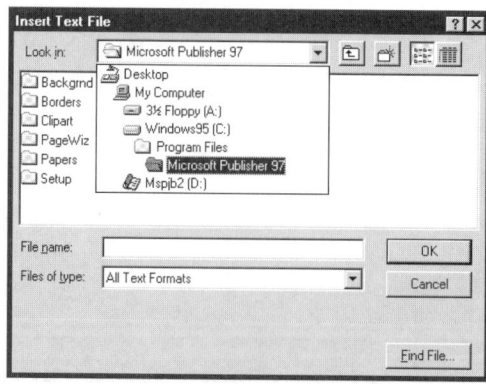

Save yourself the effort of retyping text by inserting an existing text file using the Insert Text File dialog box.

your page. These procedures work with any kind of Publisher frame (both text and pictures). To resize a text frame, follow these steps:

1. Click on any of the frame selection handles.

2. Drag toward the frame's center to make it smaller and outward to make it larger. If you select a perfectly square text frame, for example, and drag on the selection handle to the right, the box will expand to the right. The text frame will then become a rectangle.

TIP To resize a frame and retain its overall proportions, press the Shift key while dragging on a selection handle. In the example in step 2, pressing Shift while dragging would retain the perfect square shape, producing a larger or smaller square.

Erasing mistakes in real life should be as easy as deleting text frames in Publisher: To delete a text frame and all of the text within it, follow these steps:

1. Click on the text frame to select it.

2. Select Edit, Delete Text Frame. Gone!

CAUTION Don't use the Delete key on your keyboard to delete a text frame; this will simply erase the text, leaving the text frame in place.

TIP To delete more than one object on a page, select the first object. Hold down the Shift key and click on any other objects you want to delete. They are all selected as a single object. Select Edit, Delete Object and all of the selected objects disappear.

To move a frame around the page, follow these steps:

1. Click on the text frame to select it.

2. Move your mouse pointer over the edge of the box until the cursor changes into a little moving van, as shown in Figure 2.8.

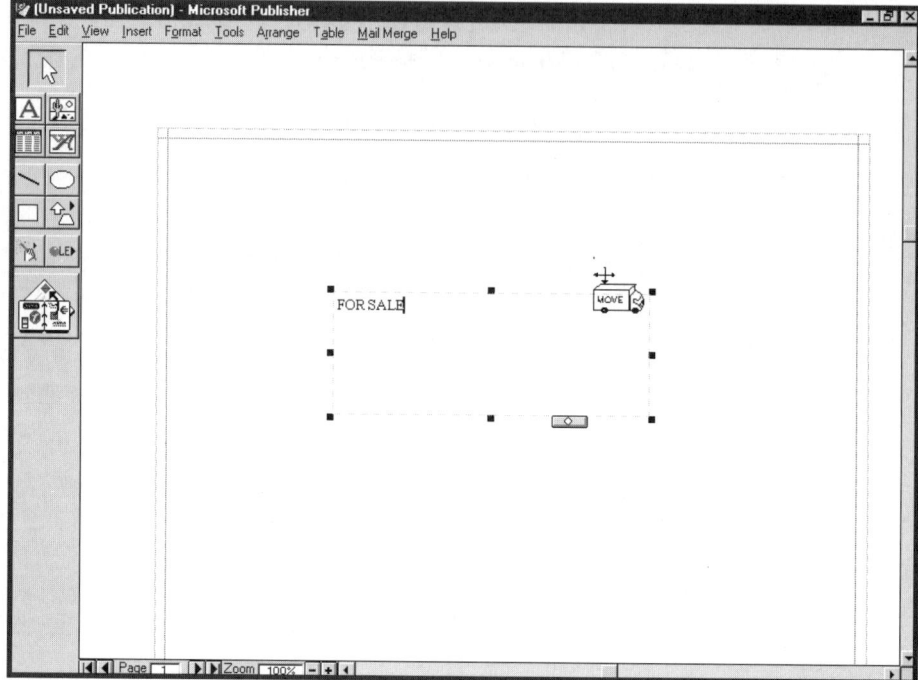

Figure 2.8

The moving van
cursor appears
when you move
your mouse pointer
over an edge of the
text frame.

3. Click and hold your mouse button to drag the frame wherever you'd like on the page.

4. When the frame is where you want it, release your mouse button, and it appears in its new location. Go ahead and practice moving the FOR SALE! text frame.

5. When you've got the hang of moving the text frame, move it back near the top of your page, and you're ready to add more text to your flyer.

Editing Text

Now it's time to create the rest of the text you'll be including. When you enter this text, you'll practice editing it as well.

1. Create a new text frame by using the Text tool.

2. Type this text. Press the Enter key for each semicolon in this list to place a return at the end of each line: **1958 Chevy Corvette**; **Per-**

fect condition; **Red and white; White leather seats; AM radio; Clean upholstery; Only 59,000 miles; Original engine!; Original paint job; Not a spot of rust; Only two owners.** The text frame should look like the one shown in Figure 2.9.

TIP

When you're creating a document like a flyer, consider where it will be read. Someone scanning flyers on a community bulletin board or finding one on their windshield in a parking lot won't spend a lot of time reading. Make your text short and to the point.

NOTE

You don't need to press Enter at the end of a line of text unless each line is a separate thought, as in this list of features. Publisher automatically wraps text for you, making paragraphs fit within the text frame as you type. Press Enter only to start a new paragraph.

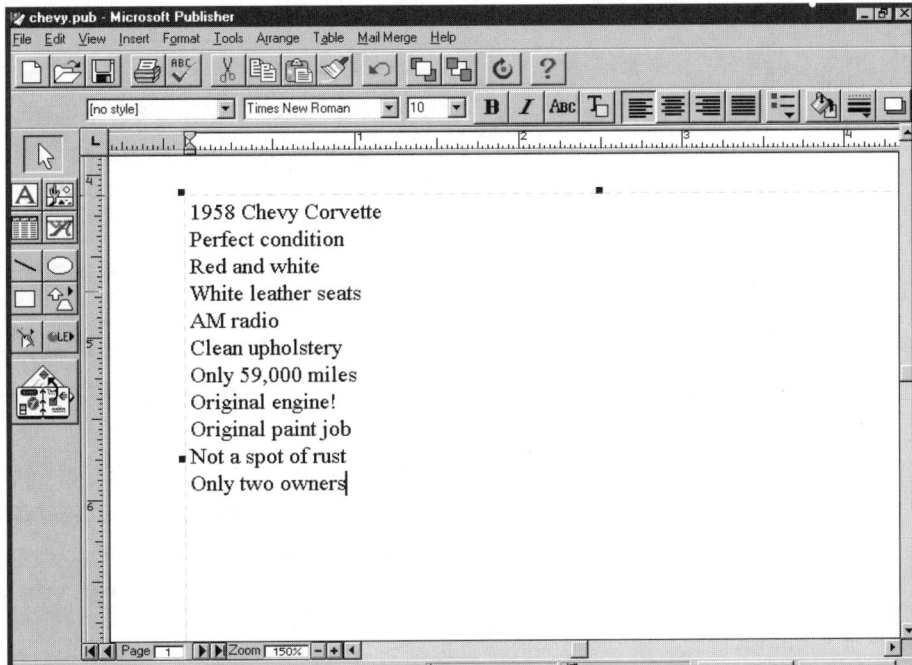

Figure 2.9

Sell your product quickly by prominently listing the best features or benefits in the flyer.

Oops. Doesn't that mileage look suspiciously low for a 40-year-old car? Let's correct the 59,000 figure to read 105,000 by following these steps:

1. Click to the left of the 5 in 59,000 to place your insertion point.

2. Holding down your mouse button, drag to the right until the numbers 5 and 9 are highlighted (this is called *selecting text*).

3. Type **105**. The selected text is replaced by the new text.

You can also use the Delete key to delete text to the right of the cursor, and then type in your new text. If you wanted to add text without replacing what's there, you would simply click to place your cursor where you want the additional text and begin typing.

Publisher offers other standard text editing commands. You can also use the Cut, Copy, and Paste buttons on the Standard toolbar or the corresponding Edit menu commands to cut text to the Windows Clipboard, or copy and paste text into a new location. Just select the text first, and then use any of these three buttons or commands (as you've probably used them in other programs).

TIP Publisher also has a Drag-and-Drop feature for moving selected text, which can be quicker than performing a cut-and-paste operation. To quickly move text, select it, hold down your mouse button, and drag the text to its new location. Release your mouse button to drop the text where you want it to appear on the page.

NOTE When you copy something, Publisher places it on the Windows Clipboard. When you paste, you are actually pasting a copy, but whatever is on the Clipboard is still there until it's replaced by the next thing you cut or copy. That means that if you copy something and want to place multiple copies of it in a document, you can simply continue using the Paste command to place as many copies as you like.

Formatting Text

Up to now you've left your text in the Publisher default entry format; that is, the *font,* or style of type, is Times New Roman, and the font size is 10. This is really boring, and the result is both a creative dead end and tiny text no one can read. Bummer.

But don't worry, you'll fix the style by working with fonts and formatting. Basically, font and font size are to text what musical style and rhythm are to a song: they can change the effect of your document from the slow, old-fashioned feel of a waltz to the zippy swing of reggae, or any other style you might prefer.

What's a Font?

A font is a design style applied to type. Look at this book. It consists of several fonts. The headings are in one font, and the body of the text is in another.

Today there are thousands of fonts from which to choose. They range from business-like to silly. Some fonts even attempt to duplicate handwritten script (the word "script" is usually in the name of these fonts).

Desktop publishers spend many hours trying to select just the right font or combination of fonts to give a publication the right feel. Often, a few fonts will be combined on a page to provide variety or emphasis. For example, look at Figure 2.10; here a font called Goudy Stout has been applied to the FOR SALE! text in the flyer. Because these two words are the attention-getters in this document, the ones that tell the reader the purpose of the flyer, they should appear in this kind of bold, eye-catching font.

Figure 2.10

Thick, bold fonts shout your message at the reader.

Figure 2.11

The fonts with little pictures instead of letters are called *symbol fonts*, because that's what they're made up of.

To apply a different font to your text, follow these steps:

1. Select the FOR SALE! text by clicking to the left of the F and dragging across the letters to highlight the phrase.

2. Click on the down arrow on the right side of the Font list box on the Formatting toolbar. The drop-down list of fonts shown in Figure 2.11 appears.

3. Use the scroll bar on the right of this list to view the different fonts installed on your system. They're likely to differ from what I have on my computer.

4. When you locate one with a similar feel to the one in Figure 2.10, click on it to apply it to the selected text. Some possible options are Impact, Stencil, Braggadocio, or my selection, Goudy Stout.

5. Select all the text you entered in the second text frame.

6. This time, select Format, Character to open the Character dialog box shown in Figure 2.12. Rather than using the individual font formatting tools on the Formatting menu, you can use the Character dialog box to make several changes to the text at once.

7. Use the Font drop-down list to select a different font for this text. Some options to try are Lucida Sans, Tahoma, or MS Sans Serif. These are clean, easy-to-read fonts that work well with short but important text.

8. Click on OK to apply the new font to the text.

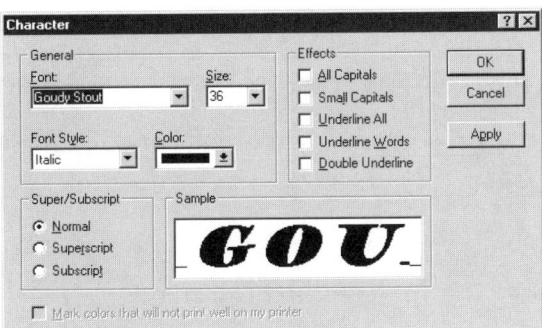

Figure 2.12

Change font, font size, style, color, and effects all in one place from the Character dialog box.

Adjusting Font Size

The next step is to adjust the size of the text. Text size is a tool you can use to place emphasis on one piece of text over another, to fit more information within a limited space, or to make your text stand out—or, in the case of fine print in sales documents and legal contracts, to make it disappear!

A rule of thumb for text size is to aim for readability: don't make text too large or too small to be read easily. Some fonts, when enlarged or reduced, are less easy to read than others. You may not know this until you play around with them in different sizes.

Instead of just trying to make things easier to read, use your understanding of the contents of your publication to put the most important information in a larger type size. Text such as "For Sale," "Free Sample," or headings that mark off the different sections of a report are candidates for larger type sizes.

 TIP Type size is measured in points. A point is a printer's measurement that basically equals $1/72$ of an inch. Most business documents use a 12-point type size. Oddly enough, different fonts of the same size can actually take up different amounts of space on the page. How do you know what you're going to get? Experiment, or use the preview feature in the Character dialog box!

Here's how you adjust text size:

1. Select the FOR SALE! text.

2. Click the arrow on the right of the Font Size list box on the Formatting toolbar.

3. Select 36 from the drop-down list.

4. Select the text in the second text frame.

5. Change the font size to 16, using the Font Size list box on the Formatting toolbar (you can also do this by selecting Format, Character, and making the choice from the dialog box in Figure 2.12).

6. If you can no longer see all of the text in the text frame, click on the bottom selection handle and drag down to enlarge the text frame until all the text is visible.

Your document should now look something like the one in Figure 2.13.

Applying Font Styles and Color

You can do a few other things to text to add some zing to it. You can use color (useful, of course, only if you're printing the document in color) or apply text styles, including bold, italic, and small capitals. To apply color or font styles, you first select the text. Then you can use tools on the Formatting toolbar to easily format the text:

1. Select the FOR SALE! text.

2. Click on the Font Color tool. The drop-down palette in Figure 2.14 appears.

3. Click on one of the colored squares in the palette to apply the color to the text. If you need more colors than the default palette shows, click on the More Colors button.

■ ■

 TIP Using several shades of a color (paler and darker versions of the color) can make a pleasing, consistent color scheme for your document. If you want to apply a shade of a

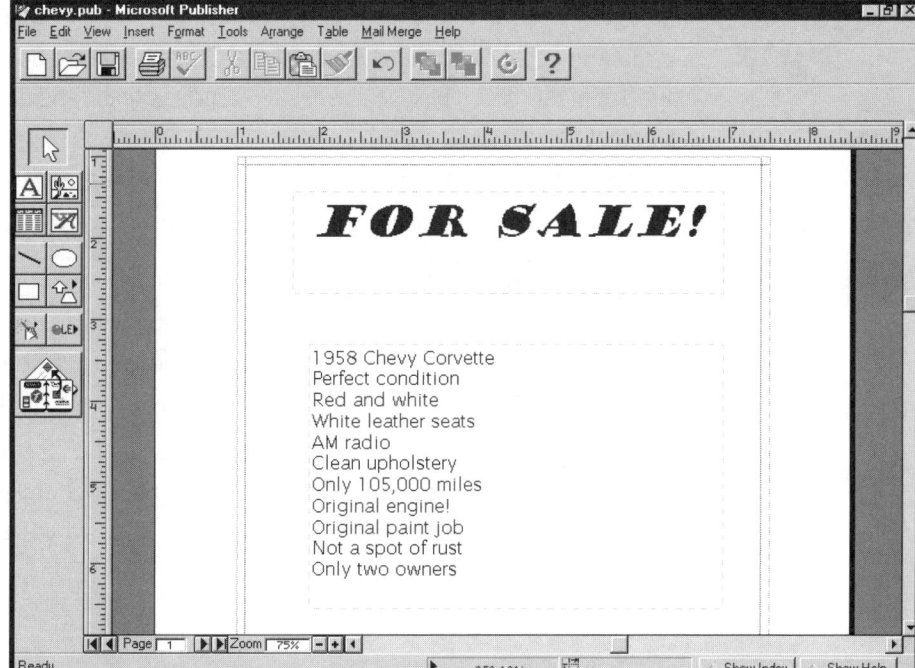

Figure 2.13

With a few easy formatting changes, your flyer begins to take shape.

particular color, click on the Patterns & Shading button on the Font Color palette. From the dialog box that appears you can select various shades of a color.

4. With the FOR SALE! text still selected, click on the Italic button on the Formatting toolbar. The text becomes italicized.

Figure 2.14

Recently used colors will appear at the top of this palette; a shortcut if you use the same colors again and again.

NOTE You can also apply color and styles from the Character dialog box by selecting Format, Character. In this dialog box, you have effects such as single and double underlining, and superscript and subscript.

Working with Bulleted Lists

Right now, you have a long list of points to make about your car. Publisher lets you insert bullets before each point to visually organize your lists. Bullets also make lists more graphically appealing and easier to read.

When you apply a bulleted list style to selected text, a bullet appears at the start of each new paragraph (that is, each place where you've pressed the Enter key to start a new line). Follow these steps to turn a list of information into a bulleted list:

1. Select the car features list.

2. Click on the Bulleted or Numbered List button on the Formatting toolbar (see Figure 2.15).

3. Click on More at the bottom of this list. The Indents and Lists dialog box shown in Figure 2.16 appears.

4. Click on the New Bullet button. The New Bullet dialog box offers various symbols you can use for your bullet (see Figure 2.17).

5. Click on a symbol that appeals to you, and Publisher will enlarge it so that you can see it more clearly. If you want to see more symbols, select a different source for symbols in the Show Symbols From list box.

Figure 2.15

This drop-down list of choices offers several popular styles of bullets.

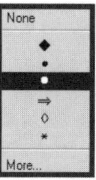

Figure 2.16

You can apply both bulleted and numbered list styles from the Indents and Lists dialog box.

6. Click on OK to place the symbol in the Bullet Type choices in the Indents and Lists dialog box.

7. Change the bullet point size to 12 by clicking on the up arrow next to the size text box.

8. Click on OK to apply the bullet style to your list. After you click outside the text frame to deselect it, your text should look something like the text in Figure 2.18.

TIP Bullets work well for lists that have no particular order or priority; numbered lists, which can be applied from the same dialog box you just used, are better for listing a series of steps, a sequence, or a list organized from lowest to highest (or vice versa).

Figure 2.17

Various fonts provide symbols that you can use for bullets.

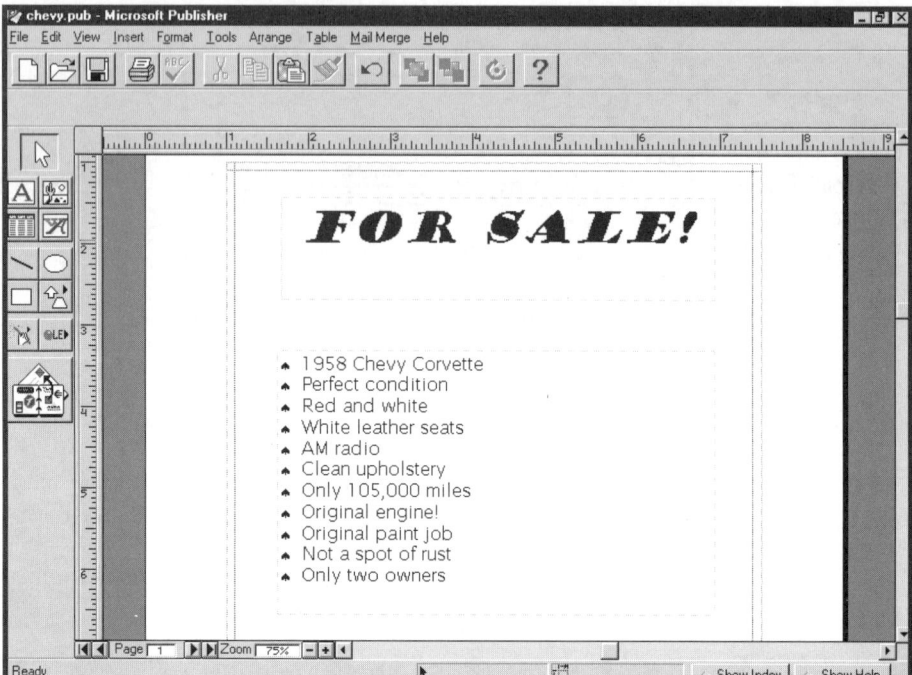

Bullets draw the
reader's eye to each
point in the list.

Save Your Work and Take a Break

OK, you've earned it. Take a quick breather before you move on from
working with text to adding some fun design elements such as borders and
pictures to your flyer. Stretch, contemplate all you've accomplished, and
come back refreshed and ready to get creative! However, before you take
your break, it's a good idea to save your document, just to be safe. Follow
these simple steps:

1. Select File, Save.

2. In the Save As dialog box that appears, use the Save in list box to
    locate the drive and directory where you want to save the file; the
    default is the Publisher directory.

3. Enter a name in the File name list box. The file extension for a Pub-
    lisher file format is .pub; this will be added to the filename you enter

automatically, as long as the Save as type list box is designated Publisher Files.

4. Click on Save to save your file.

That wasn't so bad, was it? Now, when you want to save the file again, which you should do regularly, just click on the Save button on the Standard toolbar. Any changes since the last save will be saved without the use of the Save As dialog box again.

NOTE If you want to save a file with a different name after you've saved it the first time, select File, Save As, and give the file a new name. Both the original saved file and the file with a new name will now be available to you.

Working with Columns and Borders

The fonts you apply to your text are crucial in the creation of a well-designed product that communicates effectively. It's also useful to know how to use devices to structure that text on the page. Columns let you place information side by side, and they break up long lines of text to make scanning a longer document easier on the reader. Borders can range from plain to fancy, and they set off text by surrounding the words with a visible frame and drawing the reader's eye to important points. In this section, you'll master using both columns and borders.

Modifying a Text Frame to Add Columns

Columns are a familiar fixture in newsletters and newspapers. They work very well with documents that have to present a variety of information, such as classified ads or a series of unrelated stories in the newspaper.

However, columns can also be used to place lengthy lists of information side by side, such as the one in your flyer, to make better use of space on the page. Try modifying the list of car features to flow in two columns by following these steps:

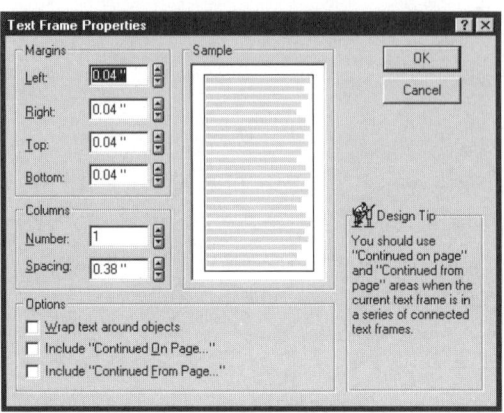

1. Right-click on the text frame which contains the bulleted list.

2. From the shortcut menu that appears, select Text Frame Properties. The dialog box in Figure 2.19 appears.

3. Click on the up arrow next to the Columns, <u>N</u>umber text box to change to a two-column setting.

4. Click on OK to apply the column setting. If your original text frame is tall, all of the bullets probably still fit in the first column.

5. To place the bullet points in two side-by-side columns and make the best use of space, resize the text frame by clicking on the bottom selection handle and dragging upward until the text flows as shown in Figure 2.20.

Applying a Border to Text

The FOR SALE! text is the key to establishing the purpose of this document and catching the reader's attention, so you might want to set it off with a border design. Borders surround the text frame with anything from a simple line to fancy design elements using pictures, such as flowers or balloons.

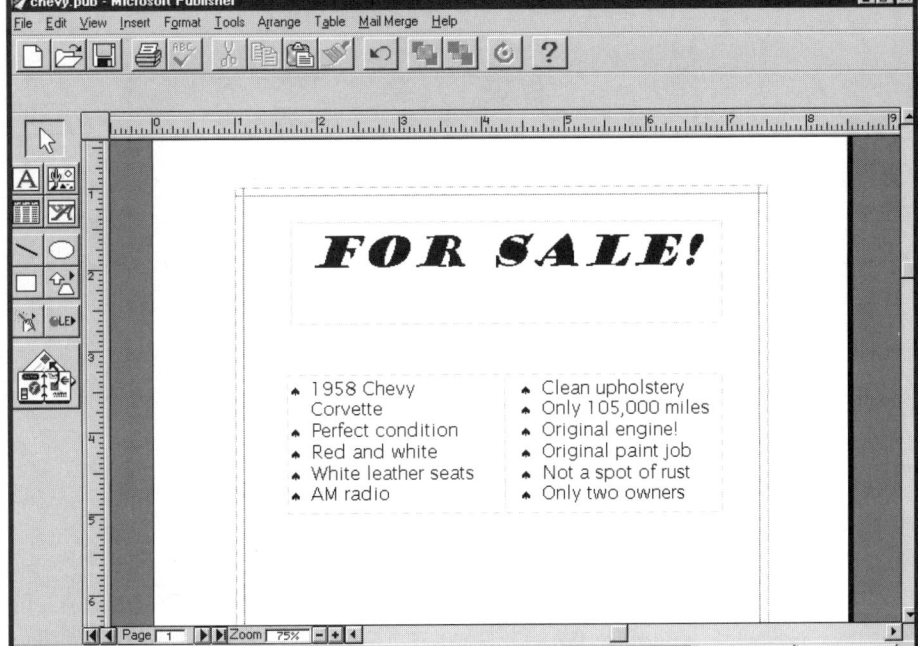

Figure 2.20

Fit more information across your page by modifying the text frame to make the best use of columns.

CAUTION Be careful that a more elaborate border design doesn't distract the reader's attention from the text within it. Match the style of the border to the message.

Applying a border to a text frame or picture frame is simple:

1. Select the frame by clicking on it.

2. Select Format, Border. The BorderArt dialog box shown in Figure 2.21 is displayed.

3. Click on the 8 pt Thickness sample.

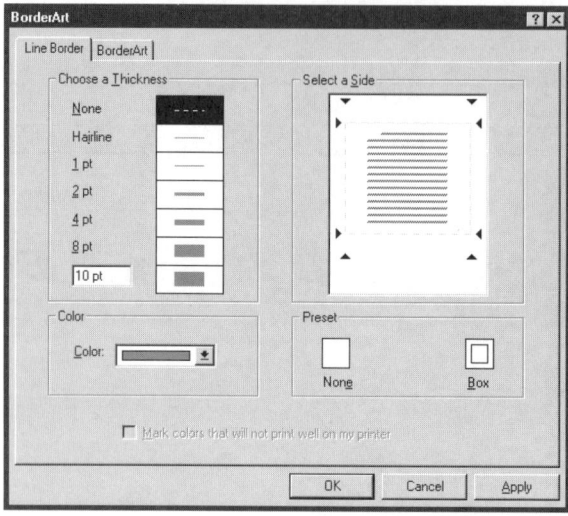

Figure 2.21

You can apply a border to the entire frame, or only to selected sides using the BorderArt dialog box.

 **NOTE** If you want to apply a border to only one side of a frame, select that side by clicking on it in the Select a Side preview. If you don't select a side, the border settings you make will be applied to the entire frame.

4. Click on the BorderArt tab to select it. It's shown in Figure 2.22.

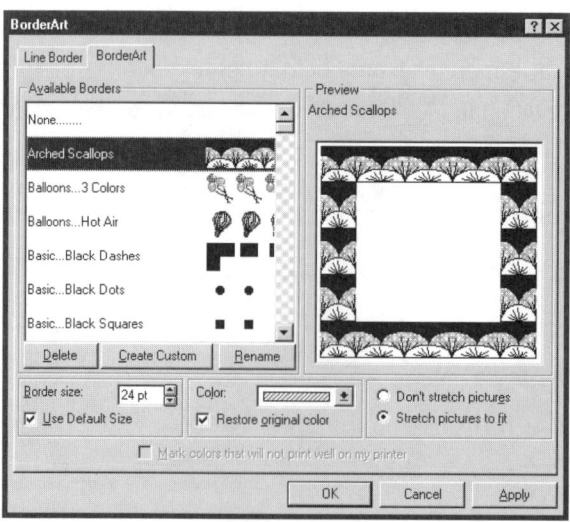

Figure 2.22

Choices of borders range from simple to silly.

5. Take a moment to scroll down the list of Available Borders until you see the one called Checkered (this resembles the finishing flag for a car race, so subliminally it suggests to the reader a car with great speed); click on this choice.

NOTE
When you choose a BorderArt style, any size setting you've made on the other tab of this dialog box may be overridden. That's because the images in BorderArt just won't show up unless the border itself is a minimum width. In this example, your 8 pt. setting changes to 10 pt. when you select the Checkered BorderArt style.

6. Click on OK.

7. Click outside the frame to deselect it, and your flyer should look like the one in Figure 2.23. You can resize the frame as you like to make the text fit, or have the frame fill more of the page from side to side.

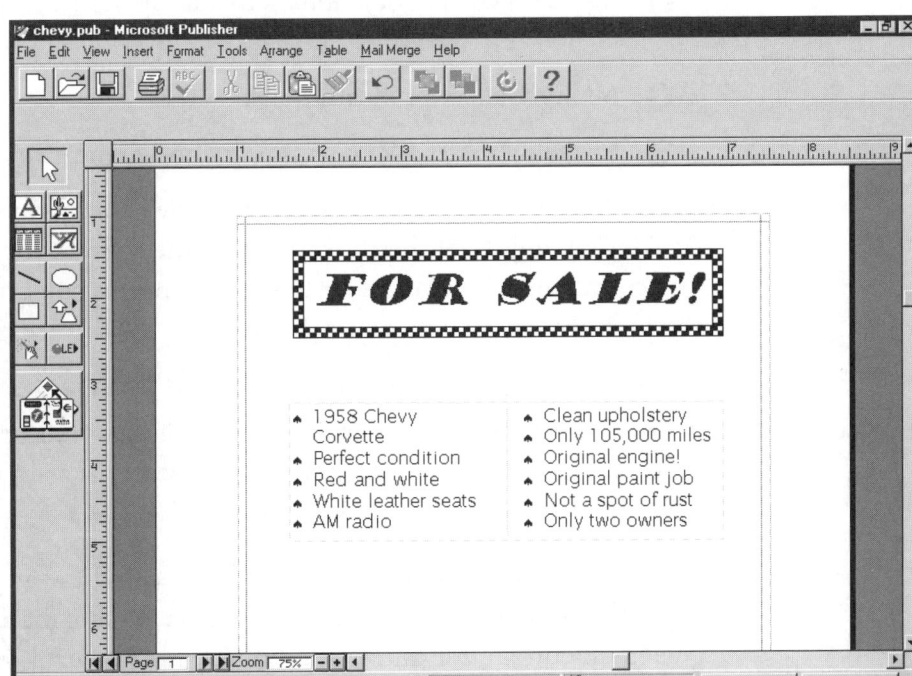

Figure 2.23

The border calls attention to the key message and suggests the thrill of car racing to the reader.

Adding Pictures

You've paid a lot of attention to the text and its format and organization on your page. You've added a border design to create a little excitement. But what about other visual elements? For example, how about a picture or two? It's said that pictures are worth a thousand words. That's what this section is all about: adding images that reinforce your message and make your publication interesting to look at.

Working with Graphics

Graphics is a universal term for visual elements in a document. Graphics can include simple line drawings, photographs, and everything in between. Actually, the border design you just applied is a graphic element. Publisher has several of these graphic elements built right in. You can use these any way you like. These include:

- ✿ BorderArt, which you've just seen.

- ✿ A Design Gallery of graphics, including headings, pull quotes, ornaments, and Web page buttons.

- ✿ A Clip Gallery of illustrations.

- ✿ Several graphics files containing photographic images.

In addition, you can insert any graphics file, from a photograph to a line drawing, in any Publisher document. Some sources for graphics files are CD collections of art you can purchase or images you can download from the Internet.

 **CAUTION**
Be careful to get proper permissions to use graphic images in your documents. Many are protected by copyright laws and require credit to the creator and a fee for use.

Graphics can be inserted in two ways. You can draw a picture frame and insert the graphic into it, or you can insert a graphic file and Publisher will give it a picture frame automatically. You can't control the initial location

of the image and its frame if you let Publisher create the frame. On the other hand, it's easy to move a graphic wherever you like after it's on your page, so how you insert a picture is really up to you.

TIP Drawing a picture frame first provides one more shortcut; after you draw the frame, you can simply double-click anywhere within it to open the Insert Picture File dialog box. You can use this to locate and insert a graphic file.

Inserting Clip Art

Try placing a graphic in the flyer by using the Clip Gallery of images that is built into Publisher. Because you're trying to sell a car, something in the automotive line ought to fit the bill.

1. Click on the Picture button on the Publisher toolbar.

2. Click on the bottom half of the flyer page and drag to draw a rectangular picture frame.

3. Select Insert, Clip Art. The Microsoft Clip Gallery shown in Figure 2.24 appears.

Figure 2.24

You can even import a clip and include it in the Clip Gallery; this same gallery is used by all Microsoft Office products.

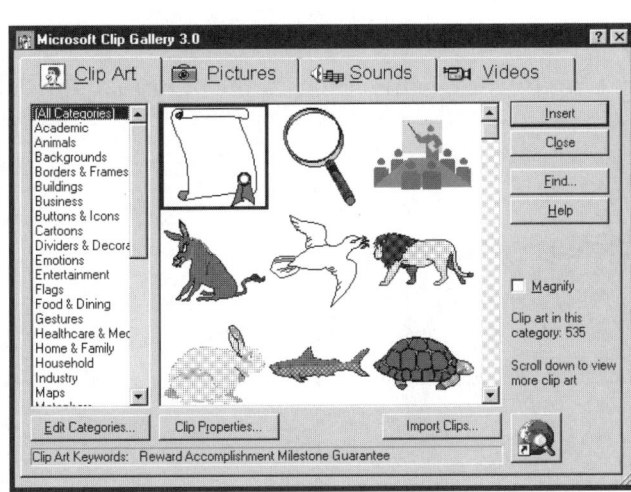

4. Use the scroll bar next to the list of categories to locate the category, "Transportation." The preview of images in the center of the dialog box changes to show only those within that category.

5. Click on the image of a '50s-style car (you may need to use the scroll bar to the right of the images to find it).

6. Click on Insert to place the picture in your flyer.

NOTE Notice that there are three other tabs in the Clip Gallery besides Clip Art: Pictures, Sounds, and Videos. Publisher provides some photos accessible from the Pictures tab; the Sounds and Videos tabs are empty, but you can place your own files in there by importing them. After you do, they'll be available to you any time you need them.

Because a frame you've predrawn isn't likely to precisely fit the dimensions of a graphic, you'll probably see the Import Picture dialog box shown in Figure 2.25 when you insert clip art. You can choose to change the frame to fit the picture or the picture to fit the frame. Be aware that if you modify the picture instead of the frame, the image may appear somewhat distorted. For now, leave the default and allow Publisher to modify the frame.

7. Click on OK to place the picture.

Now that you have several objects on the page, you might want to press F9 at this point or use the Zoom settings at the bottom of the Publisher window to

Figure 2.25

Publisher prompts you to get a perfect fit of frame to picture.

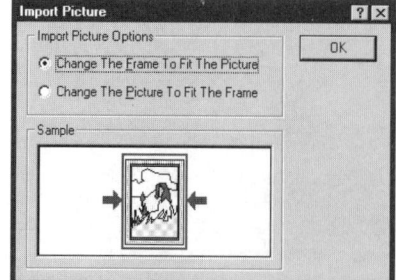

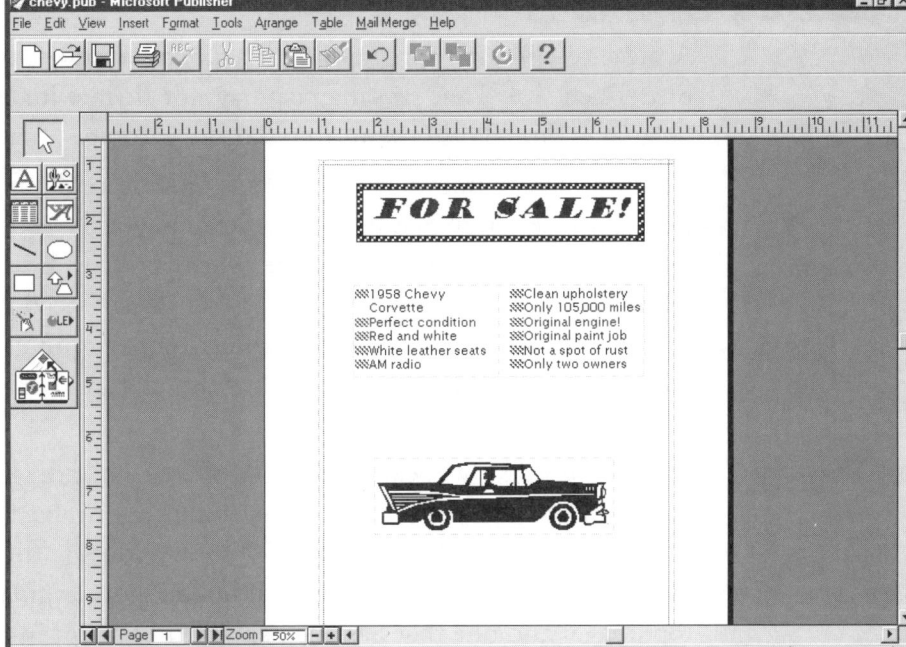

Figure 2.26

With border art and a clip art image, the flyer takes on more visual interest.

see the overall design of your document better. It should look something like the page in Figure 2.26.

NOTE Deleting a picture frame is a little different from deleting a text frame. If there's a picture in the frame you select, when you press the Delete key you delete both the frame and picture. (With text, pressing Delete only gets rid of the text, not the frame.) You can also use the Edit, Delete Object command to delete the picture and its frame.

Modifying Pictures

After you've placed a picture in a document, you have a lot of freedom in modifying its size and location, and even adding color to it. Use those abilities to make sure the graphic balances and supports the text in your publication. It shouldn't overwhelm the text.

Resizing Graphics

A piece of clip art or a graphic file will come into your publication at a predefined size. That size may or may not fit in with the design of your document. You'll often want to resize the graphic.

Resizing picture frames is the same as resizing text frames: you click and drag on the selection handles in the direction you'd like the frame to stretch. However, there's one key difference: when you stretch a text frame, the text within it doesn't change. That is, the text doesn't become larger or appear stretched out—it just has more or less room around it. With a picture frame, stretching the frame stretches the picture. This can make for an image that appears distorted.

To deal with that, you can press the Shift key while dragging on a selection handle. The picture will retain its overall proportions, but will simply become bigger or smaller. Figure 2.27 shows you the difference between a picture that has been resized without retaining its original proportions (the top image) and one that has been enlarged but kept in proportion.

If you'd like, you can modify the size of the clip art you inserted by using the selection handles. Keep it to about the size of the image shown in Figure 2.26, and retain its original proportions by using the Shift key as you resize it.

Adding Color

If you can either print in color yourself or have your publications printed in color by a printing service, you can add tremendous impact with color.

Figure 2.27

Sometimes the distorted, almost cartoon-like look on the top is appropriate— sometimes it's not.

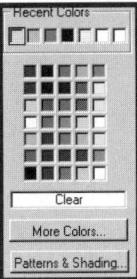

Figure 2.28

The More Colors and Patterns & Shading buttons work exactly the same as the buttons in the Font Color palette.

For selling in particular, a splash of red or yellow can draw attention to your ad or flyer ahead of the others that may surround it in a newsletter or on a bulletin board.

When you select a picture and add color, you are actually adding color to the frame itself, in effect providing a colored background to the picture. Try that now with your car clip art.

1. Click on the car picture frame to select it. A picture formatting toolbar appears just below the Standard toolbar.

2. Click on the Object Color button on the picture formatting toolbar. A drop-down palette appears—you'll recognize it from the Font Color tool you used earlier this morning (see Figure 2.28).

3. Click on a yellow color square. The background color is applied to the picture frame.

4. Click outside the picture frame to see the color applied, as shown in Figure 2.29.

Arranging Things

Things are looking pretty good for your flyer: you've used fonts and formatting intelligently to get your message across, and a border and picture to add some visual appeal. But there's something important missing. How the heck are all these anxious buyers going to get in touch with you to buy the darn thing? You need to add a phone number. To add this element, you'll get some practice at arranging elements on your Publisher page.

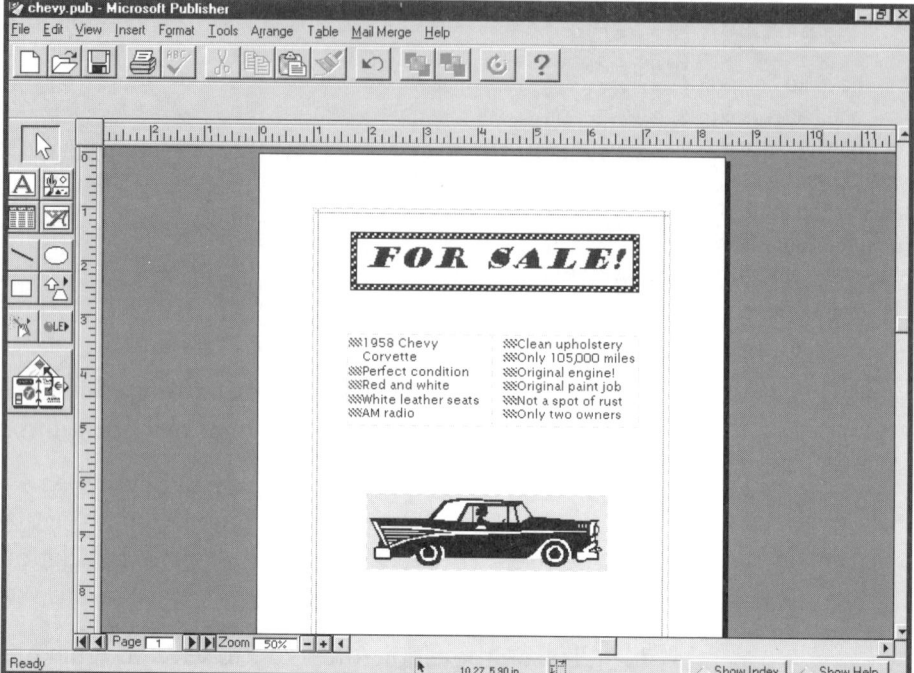

Figure 2.29

Color can make an
illustration look
crisper and more
dramatic on the
printed page.

Assuming you're going to post this flyer on a local community center bulletin board, you might want to use the gimmick of multiple tear-off versions of your phone number that people can take home with them for reference. These little phone numbers typically line up along the bottom of a flyer, like the one shown in Figure 2.30.

You can achieve the effect shown in Figure 2.30 in a few different ways. One would be to create a text frame, type a phone number in it, rotate the text frame, and then make several copies of it. You'd have to line up each text box along the bottom of the page and be sure to apply a border to each box.

You're going to try a second approach: you'll create one text frame with the phone numbers typed into it like a long list. Then, you'll rotate the single text box to fit sideways along the bottom of the page. Finally, you'll draw simple rectangles to surround each of the successive phone numbers. This method is a little easier because objects you draw, such as a square, are a bit easier to line up than text frames.

Figure 2.30

Don't ever forget to
include contact
information
where needed!

When you've finished creating and rotating these objects, you'll then group
the rectangles with the text frame, so the whole thing, the phone numbers
and the rectangles surrounding them, can be treated as a single object.
Grouping saves you from having to move each individual piece of a group
of objects separately, and maintains the relative positions of all of the pieces
of the object.

Rotating

You might want to rotate an object on a page for many reasons. You might
want text to appear like a banner across the corner of a page, as in Figure
2.31. Or you might rotate an object so that it can fit next to other objects
on the page. Some pictures—airplanes, for example—seem to take on a
sense of motion when tipped up or down on the page. You can even rotate
pictures so they reverse direction: a silhouette of a face that came in facing
left can be made to face right by rotating it 180 degrees. Start your practice
with rotating by following these steps to create a list of phone numbers:

Figure 2.31

Banners call out
important offers or
information,
catching the eye
like bunting on a
Fourth of July float.

1. Click on the Text tool and draw a text frame about seven inches long by two inches wide. Use the vertical and horizontal rulers to judge the size as you draw the frame.

2. Type **555-9876**.

3. Select the text you just typed, and format it to use the Arial font in 22-point size.

4. Press Enter two times, and then type **555-9876** again. Repeat this step until you have eight phone numbers, with a double space between each. (Of course, you could also copy the one phone number and paste it seven times, but with such short text it's often just as easy to type it; it's up to you!)

5. Select the text frame.

6. Select Arrange, Rotate/Flip.

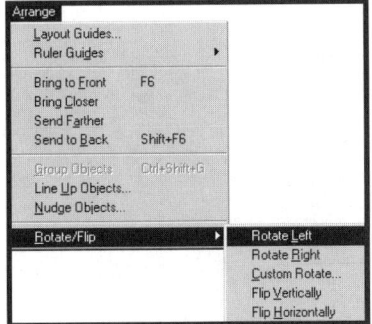

Figure 2.32

You can choose to either flip or rotate an object from this cascading menu.

7. From the cascading menu that appears (see Figure 2.32), select Rotate Left. The text box should now be sideways on the page, with the left side of the box along the bottom.

There are actually three other methods of rotating. If you want a simple 90-degree rotation to the left or right, or to flip an object 180 degrees vertically or horizontally, the method you just used is quickest because those preset increments are accessible through the commands on the Arrange menu. However, you can also move objects in much smaller increments by selecting the Custom Rotate command from the Rotate/Flip cascading menu, or by using one of these two methods:

- Select the object to be rotated and click on the Rotate button on the Standard toolbar. The Rotate Objects dialog box shown in Figure 2.33 appears. Use either the buttons to rotate to the left or right in five-degree increments; or, use the arrow buttons next to the Angle text box to adjust by increments of one degree.

- Press the Alt key and move your mouse pointer over any selection handle until the cursor changes to a circle with two arrows. Click and drag the handle to the left or right to rotate the frame as far as you like in either direction.

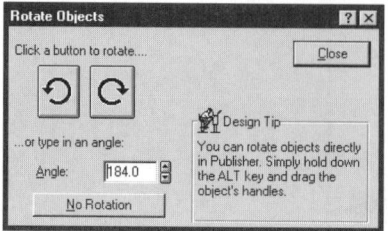

However you do it, your flyer should now look like the one in Figure 2.34.

Lining Up Things

Now it's time to draw the little rectangles to surround the phone numbers and line them up along the bottom of the page, suggesting to people that

Figure 2.34

It's a good idea to
make a phone
number bold and in
large type so it
can't be missed.

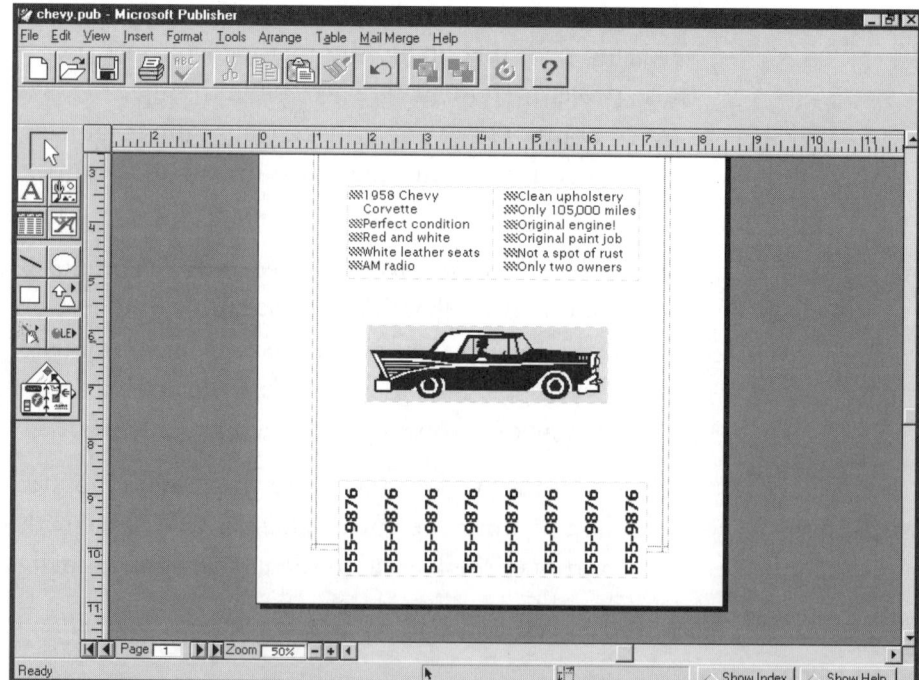

they can tear off one number at a time. You'll learn more about drawing later in this book; for now, you'll draw a single rectangle, and then copy and paste it. Then you'll work with a couple of features of Publisher to line up the boxes.

1. Click on the Box button on the Publisher toolbar.

2. Click on the desktop area outside your flyer and drag to draw a rectangle about two inches tall and half an inch wide.

3. With the rectangle selected, click on the Copy tool, and then on the Paste tool. This pastes a copy of the rectangle on top, but a little to the side of the original.

4. Click on the Paste tool six more times. You should now have eight rectangles.

5. The top rectangle should be selected. Move the mouse pointer over the rectangle until the moving van cursor appears; move the rectangle and place it over the far right phone number.

6. Repeat the previous step until you've placed a rectangle over each number.

When you move drawing objects on a page, they snap to an invisible grid; because of this, the tops of all the rectangles are probably pretty well lined up at this point. However, if they're not, you can use a little trick to line them up exactly.

1. Click on one box to select it.

2. Press the Shift key and, holding it down, click on each of the other boxes to select them in turn. Each selected object will have gray selection handles.

3. When they're all selected, choose Arrange, Line Up Objects. The dialog box in Figure 2.35 appears.

4. Click on the Top Edges option button in the Top to Bottom section of this dialog box. The Sample shows you how the objects will be aligned.

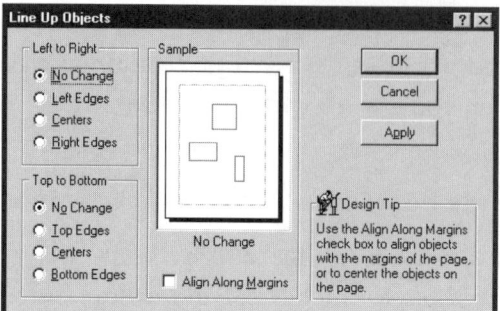

Figure 2.35

You can organize objects on a page in several ways using these settings.

5. Click on OK. If there was any variation in the alignment of the boxes from top to bottom, they should be in perfect alignment now.

Nudge, Nudge

Now, there's one more thing to look at before you make the phone number elements into a single object. In moving the rectangles into place, you may not have them evenly spaced across the page: there may be a little more space between some boxes and a little less between others. There's no short-cut here to assure perfect spacing; however, there is a feature called *nudging* that lets you fine-tune this spacing yourself.

1. Select a rectangle that's a little too far to the left or right.

2. Select Arrange, Nudge Objects. The dialog box in Figure 2.36 appears.

3. Click on the right or left arrow control to nudge the rectangle slightly in that direction. If you'd like to nudge in larger or smaller increments, you can select the Nudge By check box and enter a specific measurement.

TIP You can also select the object, and then press the Alt key and a directional arrow on your keyboard to nudge an object in that direction.

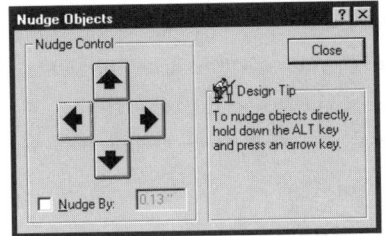

Figure 2.36

You can nudge objects up, down, left, or right.

Forming Groups

After all that nudging, I'll bet you're ready for something easy. You'll be glad to hear that grouping things is a piece of cake.

1. Click on the text frame to select it (click somewhere between the rectangles so that you don't select one of them by mistake).

2. Press the Shift key and click on the edge of each of the rectangles in turn until they're all selected.

3. Select Arrange, Group Objects.

4. With the single object selected, you can move it slightly up or down on the page; all of its elements move together and retain their positions relative to the other elements.

That's it. You can also format, rotate, or delete grouped objects just as you would a single object, making working with the various pieces much easier. To ungroup an object, just reverse the process: select the single object, and then select Arrange, Ungroup Objects. Each element that makes up the object will now return to being a separate object that you can move, delete, or format separately.

Take a Break

You're almost there, so stop complaining about those hunger pangs; you'll have some lunch soon enough. Before you do, check your document for errors and print it out so that you can see what it looks like up close. (OK, if you really must, go grab an apple now to tide you over).

> **TIP** It's probably a good idea to save your document at this point so that you don't lose anything while you've got your head stuck in the refrigerator!

Finalizing Your Document

OK—home stretch. But what you're about to do is every bit as important as making that last sprint from third base to home: you're going to check the details to make sure your flyer is ready for prime time.

Publisher contains several tools to help you check to see that you've followed the rules of good design, spelled everything just right, and have words hyphenated properly.

Using Design Checker

Design Checker is like having Publisher run through a quick checklist of good design for you. Built-in rules about things such as the number of fonts to use on a single page, the proportions of pictures, the way text fits in a text frame, and more are checked against your document. When Publisher finds something out of sync with those design rules, it notifies you with a dialog box. To see how the Design Checker works, try changing one thing on your flyer:

1. Select the picture of the car, and drag on a selection handle to resize it without retaining its original proportions.

2. To run the Design Checker, select Tools, Design Checker. The Design Checker dialog box, shown in Figure 2.37, is displayed.

Figure 2.37

If you only want to check a page or two of your document, change the Pages range.

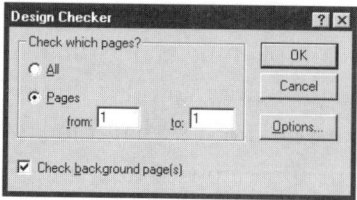

By default, Publisher checks the full range of pages in your publication. You can run a check on just a certain page or a range of pages by typing those page numbers in the from: and to: text boxes.

NOTE The Check <u>b</u>ackground page(s) item refers to Publisher's background, which is discussed in a later session. Publisher allows you to place items that repeat on all pages of the publication on the background. This works a bit like headers and footers in word processor documents. If you don't want the background elements included in the Design Check, click on the Check <u>b</u>ackground page(s) check box to deselect it.

3. If you want to look at and modify the things that Design Checker looks for in your document, you can click on the Options button in the Design Checker dialog box. This displays the Options dialog box shown in Figure 2.38.

4. Publisher will check for any item with a check mark; to stop Publisher from checking for any of these items, click on its check box to deselect it.

5. Click on OK to return to the Design Checker dialog box, and click on OK to proceed with the check.

Figure 2.38

If you know you've done some of the things on this list, save yourself time by changing these options before running the check.

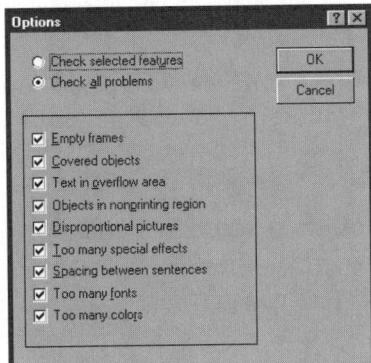

Figure 2.39

Publisher questions
whether you meant
to make this
graphic
disproportionate
in size.

The dialog box in Figure 2.39 appears. You can ignore the problem just this once or all instances of it by clicking on the Ignore or Ignore All buttons, respectively. You can get a further explanation of the problem by clicking on Explain, or you can let Publisher resize the picture to its original proportions by clicking on Change. Click on Change now, and then on Continue. Because that should be the only design problem in your flyer, you see a dialog box that says the Design Checker is complete.

CAUTION　Don't take this all too seriously: Design Checker is just a set of rules. It's not Picasso and it's not your boss. If you are aware that you did something like using four fonts on a single page and you feel that your design works, feel free to ignore Design Checker. But at least by running it, you may catch some things you didn't do intentionally, and learn a thing or two about design.

Check Your Spelling!

Come on, you knew you couldn't escape this one. So you weren't the best speller in your class in fourth grade. Just remember to run Publisher's Check Spelling feature, and you'll be all set (of course, it's still a good idea to proofread your document yourself to catch that time you typed "there" when you meant "they're").

Now, I didn't lead you astray and have you spell something wrong as you entered the text for this flyer (which isn't to say that you didn't lead yourself astray when you typed it). But to be sure you can see how stellar Publisher's Check Spelling is, go ahead and add an extra "t" to the word "Corvette." Then, start your spelling check:

1. Select the text frame containing the mistake.

2. Select Tools, Check Spelling or click on the Spelling button on the Standard toolbar. The dialog box in Figure 2.40 appears.

3. Click on Change to correct your error. Publisher tells you that Check Spelling is complete.

4. Click on OK to return to your perfectly designed, perfectly spelled flyer.

The other options available when you're running the Check Spelling feature are the following:

- To Ignore this instance of the mistake or Ignore All instances of it in the document.

- To Add the apparent misspelling to Publisher's dictionary so it won't flag it as an error in future. You might want to do this with unrecognized proper names or acronyms (like NAFTA).

- Change All changes not only this instance of the problem, but any instance of it anywhere in the document. Be careful with this one, some things are incorrect in one context but correct in another.

Figure 2.40

Publisher is even smart enough to know Detroit's finest has gone wrong when it sees it.

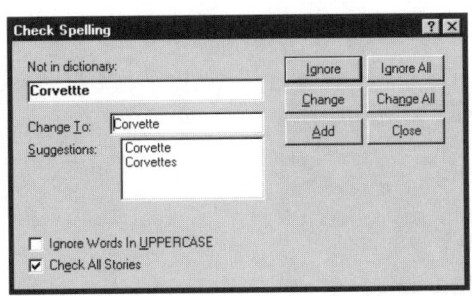

✿ Close stops the Check Spelling function and closes the dialog box without making any changes.

Hyphenation

Publisher handles hyphenation automatically by default. However, if you're finding that it's causing some odd breaks in lines in your final document, you do have some options.

Select Tools, Hyphenate. The dialog box in Figure 2.41 appears. Here you can turn off automatic hyphenation, get an opportunity to confirm each hyphenation Publisher intends to make, or change the hyphenation zone. This zone controls how ragged the right end of lines of text can be. A smaller number here makes the right margin more evenly aligned, but can result in a lot more hyphens. A larger number gives you a kind of jagged right margin, but you'll cut down on hyphens.

Printing It Yourself

OK, you're ready to print your flyer: that car's not going to sell itself. In most cases, the whole point of desktop publishing is to produce a printed product.

The basic variable in printing is whether you intend to print to a local or networked printer, or you want to send your document to an outside printing service to print for you.

When printing your own Publisher document, you need to designate the printer you want to print to, set up the quality, color, and orientation of the output, and make decisions about things such as how many copies to print and which pages in your document to print. You'll use a couple of different dialog boxes in the process.

Figure 2.41

Documents with multiple columns of text are especially susceptible to too many hyphens.

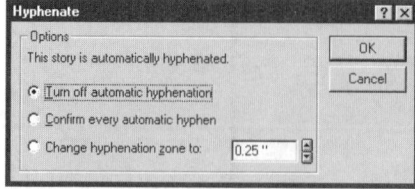

NOTE Before setting up Publisher to print, you should have installed a default printer on your computer. To do this, open the Windows Start menu and select Printers. When the Printers window opens, double-click on the Install Printer icon to run the Install Printer Wizard. You'll need the proper print driver (some are on your Windows disks, others you'll have to supply from your printer's manufacturer). This section assumes you have a default printer installed.

Using Print Setup

Before you print anything, you should check the print settings to avoid wasting paper. Just follow these steps to check out the Print Setup dialog box:

1. Select File, Print Setup. The dialog box in Figure 2.42 appears.

2. Choose the printer that you want to use. You use this command only if you have more than one printer installed on your computer and you want to print to one other than the default printer.

3. Make sure that the settings in the dialog box are the ones you want to use.

   ✿ If you were printing to legal-size paper ($8\frac{1}{2} \times 14$) or an envelope, for example, you would make that choice in the Size list box. The default, letter size, is fine for most publications you'll print.

Figure 2.42

If you want to use an installed printer other than your default, change the printer name here.

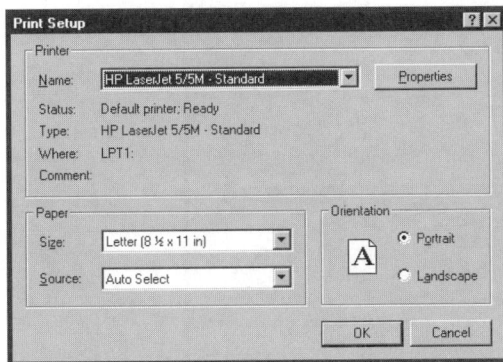

✿ Some printers are set up with one kind of paper in an upper tray and another kind in a lower tray (for example, plain bond in one and company stationery in the other). Some printers also have a special feed for envelopes. If yours does, select the proper source for the paper in the Source list box.

✿ Page orientation deals with whether the long side of the printed page is on top (landscape) or the short side (portrait).

4. Click on the Properties button in the Print Setup dialog box. The Properties dialog box appears, with even more detailed settings. The tabs displayed and their contents will vary depending on the printer you're using. An example of what you'll find on the Print Quality and Device Options tabs with an HP Laserjet 5 printer installed is shown in Figures 2.43 and 2.44.

5. Look carefully at the options your own system provides. Generally, they'll give you more control over things like the quality of output, how your printer deals with two-sided printing, and printing of post-script fonts. The defaults are usually fine, but if you have problems with printing, the answer may lie with one of these settings.

■ ■

 TIP Don't forget that Publisher has a Print Troubleshooter command on its Help menu that might come in handy if you run into problems while printing.

■ ■

Figure 2.43

Depending on the printer you're using, a Print Quality or Graphics tab may be available to set up how the printer will handle graphics, including resolution and use of bitmaps.

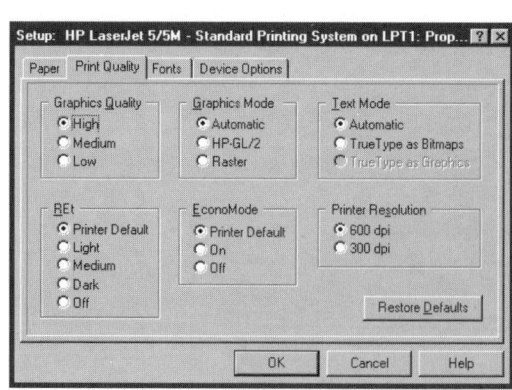

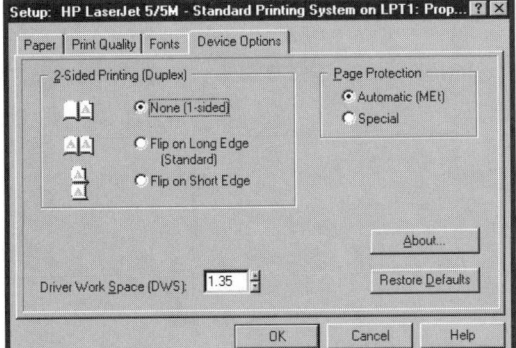

Figure 2.44

Device options will
vary, but can
include how the
printer sets up
two-sided printing.

6. Click on the Cancel button in the Properties dialog box.

7. Click on the Cancel button in the Print Setup dialog box. The default settings remain selected.

Using the Print Dialog Box

When you have your printer all set up, you still have a few more choices to make before actually printing. These choices are in the Print dialog box, and you make them by following these steps:

1. Select File, Print. A Print dialog box something like the one shown in Figure 2.45 appears. The Printer area at the top of this dialog box is the same as the information you saw in the Print Setup dialog. In fact, clicking the Properties button here takes you to the same Properties dialog box you just saw.

TIP   If you want to print the document to a file so that you can print it from another computer (whether it has Publisher installed on it or not), use the Print to file check box in the Printer area of the Print dialog box.

2. Prepare for printing your document by selecting from these choices in the Print dialog box:

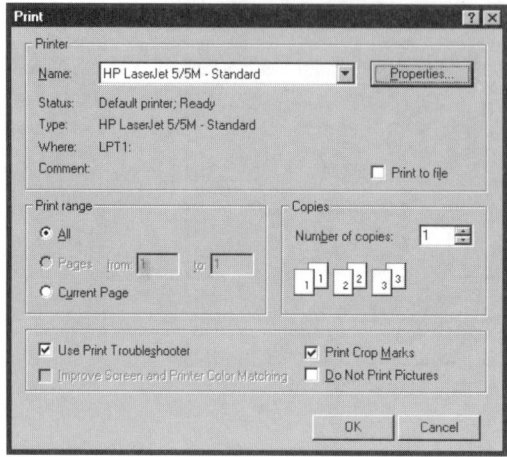

○ Print range allows you to print All of the pages in the publication, just the Current Page (the page you have displayed at the moment), or a range of pages. To use the Pages range feature, you first click on the Pages option button. Enter the first page you want to print in the from: text box and the last page of the range in the to: text box.

○ You can choose how many copies you want to print by clicking on the up and down arrows next to the Number of copies text box, or by highlighting the current number and typing a new one in.

○ If you select Use Print Troubleshooter by clicking in its check box, any problems encountered during printing cause Publisher to display associated Help topics to suggest solutions.

○ Crop marks indicate where your final document should be trimmed to be the proper size. If you want these to print, click on the Print Crop Marks check box. (Crop Marks are mostly used by professional printing services).

○ If you just want to see a draft to review text and don't need to take the time to print complex graphics, select the Do Not Print Pictures check box.

✿ The final choice, Improve Screen and Printer Color Matching, invokes a color matching system that attempts to adjust your printed colors to closely match the colors you see on your monitor. If you don't have a color printer selected, this option won't be available to you.

3. Click on OK to print your car flyer.

Using Outside Printers

What if you want to let someone else do the work for you? For example, say you want to print in very large quantities, or you'd like to take advantage of more sophisticated printing services such as color printing or higher resolution? In those situations, you may find yourself dealing with a printing service. Publisher has special tools to help you out.

PRINTING JARGON

Before you follow the steps to set up for an outside printer, here are a few terms you should know:

Resolution relates to how many dots per inch (dpi) are printed on the page. All modern printing is made up of tiny dots brought together to form text and images on the page. The more dots, the higher the resolution and the crisper the image.

Spot color is the use of black, white, gray, and up to two colors to print your document. You'll see spot color used in newspapers and in your phone book; a touch of red, for example, on a company name in an otherwise black-and-white ad.

Full color uses a large spectrum of colors and shading in printing your document, matching the colors you see on your screen.

Separations are part of the printing process; to print spot color, for example, a printer has to make color separations that are then used to create a printing plate for each color to be used.

Bleed is a term for printed elements that go off the edge of the page. If you use a banner like the one you saw earlier in this chapter, you'd be using a bleed—the image runs right off the edge of the paper.

You'll get a closer look at how some of these terms are used as you work through the Outside Printer setup.

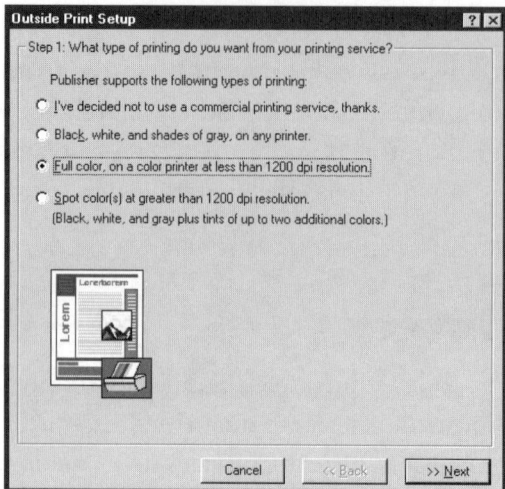

Figure 2.46

Different information appears in the bottom of the Outside Print Setup dialog box depending on what option you've selected.

Here are the steps to use the Outside Print feature:

1. Select File, Outside Print Setup. The dialog box in Figure 2.46 appears. (If you wanted to print in black and white or full color, at this point you would just click the appropriate option button and proceed by clicking on Next.)

NOTE The first choice in this dialog box, "I've decided not to use a commercial printing service, thanks." is one of the silliest things I've seen in software (and I've seen a lot). If you select it, the Next button changes to Done and your only option is to close the dialog box. In effect, you've entered a dialog box simply to say you don't want to use the feature it offers. Just ignore this setting and maybe rethink your decision to buy more Microsoft stock.

2. Click on the option button for Spot color(s) at greater than 1200 dpi resolution. The dialog box changes to look like Figure 2.47.

3. Click on the arrow next to the Spot color 1 list box and select a color from the drop-down palette.

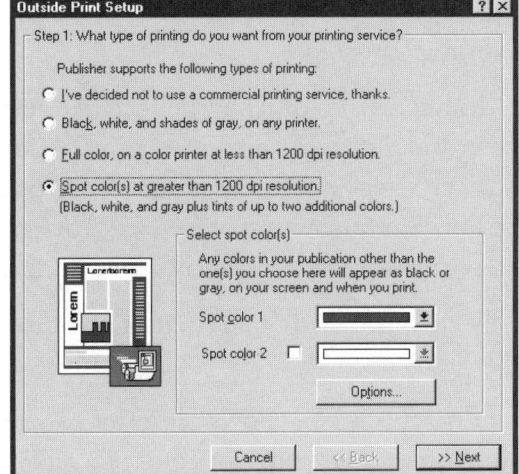

Figure 2.47

The only choice that requires a second step in this dialog box is the Spot Color choice.

TIP You can put a check mark in the Spot color 2 check box and choose a second spot color. However, a second color can add a lot of cost to your print job, so be sure you need it.

4. Click on the Next button to proceed. The second step of the Outside Print Setup appears (see Figure 2.48). (The second and third

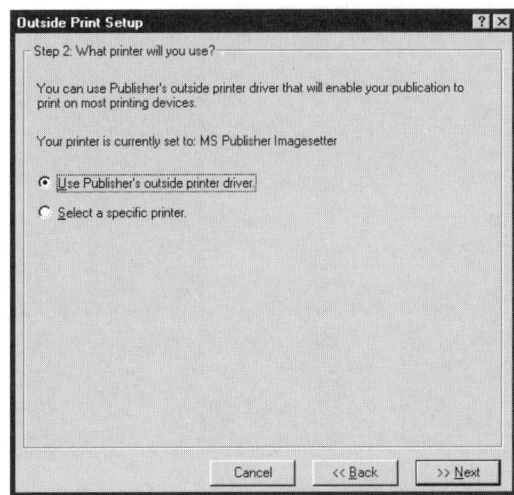

Figure 2.48

There are two simple choices in this dialog box relating to the print driver to be used.

steps of the Outside Print Setup are the same no matter which choice you make in the first step.)

5. Leave the default setting of using Publisher's outside printer driver; this choice includes the outside driver with the document in the file, so the document can be printed whether your printer has Publisher installed or not. The other option here would designate a specific print driver that a printer might request, but you won't often use this.

6. Click on Next to proceed. The final dialog box appears (see Figure 2.49).

    ❖ The first check box allows a printer to print on paper stock that is larger than your document to accommodate bleeds.

    ❖ The second choice displays markings that are useful to printers, such as crop marks and spot color names.

7. Click on Done to accept the default settings (both of these options are usually useful to outside printers, but check with your printer if you're not sure).

8. To print to a file for your printer select File, Print to Outside Printer. The dialog box in Figure 2.50 is displayed.

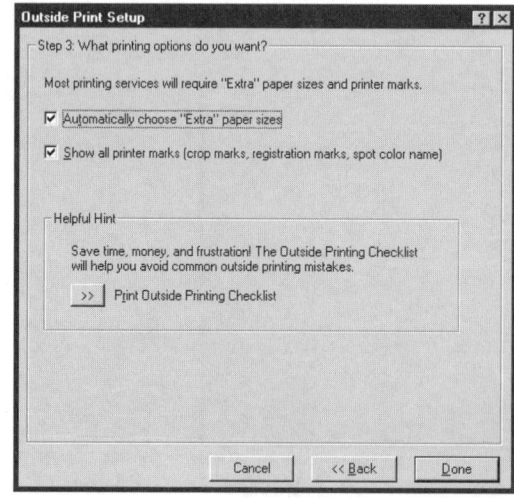

Figure 2.49

Try printing the checklist by clicking the button in the Helpful Hint area of this dialog box.

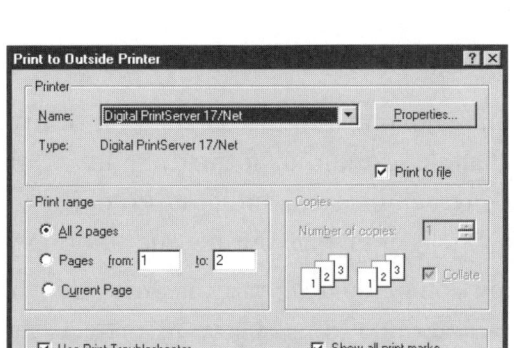

Figure 2.50

Only a few items differentiate this from the Print dialog box you've already seen.

Notice that the Print to file check box is selected by default; that's because you're printing to a file that you'll hand on to your printer. Also, two additional items, Print Color Separations and Allow Bleeds, appear among the check boxes at the bottom of the dialog box. Your printer will probably want both of these left selected.

9. Leave the defaults and click on OK to print. A Print to File dialog box appears, allowing you to designate a location and name for the file.

10. Enter a filename and click on OK from this dialog box to print to the file. Printing to the file basically saves your document and the Publisher print drivers to a file, which you can then hand on to your printer to generate the final output.

11. Publisher will suggest that you print a copy of the document and an information sheet summarizing your printing choices to bring along with you to the printer. This is a good idea. Click on Yes to print the information.

TIP Most default settings are fine when printing to a file for an outside printer; however, if you're in doubt, show your printer your document before you run through the Outside Printer setup and discuss what's needed to get the output you want.

What's Next?

In this session you've not only produced a snazzy little flyer, you've picked up skills needed to handle text and its formatting, used borders and columns, worked with pictures, and rotated and grouped objects. You've also worked through those key steps of saving your file and printing your document.

In the next session you graduate to putting out your own newsletter. In the process you'll learn about adding special text effects such as shadows and reverse type, working with tables and backgrounds, and making text flow from one text frame to another.

Making a Newsletter

- ✿ Creating exciting headings
- ✿ Discovering the wonders of WordArt
- ✿ Arranging text in a newsletter
- ✿ Connecting text frames
- ✿ Working with tables

Hopefully the creative juices that started flowing in this morning's session are still with you, because this afternoon you will tackle a more challenging type of publication. Designing a newsletter, with its many elements—a masthead, stories, graphics, table of contents and so on—is a great way to hone your page design skills.

In this session, you'll have a chance to practice many of the skills you picked up in the previous session: entering and formatting text, creating columns, and inserting pictures. But you'll also learn about some new features of Publisher: using special effects for text, including a clever little applet called *WordArt*; adding and formatting tables; and using backgrounds to insert information or graphics that you want on every page. As you work with pictures and text in the newsletter, you'll also get practice with juxtaposing text and objects using picture cropping and text wrapping.

So here's your assignment: you're a part-time volunteer at the local history museum and they've asked you to design a newsletter to promote the museum's community education programs. With Publisher in place, you're ready to begin.

Creating Exciting Headings

Basically, a heading is simply a key piece of text used to draw the reader's attention or identify a document. Many documents benefit from a heading that jumps out at the reader. Newsletters and newspapers display a masthead proclaiming the name of the publication. Advertisements and

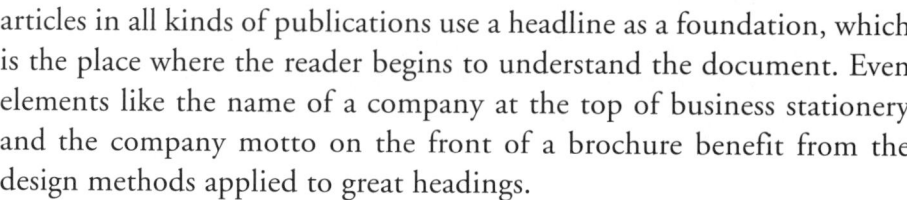

articles in all kinds of publications use a headline as a foundation, which is the place where the reader begins to understand the document. Even elements like the name of a company at the top of business stationery and the company motto on the front of a brochure benefit from the design methods applied to great headings.

Adding Variety to Headings

You can add excitement to publication headings in many ways. First, think about where you want to place the heading on the page; many headings run across the top, but they don't have to. Some designers rotate the heading and place it along the left or right edge of the document. Look at the newspaper in Figure 3.1 for an example.

Others use special text effects, such as the curved text shown in Figure 3.2, to add flair to the heading. In this variation of the same newsletter shown in Figure 3.1, a graphic element has also been added next to the heading text. The heading now runs across the top of the page in a more traditional style.

Figure 3.1

The heading of this small-town newspaper has been rotated to lie sideways on the page. It also uses reverse text.

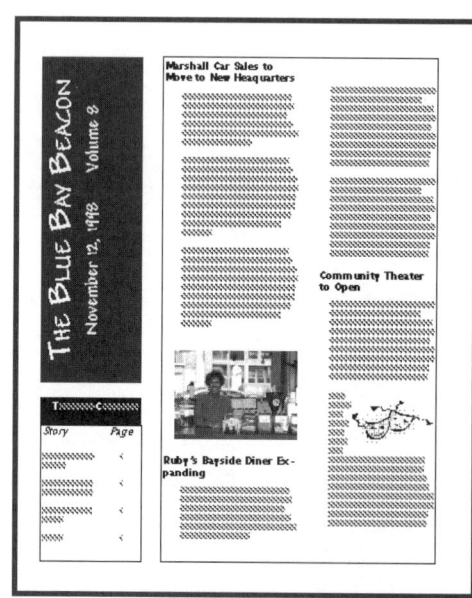

Figure 3.2

The circular graphic
continues the curve
of the heading text,
giving the
suggestion of a
wave, which is
appropriate to the
nautical title.

Color is another device often used successfully in headings. Color can suggest a mood for the publication or the setting. For example, the heading in Figure 3.1 uses a blue background (although you can't see it in the figure of this one-color book), suggesting the oceanside setting of the town of Blue Bay. In a newsletter about financial matters or gardening, try green. If you design a brochure about traffic regulations in your community, use red, green, and yellow in your heading to mimic the colors of a traffic light.

NOTE How much will the use of color cost? If you're going to send your color document to an outside printer, rather than using your own color printer, here's how the pricing will work. Black ink is the cheapest (basically, 1 color). Black ink plus one other color (referred to as *spot color*) gives you a 2-color document, which is more expensive than a 1-color document (and the payoff for adding a bit of color can be big). The big price jump occurs with four colors, usually black plus three other colors—cyan, magenta, and yellow—which look awful alone but blend on the page for a full range of tones and shades. Five-color is even more expensive for very little payoff (that one extra ink color rarely buys you much, designwise).

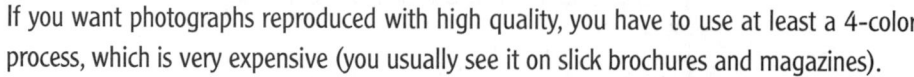

If you want photographs reproduced with high quality, you have to use at least a 4-color process, which is very expensive (you usually see it on slick brochures and magazines).

● ●

All right, it's time to try some special effects of your own on the heading of your newsletter. You'll start with a great little application you get with Publisher called *WordArt*. Open a blank Publisher document using the Full Page style to start (select File, Create New Publication, display the Blank Page tab, and choose Full Page).

Discovering the Wonders of WordArt

WordArt is referred to as an applet. *Applet* is computer-speak for a small program that larger programs (such as Publisher) use for specific functions. The WordArt applet lets you create special text effects, such as curved text. Figure 3.3 shows some of the effects you can get by using WordArt.

Figure 3.3

Text jazzes up a design when you apply WordArt effects.

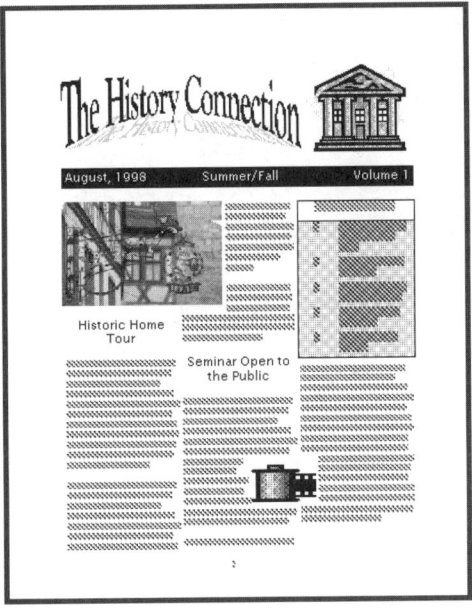

Figure 3.4

You'll bring together all of the elements of this newsletter in this session, starting with the masthead.

NOTE Does WordArt sound familiar? That may be because WordArt is a Microsoft applet that's available to all Microsoft Office applications, including Word and Excel.

Before you create the WordArt you'll use in the newsletter masthead, I'm going to give you a glimpse of the appearance of your final newsletter. Figure 3.4 shows the final newsletter, with the WordArt heading in place. To create the WordArt in Figure 3.4, follow these steps:

1. Select Insert, Object. The dialog box in Figure 3.5 appears.

2. Use the scroll bar to locate Microsoft WordArt 3.0 in the Object Type list and click on it.

3. Click on OK to open WordArt. The WordArt toolbars replace the Publisher toolbars, and an Enter Your Text Here dialog box appears (see Figure 3.6).

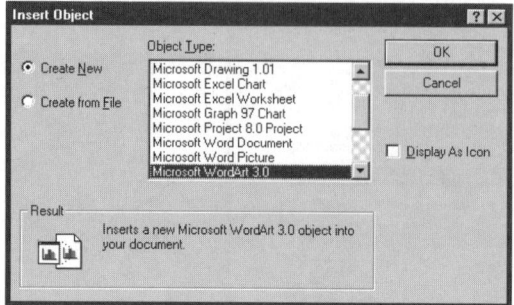

Figure 3.5

You can reach other applets through the Insert Object dialog box, such as Microsoft Graph and Microsoft Organization Chart.

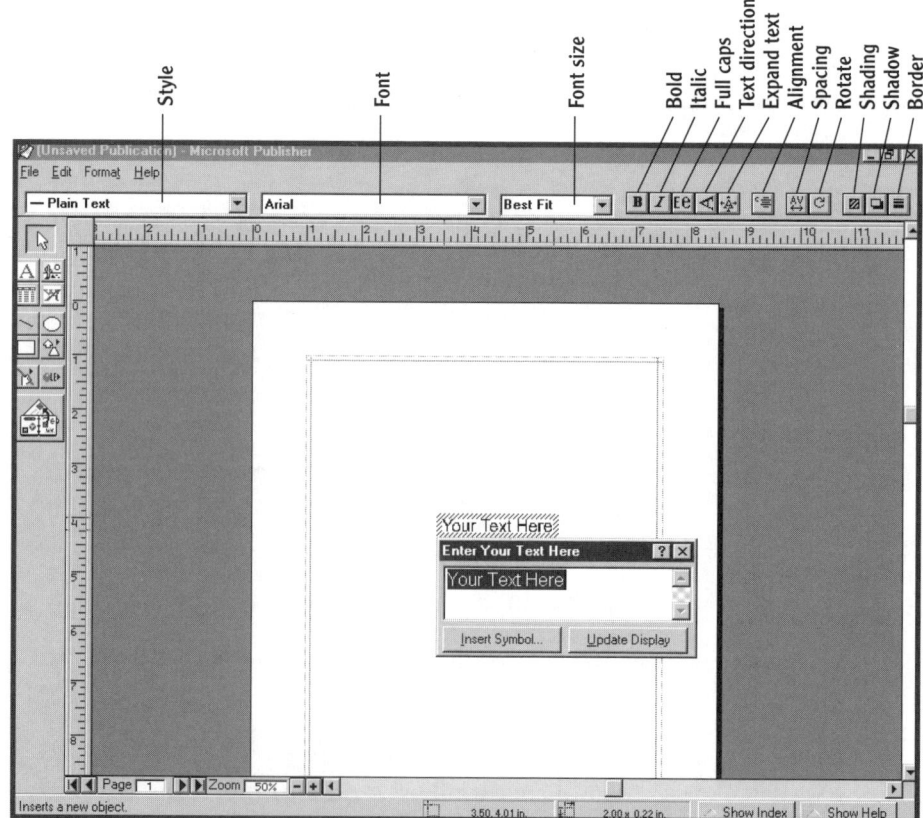

Figure 3.6

Applets open up within the larger application, taking over its interface until you close the applet.

Deflate (Bottom) style

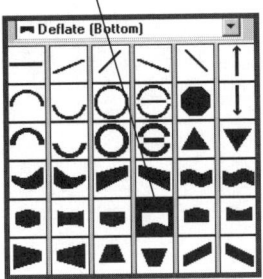

Figure 3.7

All kinds of predefined shapes are available in WordArt to give your text impact.

4. The placeholder text in this dialog box is already selected; to replace it, simply type the name of the newsletter: **The History Connection**.

5. Click on the down arrow next to the Font list box and use the scroll bar to locate the font called Goudy Old Style. (If you don't have that particular font, try a Copperplate, Baskerville Old Face, or Garamond font).

6. Click on the down arrow next to the Style list box (see Figure 3.7) and select the Deflate (Bottom) option (fourth row over, fifth row down).

7. Click on the Bold button on the toolbar to apply the Bold effect to the text.

8. Use the Font Size drop-down list to apply a 36-point font size to the text. WordArt shows a preview of how your object will look. The preview is located just above the Enter Your Text Here dialog box, as shown (slightly enlarged by using the Zoom feature) in Figure 3.8.

TIP If you want to insert a symbol in your WordArt, such as a smiling face or trademark, click on the Insert Symbol button in the WordArt dialog box to access various Symbol fonts.

9. Click on the Shadow button on the toolbar. The Shadow dialog box appears.

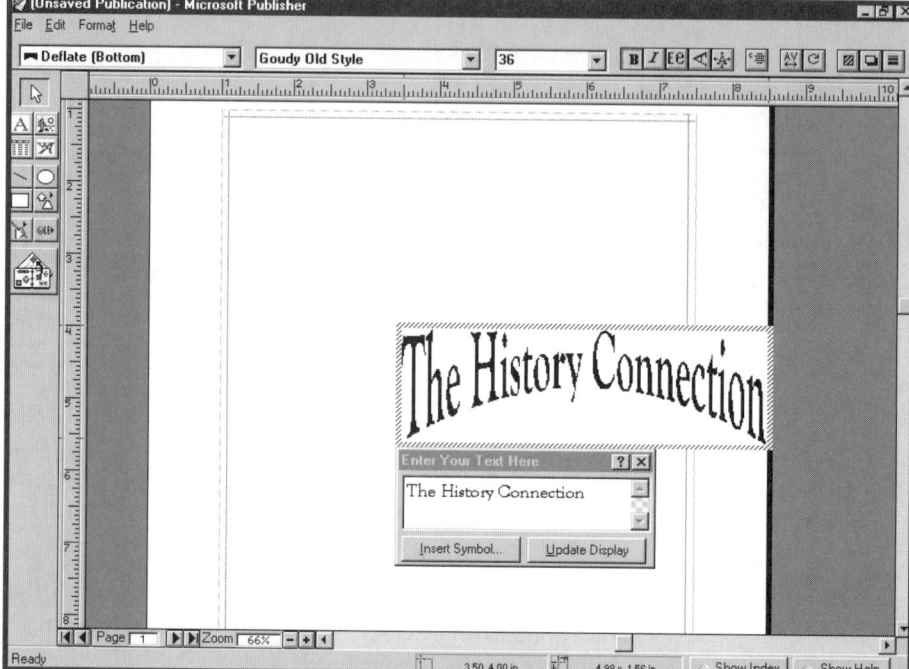

Figure 3.8

The preview gives you a good idea of how all of your WordArt formatting is coming together.

10. Select the shadow style on the far right (see Figure 3.9) by clicking on it, and then click on OK to apply it.

 **NOTE** You can also use tools on the WordArt toolbar to expand the spacing between letters in WordArt text, align the text, rotate it, or switch to full caps. Explore these options with different fonts and styles to create a wide variety of text effects.

11. Click anywhere outside the WordArt object to return to the Publisher desktop with its toolbars in place.

12. Move the WordArt object to the upper left corner of the page (refer to Figure 3.4 for guidance on placement).

Figure 3.9

Pick a shadow style that works well with the font you've chosen.

**CAUTION**   When selecting the WordArt object to move it, don't double-click on it by mistake. Double-clicking on an embedded object (that is, an object created in another program and placed in a Publisher document) re-opens for editing the application in which it was created. In this case, the WordArt toolbar would reappear.

Creating Reverse Text

I talked about the virtues of white space in the first session of this book. Typically in documents, your text and graphics are dark (usually black) and the background is white. That white space balances the text on the page. But now I'm going to turn the tables on you and suggest the use of

reverse text. Reverse text is the use of light-colored text on a dark background. This makes the text stand out on the page and it's often used in headings.

You'll create a text frame with the date and volume number of the newsletter and apply a reverse text effect to it. This line will fit under the name of the newsletter. This makes a nice underscore to the masthead, as you can see in Figure 3.10, which shows a close-up of the final masthead.

Creating reverse text is easy: you simply apply a light color to the text and fill the text frame with a dark color. White text on a black background is often used, but you can also use shades of gray, colors, or white in various combinations.

TIP

Avoid combinations that are too close when you shade. For example, yellow and white wouldn't create a very sharp contrast. Likewise, dark blue and dark green wouldn't show too well, because the colors would tend to blend at the edges of the text. Stick to very dark with very light colors, or apply starkly contrasting colors, such as dark red and yellow.

Follow these steps to create the text frame shown in Figure 3.10:

1. Click on the Text tool on the Publisher toolbar.

2. Click on your document and drag across the page to create a text frame of the approximate size of the one shown in Figure 3.10.

Figure 3.10

Reverse text becomes a powerful design element; text jumps out at the reader in clean white.

Figure 3.11

You may remember the Character dialog box from the previous session; it's used to apply a variety of formats to text.

3. Type the text **August, 1998** and press Tab; type **Summer/Fall**, and then press Tab; and finally, type **Volume 1.**

4. Select Format, Character. The Character dialog box appears.

5. Change the Font to Lucida Sans (if you don't have this font available, Arial makes a nice substitute); change the font size to 16.

6. Click on the arrow next to the Color list box (see Figure 3.11) and select white.

7. Click on OK to apply the formatting to the text. When the dialog box closes, your text seems to have disappeared. You have to change the background to something other than white for the white letters to show up.

8. Select Format, Fill Color. The Colors dialog box shown in Figure 3.12 appears.

9. Click on the solid black color block (on the far left of the bottom row), and then click on OK to apply it.

NOTE   If you don't see enough colors in these squares to fit your needs, you can click on the All colors option button at the top of the dialog box. This will give you a color spectrum and

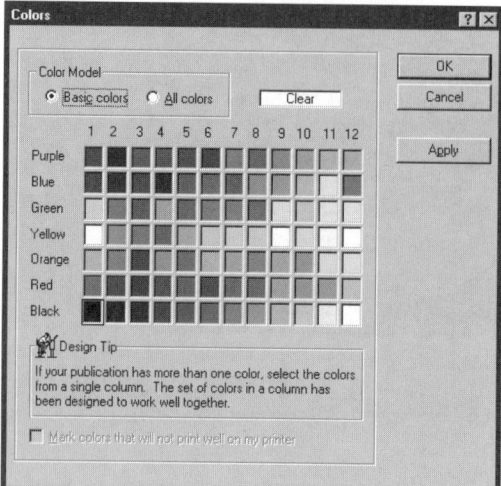

Figure 3.12

The colors of the
spectrum are
arranged in rows.

various settings from which to choose virtually any color or shade, using numerical des-
ignations for hue (color), saturation (density of color), and luminosity (brightness).

10. You might want to fine-tune the new text frame. Feel free to take a
    moment to resize the text frame, making it slightly wider or nar-
    rower in any direction so that the text looks balanced within it and
    the frame is evenly spaced across the page (again, you can refer to
    Figure 3.4 for placement).

11. You can place a line dividing the masthead from the body of the
    newsletter by clicking on the Line button on the Publisher toolbar.
    Click on one side of the page under the masthead and drag across
    the page to draw the line.

Adding Graphics: A Quick Review

You now have three of the four pieces of the masthead in place. The final
element is a piece of clip art. In this section, you'll work with graphics,
adding clip art to the masthead and then inserting the photograph that
goes along with the lead story.

You learned all about adding graphics in the Saturday morning session, but you'll get a little more practice here. Follow these steps to add clip art and a photo to your newsletter:

1. Click on the Picture button on the Publisher toolbar.

2. Click to the right of the name of the newsletter and drag to draw a square picture box (refer to Figure 3.10 to see the approximate size and position for the picture).

3. Select Insert, Clip Art. The Clip Gallery appears, as shown in Figure 3.13.

4. Click on Buildings in the Category list at the left side of the dialog box.

5. Use the scroll bar in the center preview area to locate the picture of a building with columns (see Figure 3.10).

6. Click on Insert to place the clip art in the document.

7. The Import Picture dialog box in Figure 3.14 asks you to make a choice between resizing the frame to fit the picture or the picture to fit the frame. Click on OK to choose the default of resizing the frame to fit the picture. This keeps the picture in its original proportions.

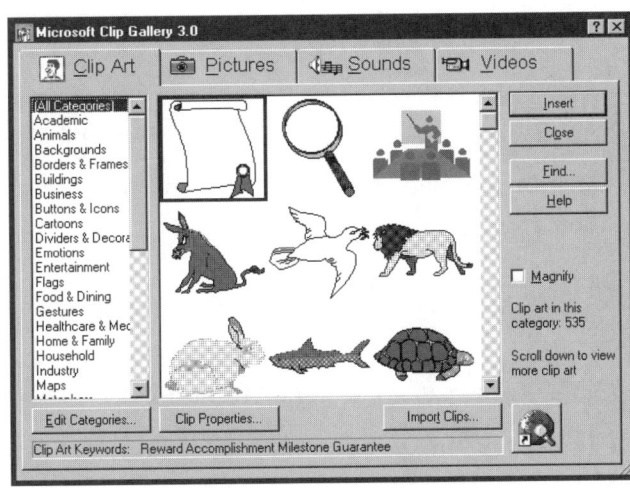

Figure 3.13

The Clip Gallery offers several kinds of media for your publications on four different tabs.

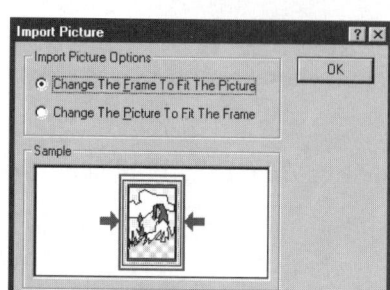

Figure 3.14

Choosing the
second option here
is likely to distort
the image.

Now you've got the four elements of the masthead in place. If you need to either resize the clip art or move it slightly so that the WordArt, dividing line, reversed text block, and clip art object balance nicely on the page, go ahead and do that now. Use the masthead in Figure 3.10 as a guide to placement.

 TIP Because you've just finished the newsletter masthead, which is used for all of your editions of the newsletter, it would be a good idea to save this file as a template at this point. That way, you can use the template to start each new edition of the newsletter without having to re-create the masthead each time.

Now it's time to insert the photograph that appears near the top of the newsletter text.

1. Click on the Picture button on the Publisher toolbar.

2. Click on the page and, holding down your mouse button, drag to draw a square picture box.

3. Select Insert, Clip Art.

4. Click on the Pictures tab to select it.

5. Click on the category name "Buildings."

6. Click on the image of a Tudor-style house.

7. Click on Insert to place the picture.

8. If the resizing message appears, accept the default of resizing the frame to fit the picture by clicking on OK.

The picture appears in your document, which should look something like Figure 3.15 at this point.

NOTE When should you resize an image to fit a frame instead of resizing the frame to fit the picture? If you have a very specifically defined area for the image on your page, you might try to resize the picture. However, it will probably appear somewhat distorted. In some cases, the distortion is minimal and it's no problem. In other cases, the picture just doesn't fit the space. Your options? You could bring the picture into the document in its original size, and then hold down the Shift key as you drag one of the handles while resizing the overall image to maintain its proportions. If that doesn't work, you could try another picture, rotate the image slightly, or crop the picture to fit the space. You'll learn more about cropping later in this chapter.

Figure 3.15

The well-balanced masthead lends a professional feel to the newsletter.

Arranging Text in a Newsletter

You've created the newsletter's masthead and placed a photograph to accompany the lead story. Now it's time to add those hot museum-related stories to your newsletter.

Remember that in Publisher you can connect text frames so that the text in one flows into a second, connected text frame. These connected text frames can be next to each other on the page or many pages apart. You can also format an individual text frame so that it has multiple columns, and the text within the text frame flows among those columns.

Think this way of the two options of flowing text among frames and flowing text in columns in a single frame: you have a handful of pens and you place them in three plastic containers, each container located in a different room of the house. Your other option is to place the pens in a single plastic container with three compartments. You still have three sets of pens, but you can't put them in three separate rooms. This gives you a little less flexibility in getting your work done. Distributing text among various frames is like placing it in three separate but connected containers. Placing it in a single text frame with columns keeps it all in one place. As you work with text in publications such as newsletters, think of Publisher pages as containers that have compartments (text frames).

Working with Text Frames

You can deal with text that will flow in columns in a few different ways. You could, for example, create three text frames of the same size, and place them side by side on the page. The advantage to this is the flexibility it gives you in flowing text to different locations in the document. For example, if the story on Page 1, Column 1, flows to the top of Column 2 on the same page, you can connect those two columns. But what if the text at the bottom of Column 2 continues, not in Column 3 of Page 1, but in Column 2 of Page 3? With three separate text frames on Page 1, you can easily connect the separate text frames to flow text in that way.

The other option is to create one large text frame and format it to have three columns. That way, the text at the bottom of each column will flow

Figure 3.16

This single text frame has three columns, but there is only a single connect button at the end of Column 3.

to the top of the next column within the text frame. Only the text at the end of the third column of this text frame can be connected to another text frame somewhere in the publication. Figure 3.16 and 3.17 show how these two scenarios would look in your newsletter.

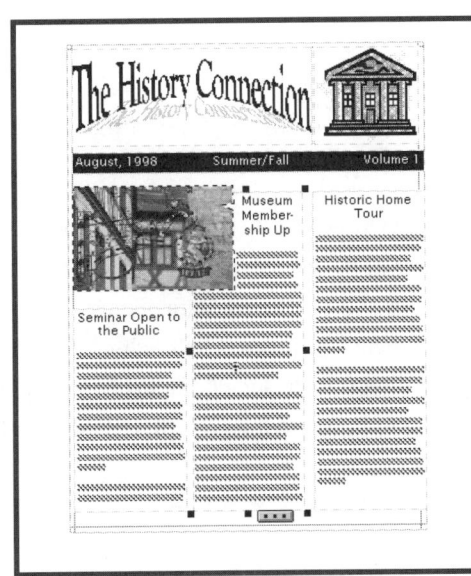

Figure 3.17

Each column contains a separate text frame with a connect button that appears at the bottom of each frame when you select it.

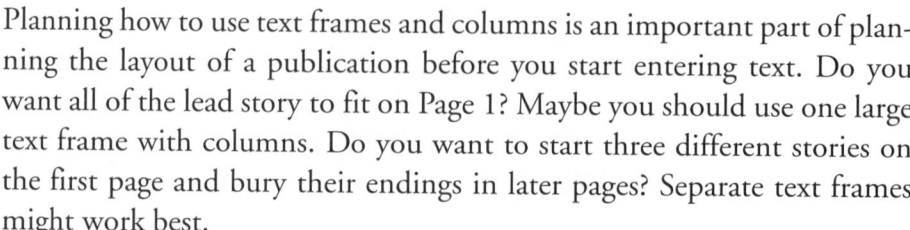

Planning how to use text frames and columns is an important part of planning the layout of a publication before you start entering text. Do you want all of the lead story to fit on Page 1? Maybe you should use one large text frame with columns. Do you want to start three different stories on the first page and bury their endings in later pages? Separate text frames might work best.

TIP
You could also use a combination of these methods. For example, create one larger text frame with two columns, and then a third text frame of a single column to form a three-column page.

NOTE
In a newsletter or newspaper-style publication, you'll often see only the beginning of several stories on the first page, rather than one long story taking up the whole page. That's because placing several stories with different headlines on the front page helps to catch the attention of more readers. The editor parcels out valuable front-page real estate to the openings of several stories and fills the less valuable back pages of the paper with the bulk of the text.

For this newsletter, you'll enter text within a single text frame, formatted in columns. You'll then flow text from this text frame to a second page of the publication.

TIP
You can add a cross reference at the bottom of a text frame to tell the reader what page it's continued on or at the top of a text frame stating where the text is continued from. Right-click on the text frame, and then select Text Frame Properties from the shortcut menu that appears. Click in either the Include Continued On Page or Include Continued From Page check box as appropriate, and then on OK. Publisher will automatically insert the correct page reference.

Creating Columns

First, you'll create a text frame and divide it into three columns. This is easy; you've already done some work with columns in the Saturday morning session. Just follow these steps:

1. Click on the Text button on the Publisher toolbar.

2. Click on the upper left corner of the photograph on your page and drag down and to the right to create a text frame approximately the size of the one in Figure 3.18. Notice that the next text frame covers up the photo. Don't worry, you'll fix that shortly.

3. Right-click anywhere in the text frame.

4. From the shortcut menu that appears, select Text Frame Properties. The dialog box in Figure 3.19 appears.

5. Change the setting for the Number of Columns to 3 using the arrow keys provided.

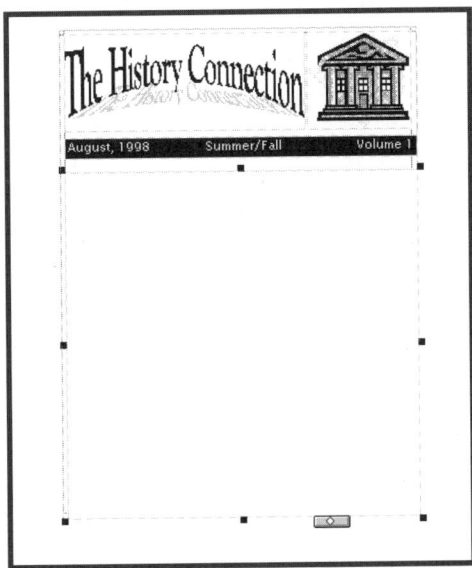

Figure 3.18

The new text frame fills out the balance of the first page.

Figure 3.19

You can also modify text frame margins from the Text Frame Properties dialog box.

6. Click on OK to apply the three-column format.

You now have three columns. Text will automatically flow from column to column, left to right. There is a connect button at the end of column 3, which you can use to connect this text frame to one other text frame.

Sending Things Back

When you created your new text frame, you covered up the photograph on your page. Objects on a page often overlap or even cover up each other. These objects can be stacked, just as you might arrange a set of playing cards in your hand as you play a card game. You stack one card on top of the other, but you leave enough showing to see each card in your hand. In your newsletter, you want the picture to be stacked on top of the text frame. To do that you must indicate to Publisher which object it should bring forward in the stack (or which object it should send back). Here's how you do it:

1. Select the text frame.

2. Select Arrange, Send to Back.

The text box is moved back in the order of objects on the page, and, as a consequence, the photo is moved forward (see Figure 3.20). You can send one object back or bring another object forward to the same effect.

Figure 3.20

The photo object comes forward when the text frame moves backward.

NOTE Did you notice that in the Arrange menu there are also commands for Bring Closer and Send Farther? These are used with more than two objects in a stack. Say you had a stack of several objects that you wanted to layer one on top of the other on your page; you might just want to move an object one place back in the stack, not all the way to the back. Use Send Farther. Or, if you want to bring an object one place farther up in the stack, you would choose Bring Closer.

Entering Text

Now you get to do some busy work. There's no way around it: you need some text to fill out the columns of the newsletter, and guess who has to type it? Here's a shortcut to entering enough text to fill the page:

1. Start by typing the headline **Historic Home Tour**. Format the heading to be a 14 point sans serif font (for example, Arial) and then press Enter twice.

2. Now, type **a long paragraph of text**—any text. Use the Gettysburg address, Hamlet's soliloquy, or your favorite joke (keep it clean, this is a family newsletter).

3. Select the paragraph you've just typed and click on the Copy button on the Standard toolbar.

4. Click at the end of the first paragraph and press Enter.

5. Click on the Paste button on the Standard toolbar. A copy of the paragraph is placed in your document.

6. Press Enter twice and type this headline: **Seminar Open to Public**. Format it as you did the other headline, Arial, 14 point.

7. This time select the two paragraphs of the first story, copy them, and paste them under the new headline.

8. Just keep on like this until you've got all three columns filled with text.

NOTE Notice that the text you add not only flows from one column to the next, but it flows neatly around the picture frame containing the photograph. This is the default for wrapping text in Publisher; you'll see how to control this feature later in this session.

TIP If you're mailing your newsletter rather than letting people pick up a copy themselves, remember to create a mailing label text box. This usually goes on the top or bottom half of the last page, along with a text box for a return address and space for postage to be affixed (or a bulk mailing permit number to be printed). Check out the last chapter of this book for ideas on handling mass mailings.

Connecting Text Frames

As you enter text you may get a message at some point that you've inserted too much text to fit in the frame; Publisher offers to create a second text

Figure 3.21

You can even create a duplicate of the current page by clicking on the last option button in this dialog box.

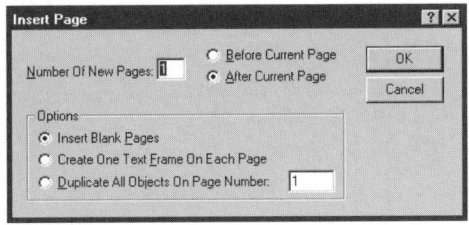

frame and flow the text into it. If you say yes to this suggestion, Publisher will create a second page in the publication, add a text frame on it, and connect the two text frames. Any text that doesn't fit in the frame on the first page will then automatically spill over into the frame on the second page.

However, you can create more than one text frame yourself and connect them any time you want, even before you've started to enter text, by following these steps:

1. Select Insert, Page. The dialog box in Figure 3.21 appears.

2. You can insert any number of pages, either before or after the one currently displayed. Accept the default of adding one blank page after the current page and click on OK.

3. Create a text frame on Page 2.

4. Use the Page navigation arrows at the bottom left corner of Publisher to move back to Page 1.

5. Click on the connect button at the bottom of the single text frame on Page 1. Your mouse pointer changes to a little measuring cup pouring some imaginary substance (a software metaphor for pouring the text).

6. Move to Page 2 and click anywhere on the text frame there. A new symbol appears at the top of the text frame, as shown in Figure 3.22, to show it's now connected to another text frame.

7. Click on the symbol at the top of the frame on Page 2; this takes you to the frame it's connected to on Page 1. Notice that the first frame now has different symbols near the bottom of Column 3, a Connect

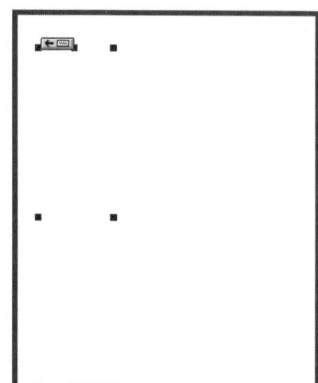

Figure 3.22

The little box at the top of this frame with its backward pointing arrow indicates that it's connected to a frame on the previous page.

Frame symbol (which now displays a little chain link to reflect its linked status) and a Go To Next Frame symbol (see Figure 3.23).

8. Add more text to the text frame on Page 1; it will automatically flow into the frame on Page 2.

NOTE To break a connection between two text frames, just click on the Connect Frame symbol on the first frame; the current connection is broken and the measuring cup cursor appears, ready for you to pour the text into a different frame.

Take a Break

OK, after pouring all of that text into different frames, you're probably about ready to pour yourself a beverage of choice. Take a break, you've earned it. But come back ready to add a table of contents to your newsletter to help your poor readers find their way.

Working with Tables

Tables are wonderful little contrivances that allow you to impose order on the chaos of numbers and words. They're made up of rows and columns that intersect in individual cells. The flexibility provided by being able to

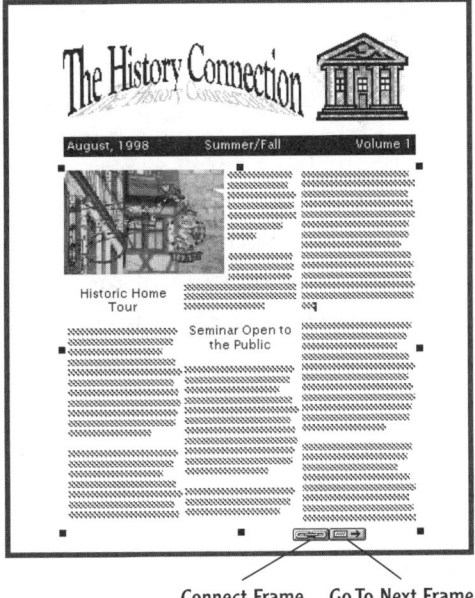

Figure 3.23

In a multipage document, the Go To Next Frame and Go To Previous Frame buttons help you find your way around.

Connect Frame   Go To Next Frame

format each of the cells or whole columns or rows of information is great: you can make the text in the first column align in the center and use a bold font and the next column can align to the right and use a normal font. Column and row headings can even be formatted differently from the text that falls under them. You can also use shading and lines to make the various sets of information easier to read (see Figure 3.24). An automatic formatting feature in Publisher makes quick work of setting up tables.

Figure 3.24

Tables provide order to sets of data, such as the numbers in this example.

	Northeast	Southwest	TOTALS
Toy Division	22.3	33.5	**55.8**
Game Division	15.4	15.3	**30.7**
Doll Division	20.3	25.3	**45.6**
Action Division	15.0	23.3	**38.3**
Video Division	40.7	32.1	**72.8**

NOTE Besides using a table, there is literally no way to vary the alignment of different pieces of a line of text across the page in a regular text frame (tabs come close, but no cigar).

Most publications with several pages use a table of contents to list the items included in the publication along with their page numbers. Books like this one include tables of contents at the front of the book. Newsletters often include a table of contents on the first page, not only to help the reader get around, but also to showcase the stories in that issue.

Adding a Table of Contents

When creating a table, you first delineate its structure (the number of rows and columns), and then type information into the individual cells. So get started by creating the table using these steps:

1. Click on the Table button on the Publisher toolbar.

2. Click on the top left corner of the third column of text and draw a rectangular box, approximately the width of the column and half its length. The Create Table dialog box shown in Figure 3.25 appears.

3. Use the arrows next to the Number of Rows and Number of Columns text boxes to set the table to have 6 rows and 2 columns.

4. Click on OK to return to your page. The blank table object shown in Figure 3.26 appears on the page. It has selection handles like other objects you've seen, which you can use to resize the table.

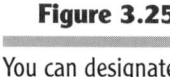

Figure 3.25

You can designate the number of rows or columns here, but you can also add or delete them later.

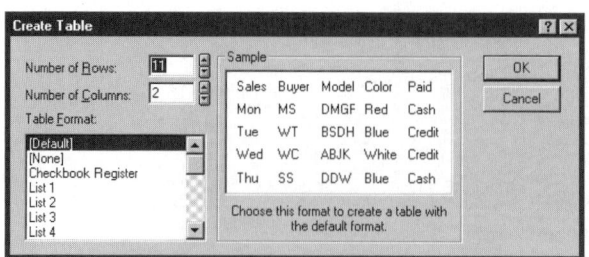

Figure 3.26

Notice that
Publisher has
placed the table in
front of the text
frame by default.

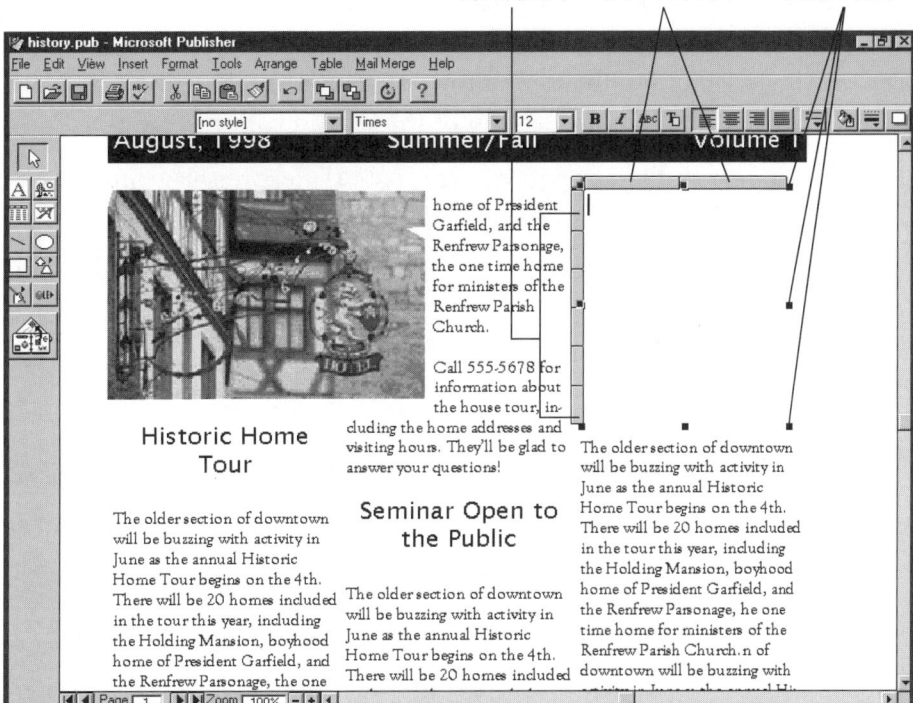

Notice that the blocks across the top and along the left edge of the table object represent the two columns and six rows you selected when creating the table. Your insertion point appears, ready to enter data in the first row.

Entering Data in a Table

The main trick to entering data in a table is learning how to move around the table from cell to cell. After you've got your insertion point in a cell, entering text is just—well, entering text, and you've got that down cold. Here are the ins and outs of moving around tables:

- ❂ Press the Tab key to move from one column to the next.

- ❂ Press Shift-Tab to move back (to the left) one column.

- ❂ Press the up or down arrow keys on your keyboard to move up or down one row.

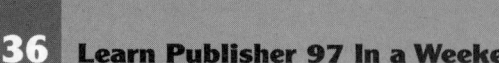

✿ Press the left or right arrow key to move backward or forward by one cell. For example, with your insertion point in the first column of the fourth row, pressing the left arrow moves you to the cell at the intersection of the second column and third row.

✿ Or you can just take the expressway and use your mouse: click on any cell you like, and there you are!

Now, follow these steps to enter the text for your newsletter's table of contents, which will list all of the stories in the publication with corresponding page numbers:

1. With your insertion point in the first cell, type **Table of Contents**.

2. Press the down arrow key and type **1**.

3. Press Tab and type **Historic House Tour Set for June**.

4. Press the right arrow key and type **1**.

5. Press Tab and type **Seminar Open to Public**.

6. Continue to enter text to match the table shown in Figure 3.27.

Notice that your text wraps automatically within cells as you type, forcing rows to expand (but not columns). This causes the overall length of the table to expand as you enter information.

Figure 3.27

The page numbers indicate the page in the newsletter where each story begins.

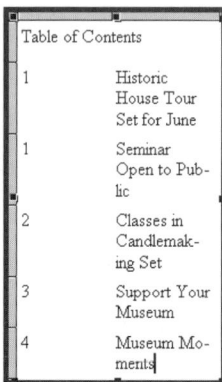

Formatting a Table

You could format the individual elements of a table by using Format menu commands for border and text alignment or you can use the buttons on the Formatting toolbar. However, why not get a head start? Use Publisher's AutoFormat feature. It's quicker, and provides a wide variety of table formats to choose from.

1. Select Table, AutoFormat. The dialog box in Figure 3.28 appears.

2. Scroll down the list of table formats until you see three Table of Contents styles. Click on each in turn to see a preview.

3. Click on the Table of Contents 2 format, and then on OK to apply it. Your table now looks like the one in Figure 3.29.

TIP Notice how the AutoFormat feature has treated the words "Table of Contents" as a single cell at the top of the table. Since this is the title of the table of contents, Publisher has made the cell containing it wider, to stretch across both columns. You can do this yourself: just click and drag your mouse to select two or more cells, and then select Table, Merge Cells.

Now the table looks pretty good, but you're going to tweak it just a bit to make that first column a little narrower (those solitary numbers don't need all that space, and the text in the second column breaks in odd ways). While you're at it, you'll also change the text font to be consistent with fonts you've already used elsewhere in the document:

Figure 3.28

The sample feature gives you a preview of how each style will look.

Auto Format		? X
Table Format:	**Sample**	OK
List with Title 1	*Table of Contents*	Cancel
List with Title 2	Chapter 1 — 1	
List with Title 3	Chapter 2 — 4	
Numbers 1	Chapter 3 — 10	
Numbers 2	Chapter 4 — 17	Options>>
Numbers 3		
Numbers 4		
Numbers 5		
Numbers 6	Use this format for a short table of	
Table of Contents 1	contents, as for a newsletter.	
Table of Contents 2		

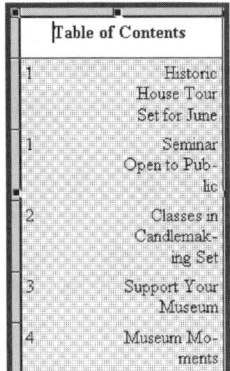

Figure 3.29

The AutoFormat feature has done its magic.

1. Move your mouse pointer between the two column markers at the top of the table; your cursor changes to two arrows pointing in opposite directions, with the word "Adjust" underneath.

2. Press and hold down the Shift key, and then click and drag the cursor to the left to make the first column narrower (but not too narrow to fit the page numbers). Release your mouse, and the column resizes.

3. Click on the right edge of the column marker for the right column of the table and drag to resize it so that the table fits across the entire first newsletter column.

4. Select Table, Highlight Entire Table.

5. Click on the arrow next to the Font list box on the Formatting toolbar and select Lucida Sans as the new font for the table (or whatever font you applied to the reverse text frame in the masthead).

6. Click next to the first number in column 1 and drag your mouse down to highlight all of the numbers in the column.

7. Click on the Center alignment button on the Formatting toolbar to center the numbers in the column.

8. Click outside your table. It should now look like the table in Figure 3.30.

Figure 3.30

Centering the page numbers keeps them from running too close to the left edge of the table frame.

Table of Contents	
1	Historic House Tour Set for June
1	Seminar Open to Public
2	Classes in Candlemaking Set
3	Support Your Museum
4	Museum Moments

You can now fine-tune your table of contents by trying any of these steps:

- Use the table's resizing handles to make its right side line up more precisely with the edge of the reverse text bar above it; this makes the page more balanced.

- Place your insertion point before words that break in the middle, such as Candlemaking in the fourth row, and press Enter to force a return, avoiding so many hyphens. You can also work with the Hyphenation feature in the Tools menu to modify how words are breaking.

- Move the table up or down on the page so that its top edge aligns with the top of the photo that's placed across the page from it.

These kinds of small changes can make the difference between a polished-looking document and a sloppy one.

Working with Text and Pictures

Not bad. You've got a pretty good-looking newsletter, but there are a few more skills you need to pick up before you can head out for that Saturday night on the town. You need to learn how to tweak the way that pictures and text fit together on the page. To do that, I'm going to ask you to add one more picture to the newsletter.

Wrapping Text around Images

To see how text wraps around images, follow these steps:

1. Draw a small picture box on the Publisher desktop (in the gray area outside your document; make it a couple of inches wide and three-quarters of an inch high).

2. Select Insert, Clip Art and choose the piece of clip art in the House-hold category that looks like a roll of film.

3. When asked whether to adjust the frame or picture, adjust the picture to fit the frame. So, now you've got a little picture floating on your desktop. What would happen if you just plopped that picture in the middle of your text? Let's see.

4. Move your mouse pointer over the picture frame until you see the moving van cursor.

5. Click and drag the picture onto the newsletter, dropping it somewhere between the second and third columns. It should look something like the image in Figure 3.31.

Notice a few things about what just happened. First, the picture appeared in front of the text, not behind it. Second, adding a picture used up some room on this page, which meant pushing some text off the page to make room. Since you had already connected this text frame to one on the second page, surplus text just poured onto the second page. Finally, the text near the clip art automatically wrapped around the image, falling outside the selection handles for the picture frame.

By default the text has wrapped around the edges of the picture frame. You can change this setting so that the text wraps around the picture itself rather than its frame; this moves the text slightly closer to the image in places and forms a more jagged text edge around the object. To see how this works, with the picture selected, click on the Wrap Text to Picture button on the picture formatting toolbar. Now the text moves in around the edges of the picture itself. Click outside the picture object to see this more clearly, as shown in Figure 3.32.

Crop Picture tool

Wrap Text
to Picture tool

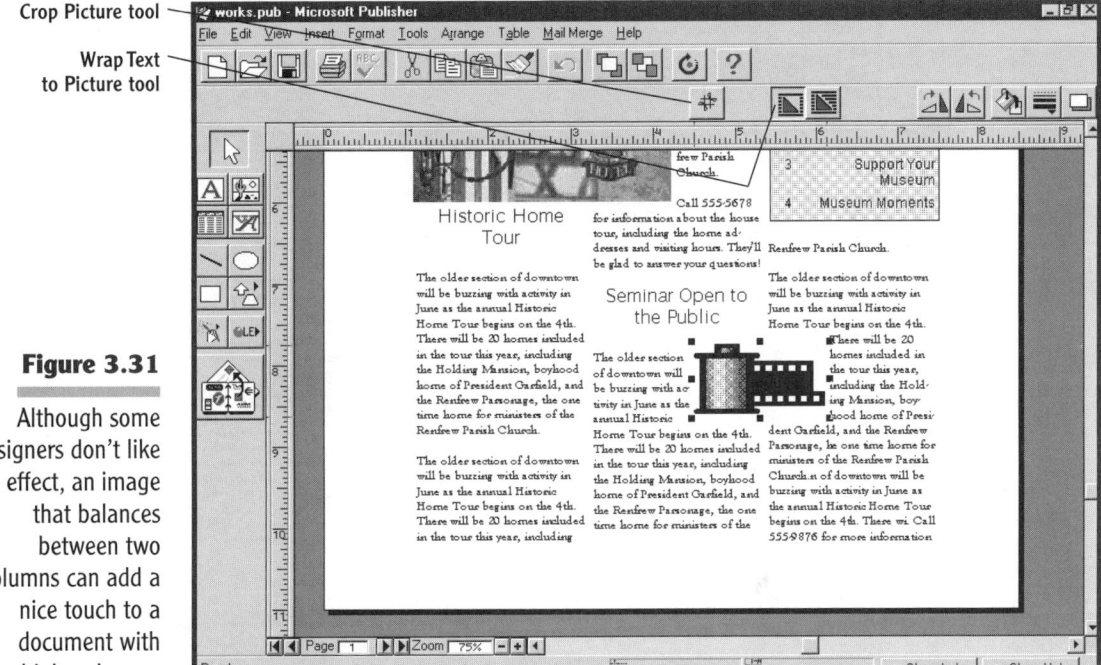

Figure 3.31

Although some designers don't like this effect, an image that balances between two columns can add a nice touch to a document with multiple columns.

NOTE You can also modify text wrapping for a selected picture by selecting Format, Object Frame Properties. Choose one of the two option buttons in the dialog box that appears to wrap text the way you prefer. Using this method, you can also modify the setting for how closely the text abuts the picture.

Cropping Pictures

Adjusting text wrapping is one way of modifying the way text and pictures fit on a page. However, you can also use picture cropping to fine-tune how text and images fit together. Sometimes a picture isn't quite right the way it comes into your document. Perhaps it takes up more space than you want to allow, or there are areas of the image that you'd prefer not to include.

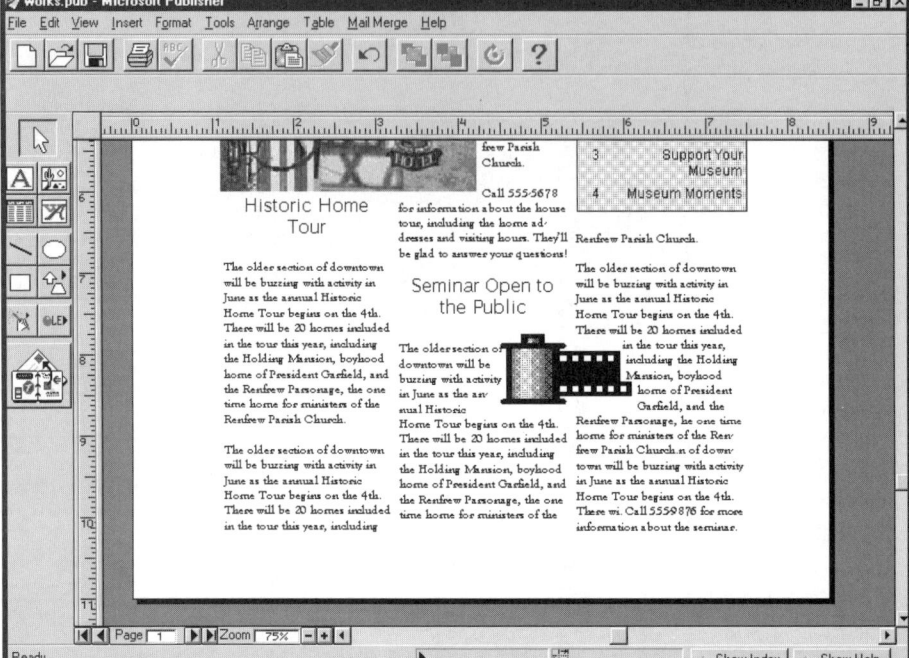

Figure 3.32

Wrapping text a little more closely can sometimes help you fit more text on a single page.

For example, the picture of the roll of film that you just placed on your front page has a long piece of film scrolling out to the right. If you cut off a bit, you can save a little space, fit more text on the page, and still get your visual point across. You can accomplish this by using cropping:

1. Select the picture.

2. Click on the Crop Picture button on the picture formatting toolbar (shown in Figure 3.31).

3. Move your mouse pointer down to the right edge of the picture until it turns into two crossed scissors as shown in Figure 3.33.

4. Click on the right edge of the picture and drag to the left, maybe a quarter of an inch, but leave a bit of film showing in the picture.

5. Release your mouse button and the picture has been cropped to cut off the right edge.

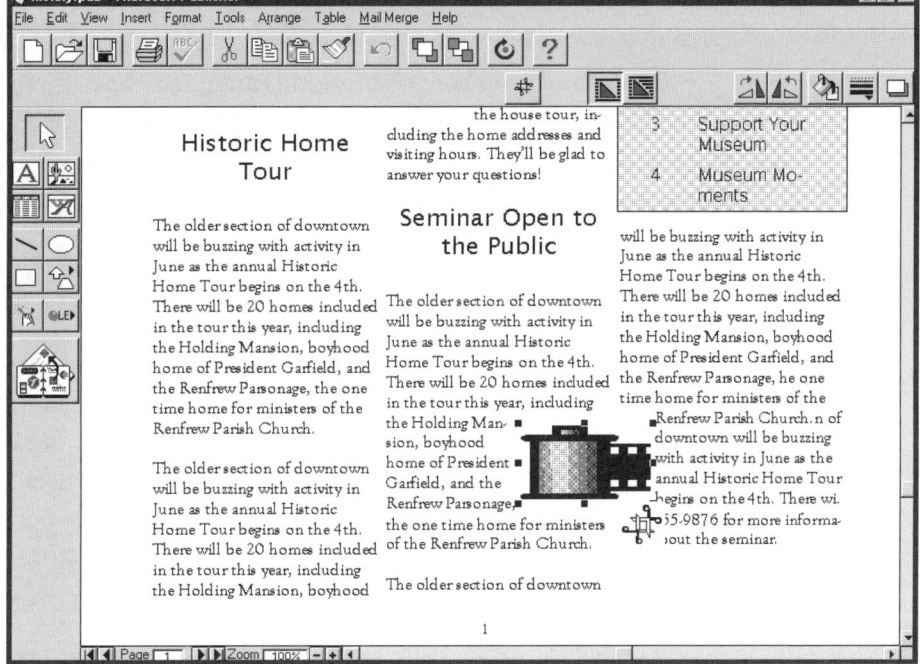

Figure 3.33

The tiny pair of scissors allows you to slice off portions of pictures in a procedure known as cropping.

CAUTION Unless you use the Undo feature immediately following the cropping action, you can't get the rest of the cropped image back. If you've moved beyond the point when you can undo your action and you decide you don't like the effect, you have to reinsert the image and repeat the procedure to recrop the picture.

Modifying the Background

There's one more thing to cover before you quit for the day. (But keep in mind that when you finish this last short section, you're halfway through learning Publisher!) You should know something about the Publisher background.

The *background* is very similar to the header and footer zones in word processor-generated documents. The background is a place to put anything that you want to appear on every page of your document, such as a company logo or page number or date. Place whatever text or graphics you want, wherever you want them on the page (taking care not to have them overlap objects on the foreground). When you return to the foreground, those objects will appear in the same location on every page. To display and work with the background, follow these steps:

1. Select <u>V</u>iew, G<u>o</u> to Background. Assuming you haven't placed anything on the background, you should simply see a blank page.

TIP Don't worry—your newsletter hasn't disappeared. To redisplay the foreground of your document (which is where you've been working all along), you can select <u>V</u>iew, G<u>o</u> to Foreground.

2. Draw a small text box near the middle bottom of the page, as in Figure 3.34.

3. Select <u>I</u>nsert, Page <u>N</u>umbers. The message in Figure 3.35 appears.

4. Click and drag to highlight the number symbol Publisher has inserted, and then click on the Center alignment button on the Formatting toolbar.

5. Select View, Go to Foreground. When you scroll to the bottom of the page, you'll see a page number, as in Figure 3.36.

Figure 3.34

Place this box to fall outside the area of the text on the foreground.

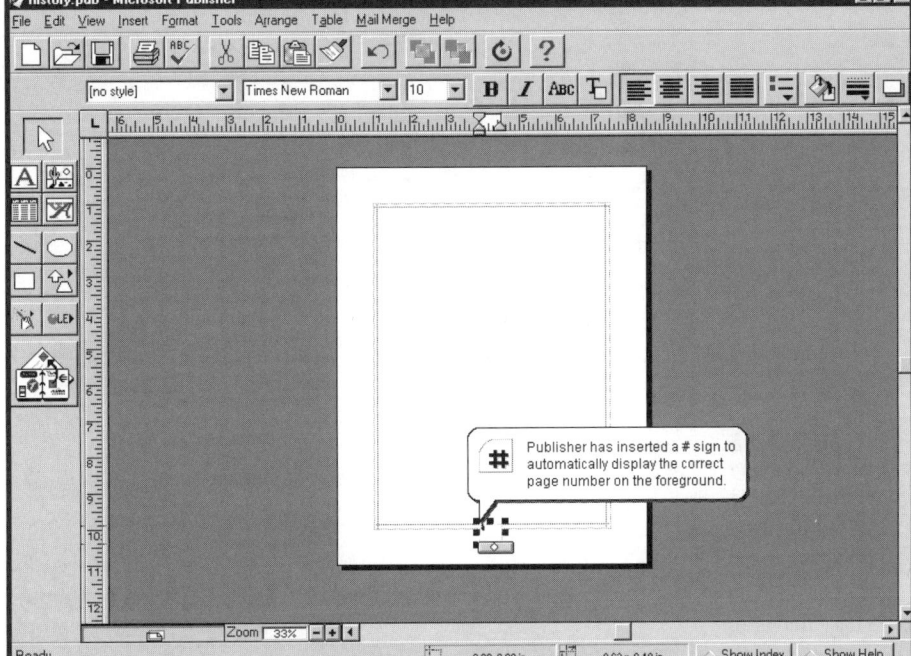

Figure 3.35

Publisher inserts a hot spot for page numbers; it will then number each consecutive page automatically for you.

What's Next?

In this chapter you worked with a more complex publication that included columns, a masthead, graphics, and a table. You learned about special text effects, such as WordArt and reverse text. You discovered how to create and format tables in Publisher. Finally, you worked with bringing objects forward or backward on a page, and with text wrapping and picture cropping to help you tweak the way text and pictures fit together on a page.

In tomorrow morning's session you'll start to use Publisher's Drawing feature to design an invitation, and then work through the Mail Merge feature to produce a personalized version of that invitation for a list of addressees. For now, party if you must, but come back in the morning, refreshed and ready to tackle the next Publisher task.

Figure 3.36

If you don't like the position of the page number, you must return to the background to move it.

Window contents:

history.pub - Microsoft Publisher

File Edit View Insert Format Tools Arrange Table Mail Merge Help

Historic Home Tour

The older section of downtown will be buzzing with activity in June as the annual Historic Home Tour begins on the 4th. There will be 20 homes included in the tour this year, including the Holding Mansion, boyhood home of President Garfield, and the Renfrew Parsonage, the one time home for ministers of the Renfrew Parish Church.

The older section of downtown will be buzzing with activity in June as the annual Historic Home Tour begins on the 4th. There will be 20 homes included in the tour this year, including the Holding Mansion, boyhood

...the home addresses and visiting hours. They'll be glad to answer your questions!

Seminar Open to the Public

The older section of downtown will be buzzing with activity in June as the annual Historic Home Tour begins on the 4th. There will be 20 homes included in the tour this year, including the Holding Mansion, boyhood home of President Garfield, and the Renfrew Parsonage, the one time home for ministers of the Renfrew Parish Church.

The older section of downtown

Museum

4 Museum Moments

will be buzzing with activity in June as the annual Historic Home Tour begins on the 4th. There will be 20 homes included in the tour this year, including the Holding Mansion, boyhood home of President Garfield, and the Renfrew Parsonage, he one time home for ministers of the Renfrew Parish Church.n of downtown will be buzzing with activity in June as the annual Historic Home Tour begins on the 4th. There wi. Call 555-9876 for more information about the seminar.

1

Page 1   Zoom 100%

Designing Invitations

- ✿ Creating a multi-page document
- ✿ Working with drawings and Design Gallery
- ✿ Combining text with drawings
- ✿ Arranging drawings on the page
- ✿ Using Mail Merge to send your invitations

The good news is you could stop right now and have a fair under standing of how to use Publisher and all that you can accomplish with it. But why stop? The goodies you'll pick up in this and the next session take you from being a fair desktop publisher to being an accomplished one. And because you're not the kind to do anything halfway, let's get going.

In this session you'll learn how to draw things for yourself with Publisher's drawing tools as well as get help with visuals from the Design Gallery. You'll explore the art of placing objects on a page for the best balance. Along the way you'll get some more practice working with WordArt and reverse text, skills you picked up in the previous session.

You'll then explore the function called *Mail Merge*. Mail merge may not sound like a barrel of laughs, but it's really a great little feature. Mail merge lets you take a document and a list of names and addresses and combine them to make a personalized mailing (you know, like the ones that tell you that you, John Smith, have just won a million dollars). Personalizing mass mailings and form letters is a way of providing more impact in your correspondence to customers or friends.

Creating a Multiple-Page Document

For this session you're going to create an invitation to the opening of a small business. The skills you'll use to design this are easily transferable to any kind of invitation or announcement for business, or even a personal event like a party or wedding invitation.

Figure 4.1

Publisher offers
several styles
of multipage
documents
using different
paper folds.

Up to now you've started new documents with a full ($8^1/_2 \times 11$) blank page. For this session, in which you'll create an invitation to the grand opening of a café, you'll use a folded-page design, the Tent Card. This gives you two pages to design, the front of the card and the inside page. Start this session by opening this blank document:

1. Select File, Create New Publication. The New Publication dialog box appears. Click on the Blank Page tab (see Figure 4.1).

2. Click on the Tent Card option, and then click on OK to create the document. You see the message shown in Figure 4.2.

3. You will be designing information for two pages of this tent card, so click on Yes to create the second page now. The blank first page appears, as shown in Figure 4.3.

Figure 4.2

You can always add
a page later, or
have Publisher do it
for you now.

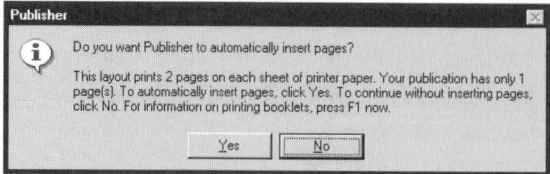

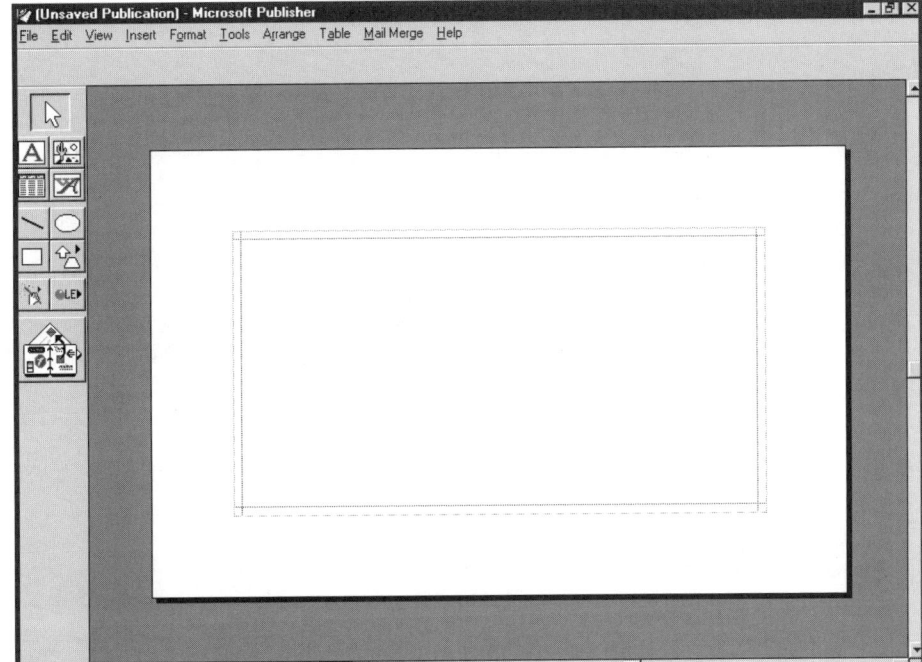

Figure 4.3

This page is in landscape orientation.

To see how this blank document will evolve as you go through the steps in this session, look at Figures 4.4 and 4.5. The former is the finished front of the card, and the latter is the inside greeting. The design combines text, WordArt, Design Gallery objects, and drawings. The feeling here is clean and modern, with key information emphasized through the use of reverse text and positioning of text and graphic objects on the page. You'll start this invitation by adding some drawings.

Working with Drawings and Design Gallery

You remember drawing: you did it in kindergarten and loved it. You drew squares, circles, stars, and lines on creamy, thick construction paper. But you're a big boy or girl now—it's time to learn to draw on a computer with a mouse. It's just as much fun, and just as easy.

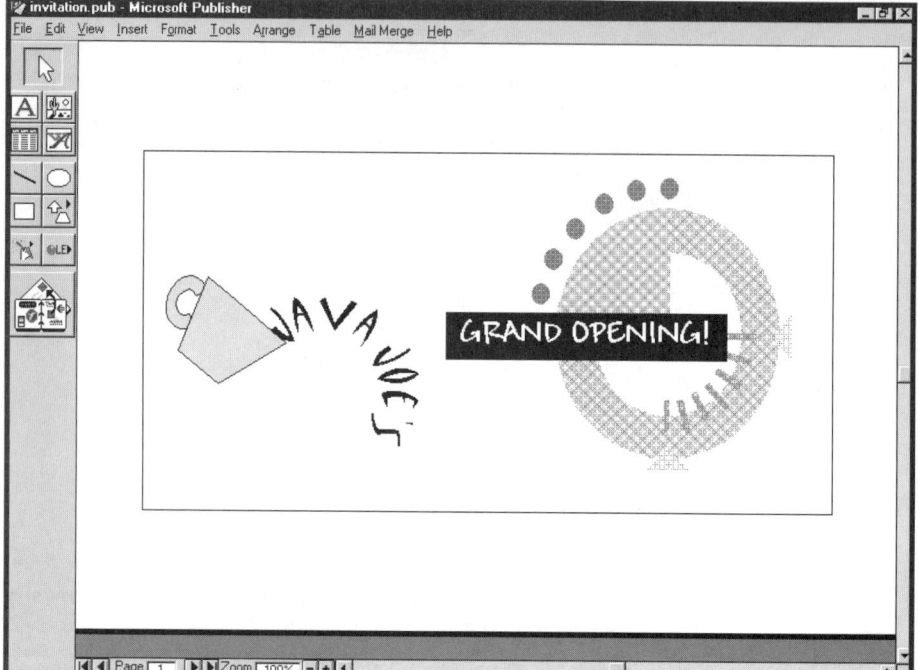

Figure 4.4

The name of the
café spills out of a
coffee cup object
that you'll draw.

Using Drawing Tools

Several drawn objects are in this invitation: the coffee cup (actually two drawings placed together) and the two intersecting lines on the second page. Each page of the invitation also has a rectangle on it to frame the contents. These drawings use some of the drawing tools shown in Figure 4.6. They are located on the Publisher toolbar.

Notice the cascading menu displayed for the Custom Shapes tool. This offers a wide variety of drawing shapes such as starbursts, arrows, a heart, and a cube.

All of these tools are used in pretty much the same way: you click on the tool to select it, and then click on the desktop and drag to draw the shape. Publisher takes care of the hard part, forming the shape. You just drag to create a drawing of the approximate size you want. Try this now to draw the rectangle surrounding the text and graphics on the first page:

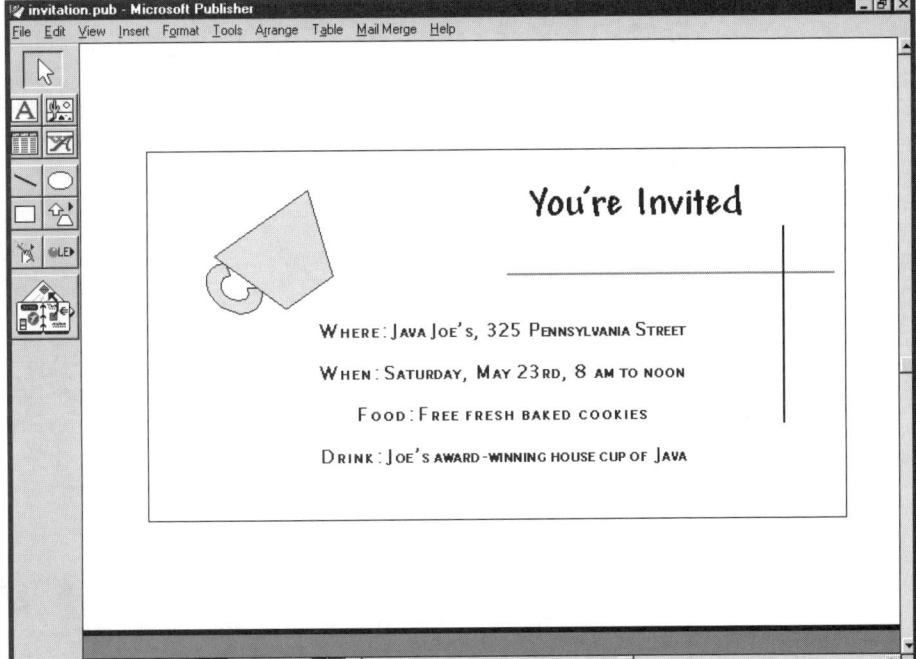

Figure 4.5

The coffee cup theme carries to the inside page.

1. Click on the Box tool.

2. Using the blue and pink guidelines as a reference, click in the upper left corner and drag down and to the right to draw a rectangle surrounding the page area, as shown in Figure 4.7.

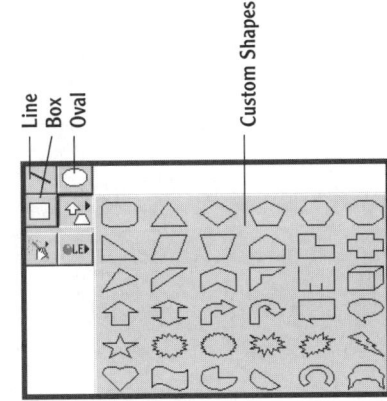

Figure 4.6

The Custom Shapes tool expands to show a cascading menu of predesigned shapes.

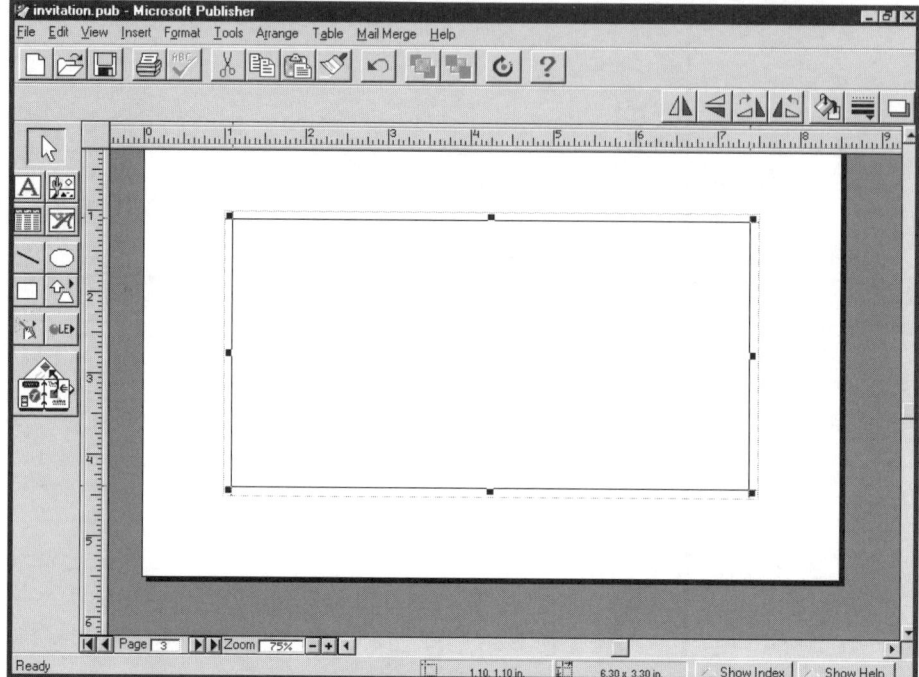

Figure 4.7

Make the rectangle about as big as the inner of the two guidelines.

3. When the box looks about the right size, release the mouse button to complete it.

TIP Don't worry, if you didn't make the rectangle quite the right size or place it quite right. You can always resize it using its selection handles or move it on the page. If you're just completely unhappy with what you did and want to start again, just select the drawing, hit delete, and start over again.

4. Click on the Custom Shapes button to display the cascading menu.

5. Select the cup-like shape, third from the left in the second row of shapes.

6. Click about half an inch from the upper left corner of the rectangle and drag down and to the right to draw a shape similar to that in Figure 4.8.

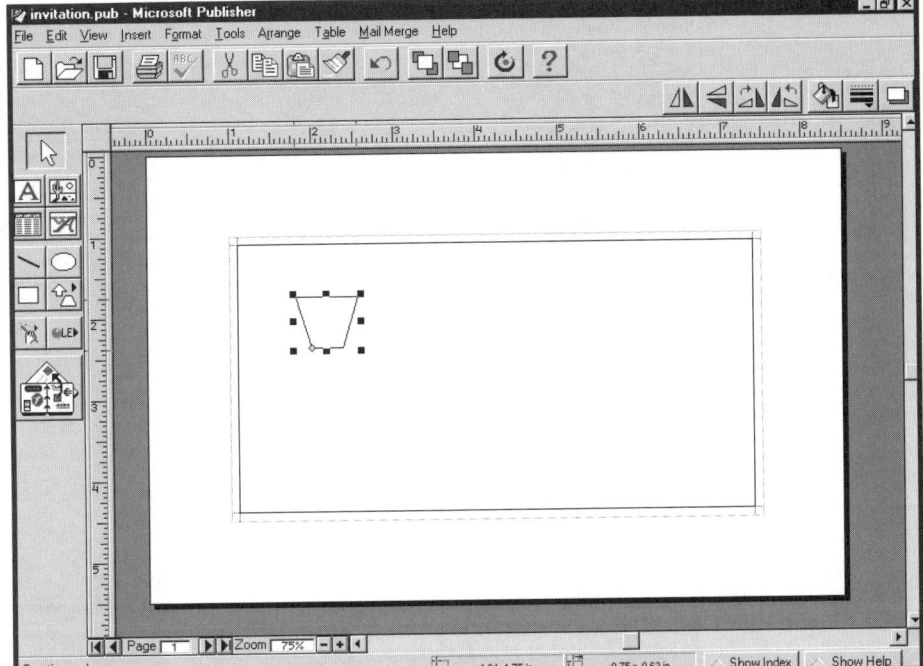

Figure 4.8

Selection handles appear around drawn objects, just as with text and inserted graphics.

7. Click on the Custom Shapes tool again; this time click on the fifth shape from the left in the bottom row (it looks like a little horseshoe).

8. Click next to the cup shape and draw a small object like the one in Figure 4.9.

You've now created the drawing objects you need for the front of the invitation. However, that coffee cup needs some tweaking to look like something that can hold java. The next task is to work with the drawings to make them look like a coffee cup.

Modifying Drawings

Working with drawings is a little more hands-on and creative than other things you've done in Publisher. It's often a process of constant creation and refinement. You draw one shape, try to combine it with another, and realize it needs to be slightly smaller or rotated a bit to the left. Maybe a different

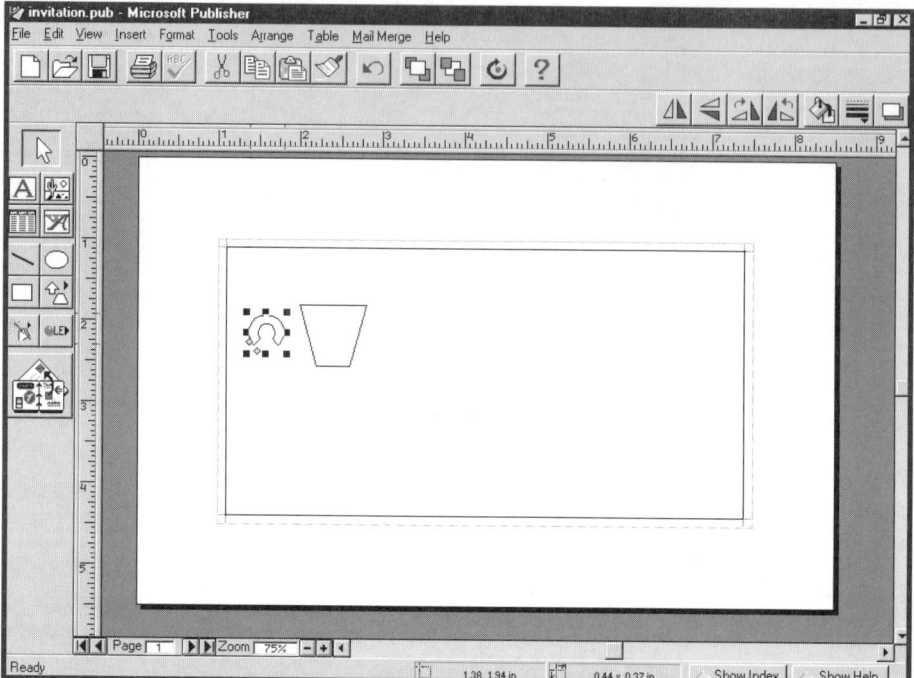

Figure 4.9

You can build drawings of common things by mixing and matching shapes.

shape would work better. You can build more complex drawings out of a combination of drawn shapes, and move those objects in relation to each other until they look just right. In fact, desktop publishing in general sometimes seems like a process of nudging, pushing, pulling, and poking things until they feel right on the page. So it's time to take the shapes you've drawn and make something of them.

You can do several things to drawings after they're on the page. You've already done some of these actions to objects such as WordArt and clip art, so this should be pretty familiar. In working with drawings you can:

- Use selection handles to resize drawings (use the Shift key if you want to retain their original proportions as you stretch a handle in any direction).

- Move drawings around the page by selecting them and looking for the little moving-van cursor, and then dragging them where you want them.

✦ Rotate or flip them in any direction using the Rotate tool on the Standard toolbar, or the Arrange, Rotate/Flip command.

✦ Fill drawings with color using the Fill Color button on the picture formatting toolbar that appears whenever a graphic is selected; or select the Format, Fill Color command.

✦ Arrange drawings on a page to stack them one on top of the other using the Arrange, Send to Back or Bring to Front commands.

✦ Group drawings so that they can be worked with as a single object using the Group command in the Arrange menu, or by pressing Shift while selecting objects to temporarily group them.

✦ Modify line styles of either single lines or the line that defines the outside of a drawn object.

You've worked with most of these functions in previous sessions. If you need to use the resizing or move functions now to have your drawings match up more precisely with the shapes I've drawn, go ahead. If you're happy with the way you've drawn these objects, it's time to rotate the elements of the coffee cup to work together as a single object.

1. Select the cup shape.

2. Click on the Rotate tool. The Rotate Objects dialog box in Figure 4.10 appears.

3. Click on the right-facing arrow button to rotate the cup until the Angle setting reads 330.

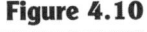

Figure 4.10

You saw the Rotate Objects dialog box in the Saturday Morning session, where you first rotated objects.

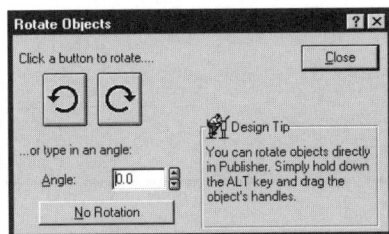

TIP If you'd like to preview the rotation angle on the page, just click on the title bar of the dialog box and drag it to the side so that you can see the object more clearly as you adjust the rotation.

4. Click on Close to close the dialog box.

5. Select the handle object.

6. Click on the Rotate tool.

7. In the Rotate Objects dialog box that appears again, click on the button with the left arrow until the Angle reads 75.

8. Click on Close to close the dialog box and click anywhere outside the object to deselect it. Your two objects now look like those in Figure 4.11.

9. Click on the handle object to select it, if it's not already selected.

10. When your cursor changes to the moving-van symbol, click and drag the handle to place it on the left edge of the cup, as shown in Figure 4.12.

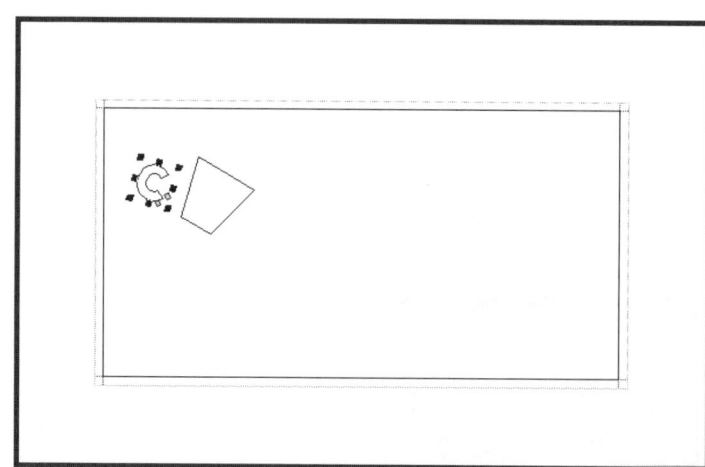

Figure 4.11

Do you see where you're going with this? Now you just have to place the two pieces together.

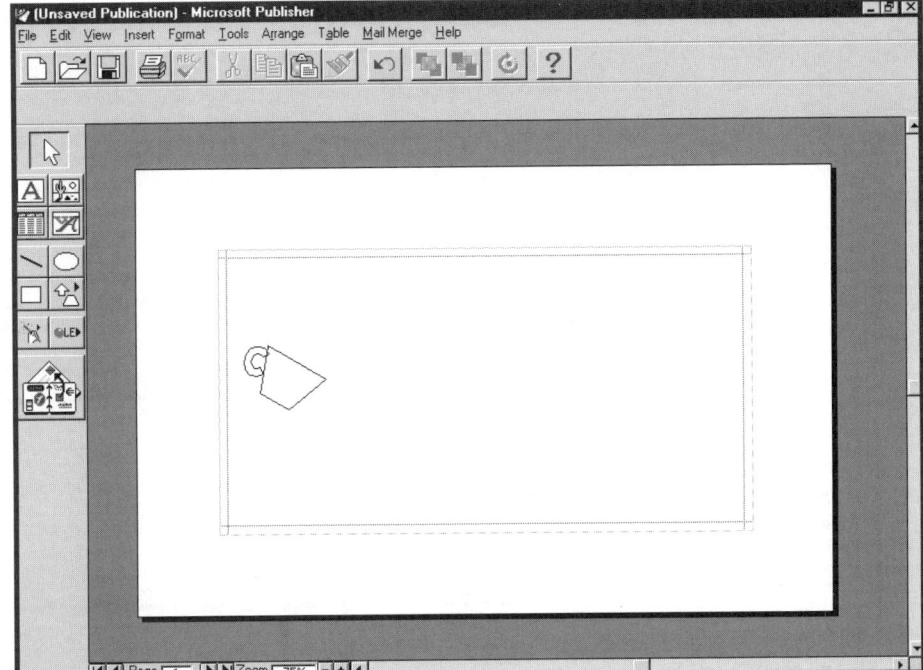

Figure 4.12

Place the handle so its edges just abut the cup shape.

11. Click on the handle object, and then, holding down the Shift key, click on the cup.

12. Select Arrange, Group Objects.

13. Select the grouped cup object and using the Object Color button on the picture formatting toolbar, select an orange color to fill the objects.

TIP ■

If the edges of the handle seem to poke into the cup, use the Arrange, Bring to Front or Send to Back commands so that the cup is in front and the handle ends at the cup's edge.

■ ■

14. Move the cup object on the page so that it is in the position of the cup in Figure 4.13.

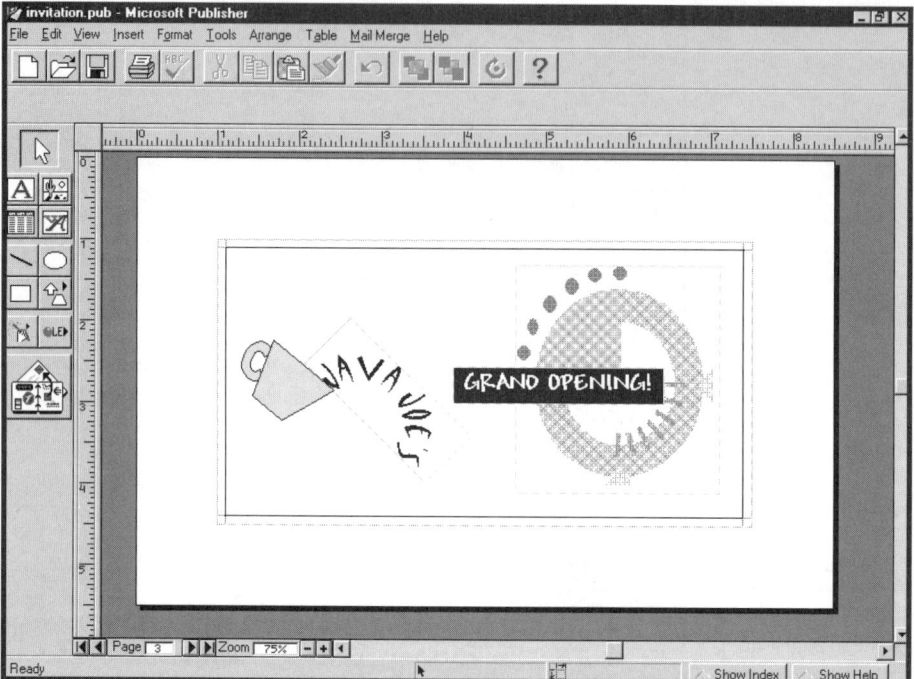

Figure 4.13

Just a reminder of
how the final page
will look and where
the cup will sit.

NOTE Publisher enables you to edit parts of a drawing; you do this using a small gray circle (or with some objects, more than one circle) that appears at the corner of the drawing near selection handles. You can place your mouse pointer over the gray circle until your cursor changes to an adjust cursor. Click and drag to modify the shape.

TIP Always remember to save periodically so that you don't lose any work you've accomplished along the way.

Combining Text with Drawings

You've gotten the hang of creating drawings and arranging them on the page. Now it's time to turn to the text part of the invitation for a moment.

Two text elements are in the finished front page of the invitation shown in Figure 4.13: a WordArt object and a text box with reverse text.

Working with WordArt

Follow these steps to create a WordArt object now:

1. Select <u>I</u>nsert, <u>O</u>bject.

2. From the Object <u>T</u>ype list, click on Microsoft WordArt 3.0, and then click on OK.

3. In the WordArt environment shown in Figure 4.14, type the text **Java Joe's** and apply the Arch Up (Curve) style.

4. Format the text to use the Matisse ITC font in 30-point size. (If you don't have Matisse, try Curlz MT, Comic Sans MS, or Beesknees ITC).

5. Click outside the WordArt object to return to the Publisher environment.

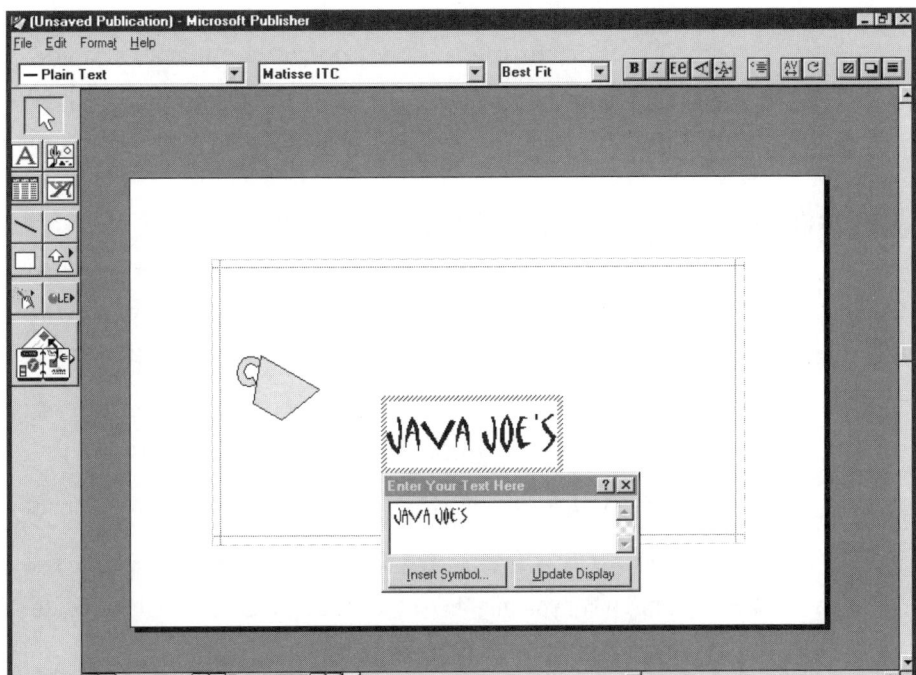

Figure 4.14

Remember, WordArt provides its own toolbar while you're working on a WordArt object.

Adding Reverse Text

Now it's time to try and create the reverse text effect to make the text Grand Opening jump out at the reader. Just follow these steps:

1. Click on the Text tool and draw a text frame about two and a half inches by three-quarters of an inch anywhere on the page.

2. Enter the text **Grand Opening** and select it. Format it with the Mead Bold font in 26-point small capitals (you can use the Small Capitals button on the Formatting toolbar for this last step).

 TIP Some alternative fonts to Mead Bold would be Tempus Sans ITC, Lucida Handwriting, or Comic Sans. The idea is to pick fonts that look relaxed and casual, to convey the informal, comfortable feeling of a café.

3. Using the Text Color tool, make the new text yellow.

4. With the text frame selected, click on the Fill Color button on the Formatting toolbar and select a black fill color.

You should now have elements for your page that look something like Figure 4.15.

Arranging Text and Drawings

To get the effect of the WordArt text spilling out of the cup that you saw in the final invitation, you'll have to rotate the WordArt object and position it just right on the page. Follow these steps to get there:

1. Move the WordArt object up near the right edge of the cup object, so the "J" in Java is next to the lip of the cup.

2. Click on the Rotate button. The Rotate Objects dialog box appears.

 TIP At this point you might want to move the dialog box to one side so that you can see how your settings affect the text onscreen.

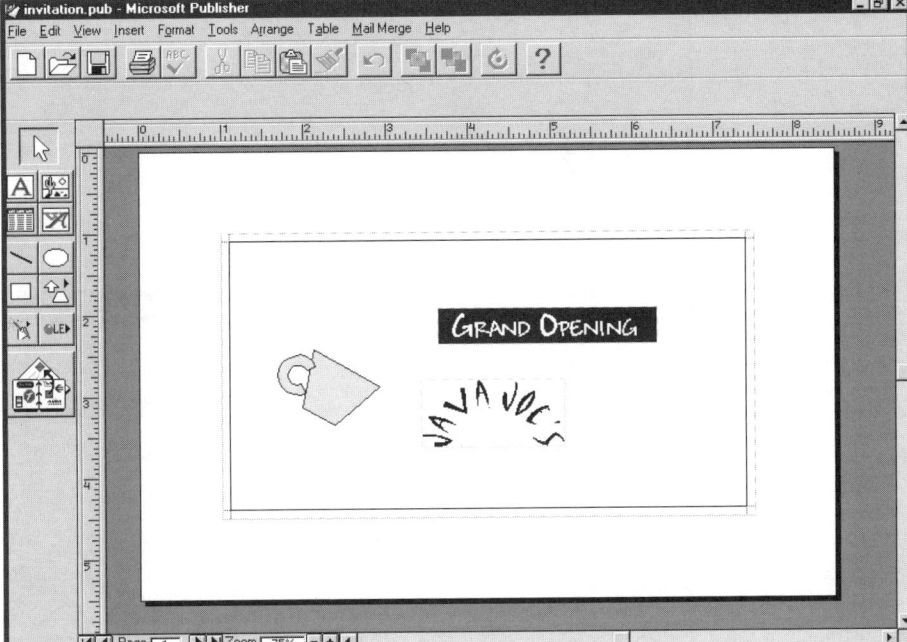

Figure 4.15

Most of the final elements are on the page; now you have to arrange them a bit.

3. Click on the right-arrow button to rotate the text to an angle of 330, as shown in Figure 4.16.

4. Click on Close. The text is at the correct angle, but you may have to move it a bit to line up with the lip of the cup, as I've done in Figure 4.17.

Using the Design Gallery

Publisher has very thoughtfully provided a collection of design elements called *Design Gallery*. Think of this as your personal grab bag of interesting elements that you can use to spice up your work. These elements come in several categories, such as Headlines, Ornaments, Titles, and Web Page Buttons. Within each category are three styles of design: Jazzy, Modern, and Plain. By selecting different categories in different styles, you have a

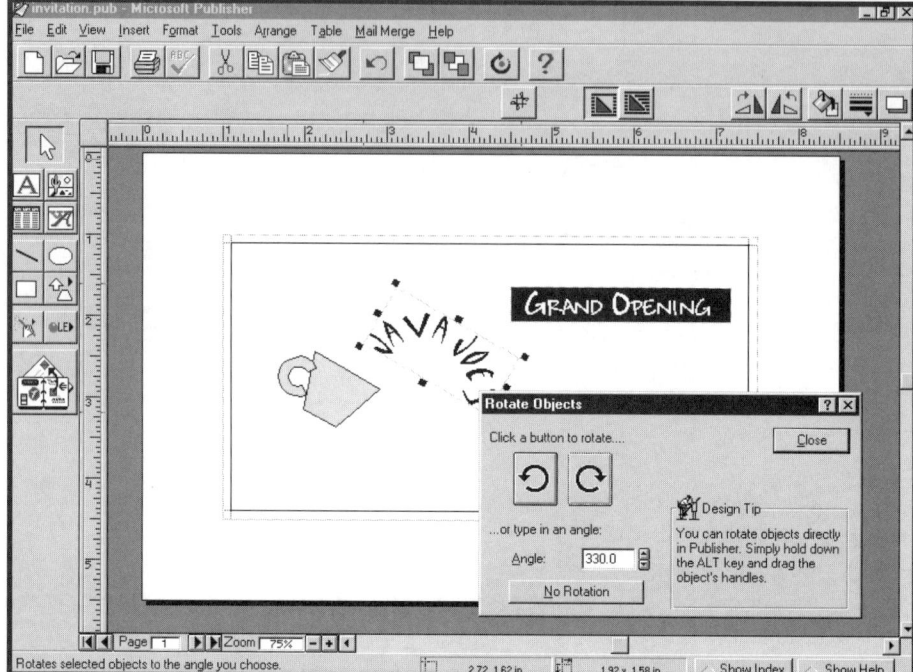

Figure 4.16

Watch the angle preview on your page as you make adjustments in the dialog box.

Figure 4.17

Use your eye to place the curve of the text at the lip of the cup, like liquid pouring out of it.

few hundred items to play with. Appendix B shows you samples of the four different styles as well as some ideas of how to use them.

TIP

Several of these elements have text placeholders. For example, you can choose a Title element and use the text placeholder to add your own title to it. The element provides a nice design to emphasize your text.

You'll add an element from the Design Gallery on the front of your invitation for visual interest. Just follow these steps:

1. Click on the Design Gallery button, which is the large button at the bottom of the Publisher toolbar. The Design Gallery dialog box shown in Figure 4.18 appears.

2. Click on various categories to see the variety of things available. After you've taken a look at what's there, click on the Ornaments category.

3. To change the style of the designs, click on the <u>M</u>ore Designs button to see the drop-down list shown in Figure 4.18. Here you can choose among Jazzy, Modern, or Plain Designs.

4. Select Plain.

Figure 4.18

You can mix and match drawings, clip art, and Design Gallery elements if you like.

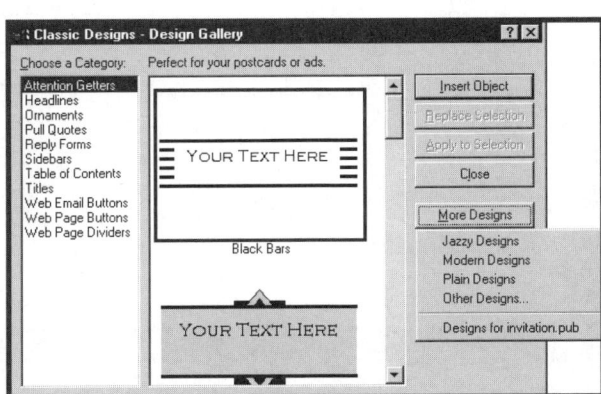

NOTE

If you have a graphic file that you'd like to add to the Design Gallery, select Other Designs from the More Designs drop-down list and locate the file by using the dialog box that appears. If you'd like to add an element you've created in this publication to the Gallery, such as the coffee cup drawing, first click on the object in your document. Open the Gallery and click on <u>M</u>ore Designs. Select the command that now appears at the bottom of the drop-down list, Add Selection to Design Gallery. This enables you to start a new design set for the Gallery and add this selection to it. You can then select that design set by choosing it from the More Designs drop-down list.

5. Use the scroll bar to the right of the design samples until you see the design called "Compass," shown in Figure 4.19.

6. Click on the <u>I</u>nsert Object button to place the object on the page.

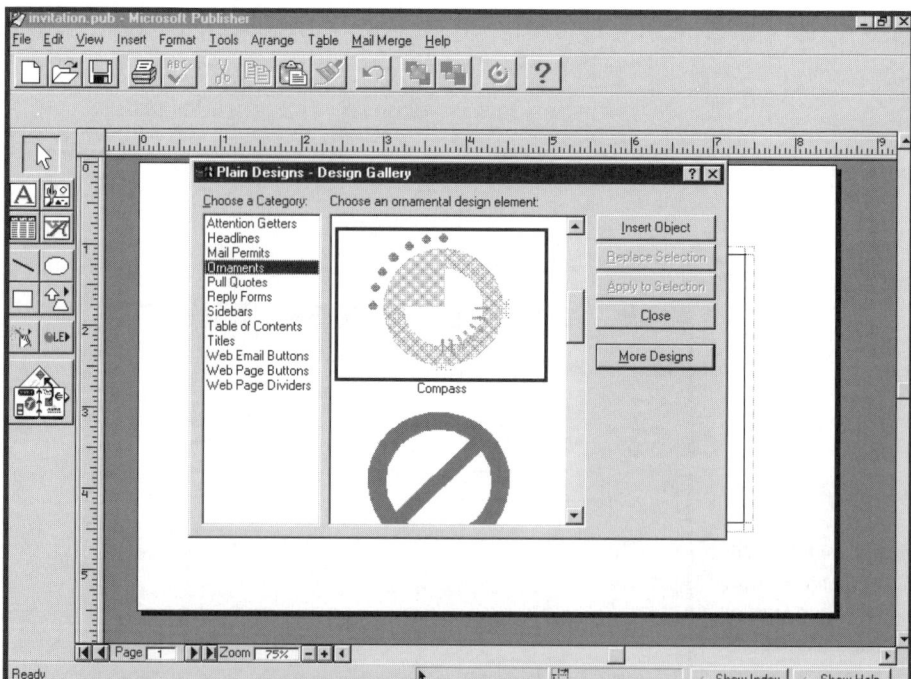

Figure 4.19

This modern geometric form fits in with the look of the invitation.

Arranging Drawings on the Page

Now, following my directions about how to place things on this page is one thing, but when you're on your own, how do you figure out how to arrange items on a page? Here are a few guidelines to consider:

- When combining text elements with design elements, either drawings or elements from the Design Gallery or the Clip Gallery, consider the purpose of the text. In this example, the name of the café pours out of the coffee cup, sending the message to the reader that this café specializes in coffee.

- If you're placing text over a design element, as with the Grand Opening text, make sure it shows up clearly against the background. Filling in the text frame with a dark color and using reverse text often makes the text object stand out.

- Try to have text continue or add to the design shape or direction of the graphics. For example, using curved WordArt text to spill out of the cup provides the feeling of motion that liquid pouring out of a cup would have. Conversely, placing the Grand Opening element along the edge of the 45-degree angle within the circle of the Design Gallery element reinforces the geometric feeling of the invitation.

- Don't forget to make use of white space. Although there's a lot going on designwise on the front of this invitation, there's still enough white space to give it a clean, modern feeling.

You now need to do three things to get the Design Gallery element to look like the one on the finished design shown in Figure 4.20:

1. Resize the object so that the frame around it measures about three inches square.

2. Move it to the right side of the invitation.

3. Move the Design Gallery element to the back (Arrange, Send to Back) so that the Grand Opening text frame shows up in front of it. (You may also need to move the text frame object so that it's placed near the middle of the design element, as shown in Figure 4.20).

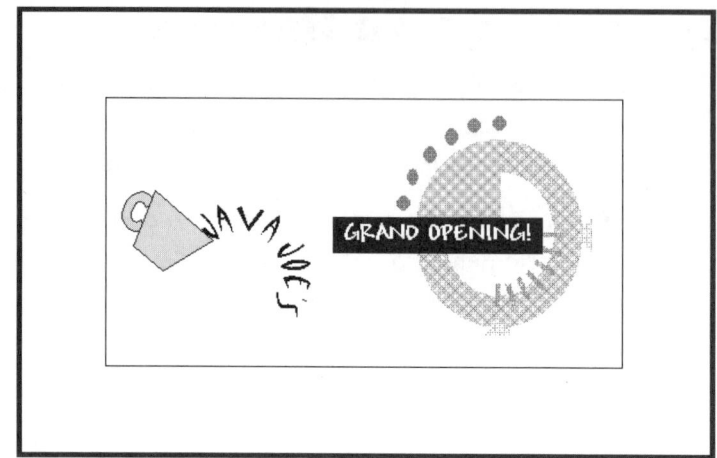

Figure 4.20

You'll often have to modify objects you place on the page to make them balance with other objects.

Creating the Second Page

You've created all of the elements for the front of the invitation. Now you'll get a crack at reviewing some of the same skills you've just used to quickly create the inside of the folded-card publication. Figure 4.21 shows the contents of the inside page.

As you can see from the callouts on Figure 4.21, basically six objects are on this page. Once again, there are two text elements, both created in text frames. A copy of the coffee cup you created is on the first page, rotated to the left. A rectangle makes a hairline frame around the other elements. Finally, two simple lines have been drawn and placed at angles to each other to both underline the first text element and frame the second. Again, the design is simple and modern, so it reinforces the feeling of the cover of the invitation.

 **NOTE** Notice that I've chosen to use the Mead Bold text on the You're Invited text item to connect it to the Grand Opening text on the first page. However, I've gone with a simpler sans serif font (Lucida Sans) for the wordier second text object rather than using one of the more casual styles of text from the first page. That's because there's a lot more text here, and a more straightforward font makes it easier to read.

Copy of coffee cup from first page   Rectangle drawn with Box tool

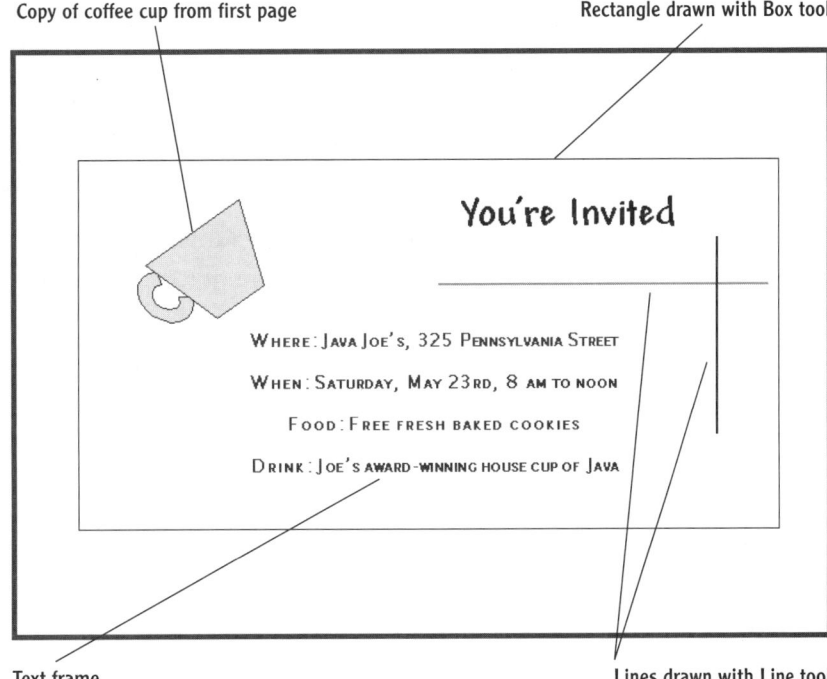

Figure 4.21

Recognize your coffee cup? This is just a copy of the one on the first page.

You're Invited

WHERE: JAVA JOE'S, 325 PENNSYLVANIA STREET

WHEN: SATURDAY, MAY 23RD, 8 AM TO NOON

FOOD: FREE FRESH BAKED COOKIES

DRINK: JOE'S AWARD-WINNING HOUSE CUP OF JAVA

Text frame   Lines drawn with Line tool

OK. You knew this moment would come: I'm going to send you out on your own to build the second page of the invitation. You have the skills, you know the procedures. Here are the details—get to work!

- Copy the cup from the first page (it should be grouped so that you can copy both the handle and cup as a single object), paste it on the second page, and rotate it to the left at a 35-degree angle.

- Use 28-point Mead Bold for the You're Invited text; leave the text black and set the fill color for the text frame to yellow. Center the text in the frame.

- Make the larger text block in the center Lucida Sans 12-point text, and apply both the Bold and Small Capitals styles to it. Center this text in its frame and adjust the line spacing to 2 spaces after each line (Format, Line Spacing).

✦ Use the Line tool to draw a horizontal line approximately three and a quarter inches long; then draw another line approximately two inches long and rotate it to a 90-degree angle. Format these lines to be two settings thicker than Hairline (with the lines selected, use the Border tool to choose the thickness setting for the line).

✦ Using the Box tool, draw a rectangle to surround the other objects (use the guidelines as a measure of its size) and use the line thickness setting one size above Hairline for a line style.

Just use Figure 4.21 as a guide to how to place these elements on the page. Now that you've put all of your hard-learned skills to good use, your invitation is complete.

TIP You'll need to use your resizing skills and object-moving skills to get everything to look as it does in Figure 4.21. Don't forget to save your publication along the way.

Take a Break

The second part of this session, mail merge, is a real change of pace. So, before you tackle it, go off and clear your head. Take a walk around the block, play with the cat, read a poem. Whatever you do, come back ready to set up a personalized mailing in which Publisher will handle everything but stuffing the envelopes and licking the stamps.

Using Mail Merge to Send Your Invitations

If you've ever had to type a separate letter and envelope to each and every customer or friend in your Rolodex, you'll recognize mail merge as the best invention since cappuccino.

Here's how mail merge works. You have a list of information, typically names and addresses. You have a form document (a form letter, an envelope, an invoice, or whatever). Publisher takes unique information in the list and inserts it into a copy of the document. You can generate hundreds

of form letters and accompanying envelopes, for example, all with different addresses, all from a single letter and an address list.

You can create the list in Publisher with the steps in the following section, or you can use a list that you have already created in a database program such as Access or a word processor such as Word for Windows. The form document you'll use for this first mail merge is the invitation you have just created, which you should still have displayed in Publisher.

Creating an Address List

The first step to the mail merge procedure is to create a list of information to combine with your document to personalize it. Publisher enables you to build an address list, with entries for almost every common piece of contact information, including name, address, phone, and e-mail address. This address list is called a *data source* in mail merge lingo.

TIP You can also perform a mail merge using an existing data source created in Publisher or another program; you'll learn how to do that in the next section.

1. Select <u>M</u>ail Merge, <u>C</u>reate Publisher Address List. The New Address List dialog box in Figure 4.22 appears on your screen.

Figure 4.22

Publisher has provided fields to enter all kinds of common contact information in this form.

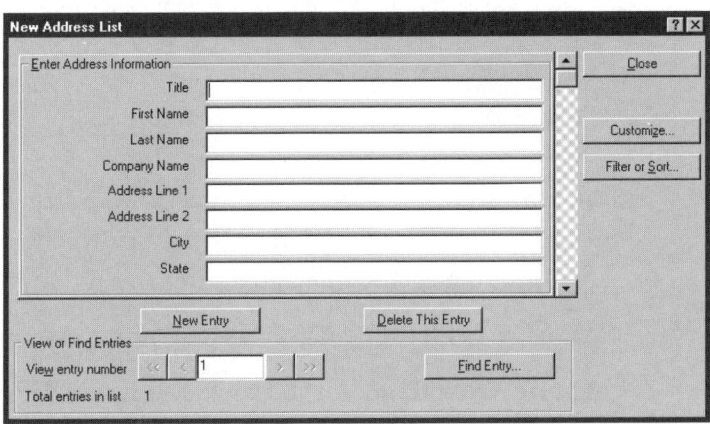

NOTE You can also get to this dialog box by selecting Mail Merge, Open Data Source, and then choosing Create an address list in Publisher from the Open Data Source dialog box.

2. Type the following information in the appropriate fields, leaving any fields not mentioned here blank:

Title: **Mr.**

First Name: **Glenn**

Last Name: **McDowell**

Company Name: **McDowell Dry Cleaners**

Address Line 1: **98 Main Street**

City: **Mencken**

State: **GA**

ZIP Code: **44578**

TIP When you use a data source for names and addresses it's a good idea to use two name fields (First Name and Last Name) as Publisher has here, rather than a single name field. That way if you want to use just the first name alone in a greeting or to mention the person by first name in the context of the document, you can place that field on its own.

3. Click on New Entry to save the first record in the address list and get a blank form to enter the second. The View entry number field at the bottom of the dialog box now indicates that this is the second record. Enter the information listed below, clicking on New Entry after entering each name and address set to enter five more records:

Ms. May Lee Hong, 225 Maple Avenue, Atlanta, GA 43267

Mr. Albert Graham, 4956 Duck Tail Lane, Ridgefield, GA 44755

Mr. Liam Allard, 89A Sharon Blvd., Mencken, GA 44578

Mrs. Anna Perewski, 3897 Peebles Court, Ridgefield, GA 44756

Dr. Pierre Minion, Medical Arts, 7 Route 37, Atlanta, GA 43269

NOTE You can use various buttons in this dialog box to locate certain records. The View entry number field has arrow buttons to move among the records in the order in which you entered them. The Find Entry button opens a search dialog box to find a record with specific text. The Filter or Sort button takes you to a dialog box in which you can either sort the entries to appear in a different order such as alphabetically by last name, or to filter out any records not meeting certain criteria from the mail merge. Use the Customize button to change the fields that appear in your address list form (for example, if you want to add a country field for international mailings).

4. Click on Close to display the Save As dialog box. In this dialog box enter a name for the data source file and click on the Save button. This saves your address list so that you can use it as the data source for other mail merges.

NOTE You don't have to use all of the fields in the New Address List form. In fact, you can use some fields for some records and other fields for others (for example, some addresses may have a second address item, such as a post office box, and others may not). You'll see how Publisher draws on the data you've entered here shortly.

Entering Merge Fields

You're now ready to insert a *merge field* into the invitation document. Publisher uses a merge field as a placeholder in the form document for corresponding data in the data source. A merge field is basically an instruction to Publisher to go retrieve that type of data and place it in that spot. For example, placing a name field in the greeting of a letter tells Publisher to place a unique name from the data source at that spot in each successive copy of the letter that it prints. Here's how you place merge fields in a document:

1. Select Mail Merge, Insert Fields. The Insert Fields dialog box appears.

2. Click on the Text tool and draw a text box like the one shown in Figure 4.23, just below the You're Invited text frame. (If you need to drag the dialog box to one side so that you can draw the text frame, feel free to do that.)

3. Click on the field titled First Name, and then click on Insert to insert the field into the text frame.

At this point you could continue to draw text frames anywhere on your document and insert as many fields as you like. Figure 4.24, for example, shows a typical form letter with the address and greeting in merge field format. After fields are inserted, you can also add text or spaces around them.

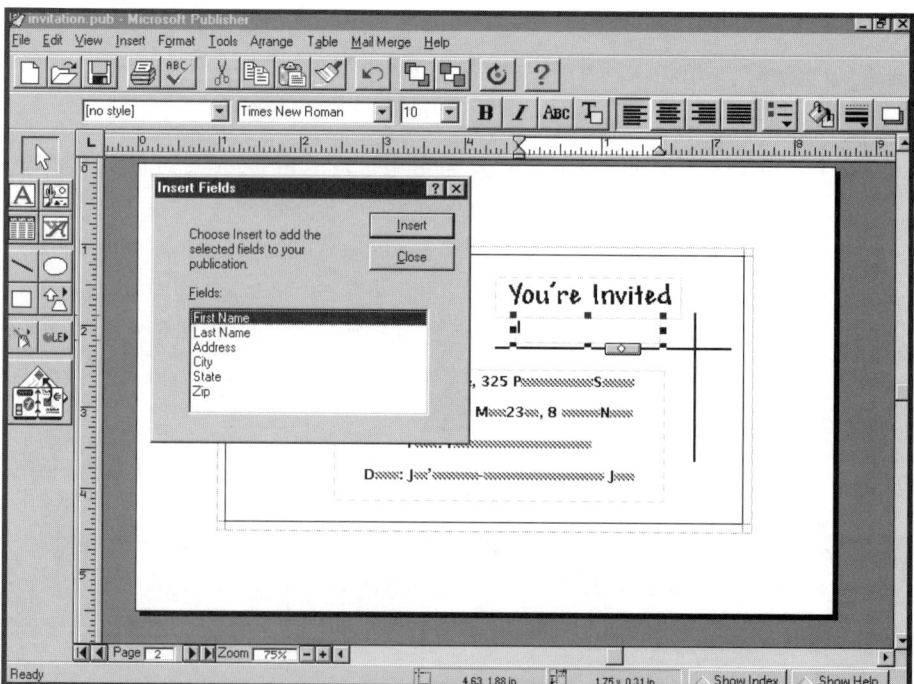

Figure 4.23

While in the Insert Fields dialog box you can add text frames to the page or even move among pages.

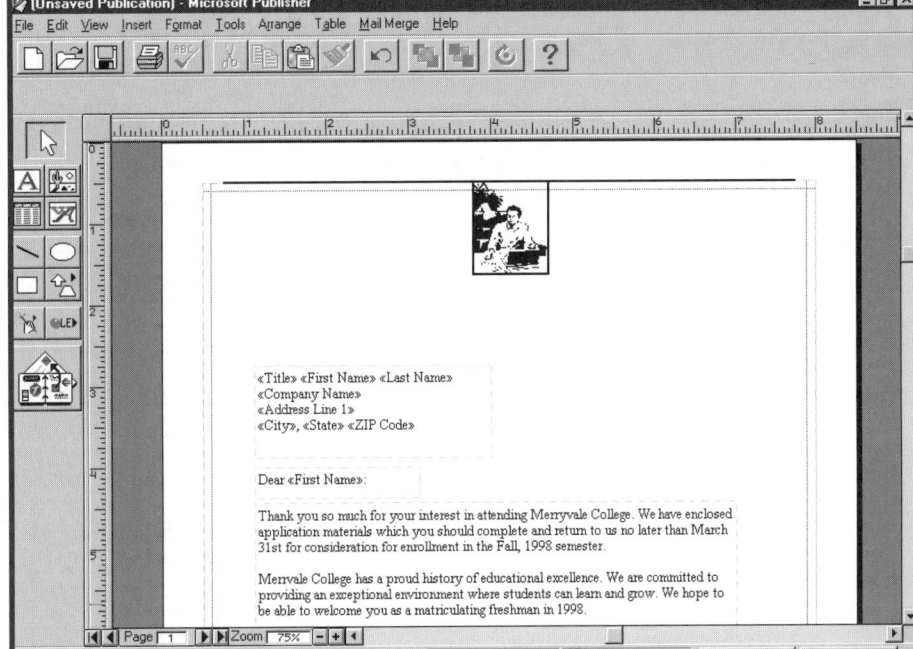

Figure 4.24

This form letter
pulls on an address
list for its inside
address and
greeting.

When you're done, click on Close to close the dialog box and return to
your document.

CAUTION People often forget small details when placing merge fields. For example, don't forget to
type in the comma after the City field or place a colon after the greeting (Dear <<First
Name>>:). Remember to add spaces where appropriate, for example, between the Title,
First Name, and Last Name fields.

Formatting Merge Fields

You can apply formatting to the field you've just inserted in your invitation
so that the actual first names that get inserted in the document during the
merge have the style of text you prefer.

1. Select the field name <<First Name>>.

2. Format the text as Lucida Sans, 12 point, Bold.

3. If you want to move the text frame slightly so that it lines up with the text above it, do that now.

Viewing Your Mail Merge

Now that you've selected a data source and placed a mail merge field into your document, there's nothing left to do but view the results.

1. Select Mail Merge, Merge. The dialog box in Figure 4.25 appears with the first name in your list displayed on the invitation (if you can't see the name, move the Preview Data dialog box aside).

2. Click repeatedly on the button with two right arrows on it to see the various first names from your address list inserted in the invitation.

3. When you've finished previewing all of the records, click on Close.

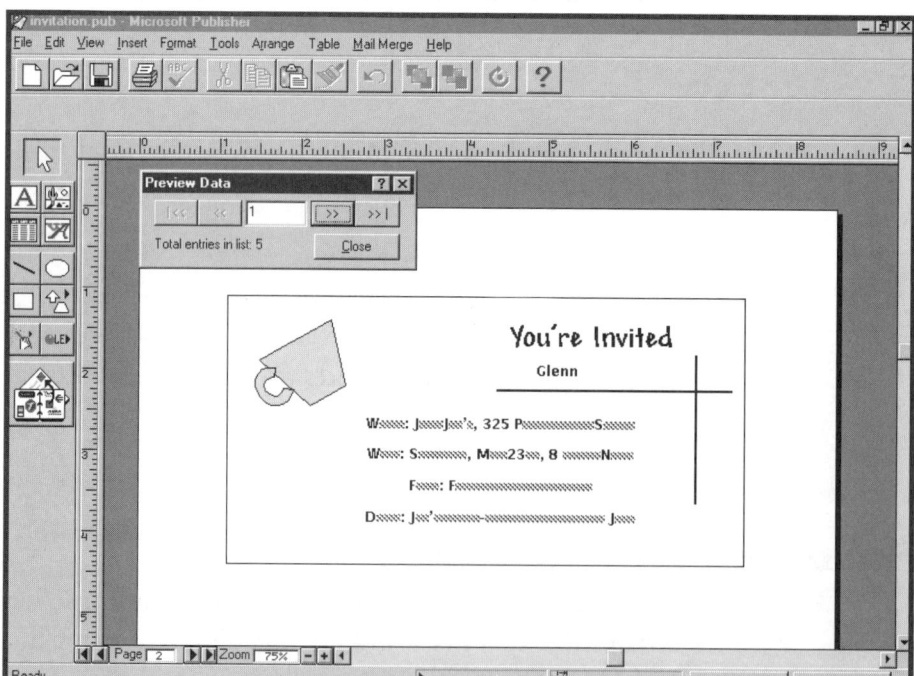

Figure 4.25

The first name in your list appears on the personalized invitation.

Printing a Mail Merge

At this point you've created a set of merge documents. All that's left is to print those documents.

1. Select File, Print Merge. The Print Merge dialog box (Figure 4.26) appears. The Print range area of this dialog box shows options of printing All Entries or a range of Entries—showing from 1 to 5—but you can change it as you wish.

2. To print the entire invitation you can accept the defaults and click on OK. (For more details about printing options, refer to the Saturday Morning session).

TIP There's also a very handy little button here: Test. Pressing this makes Publisher print one test document so that you can see how things will look before printing the whole set of entries. With larger mailings, this can save you a lot of wasted paper—if you don't like what you see the first time, you don't have to see the same mistake repeated in multiple pages of printout.

NOTE The Don't print lines that contain only empty fields check box is useful if you have inserted a field in your document, such as company name, that is empty in some of your

Figure 4.26

Instead of printing a page, you're printing entries from the address list on separate pages.

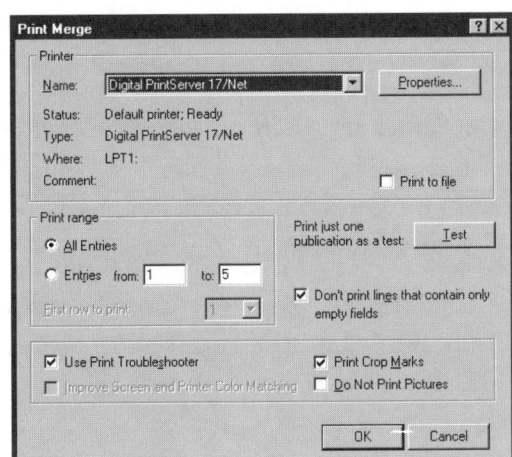

entries but not in others. If an address contains no company name, Publisher won't print a blank line when this check box is selected.

• •

Generating Envelopes

You've used the mail merge function to personalize your invitation. Now it's time to create envelopes to go along with the invitation. You'll use the Envelope Wizard to speed things along.

NOTE   There's also a Label Wizard, in case you'd like to use mailing labels instead of envelopes. The procedure is pretty much the same as that described here for envelopes.

You can save the invitation merge document with the field information intact at this point. This will let you print or view it again later without going through the setup process again.

Starting the Envelope Wizard

To start the Wizard you'll need to open a new document.

1. Select File, Create New Publication. If asked about saving the invitation merge file, say yes or no, whichever you like.

2. When the New Publication dialog box appears, click on the PageWizard tab.

3. Click on Envelope, and then on OK. The first Wizard dialog box, shown in Figure 4.27, appears. Publisher Design Assistant suggests that, because you've used a certain style with Wizards in the past, you might want to use that style again.

4. Leave the default option of using your previous style (yours may be different from mine), and click on Next to proceed. The dialog box that appears, shown in Figure 4.28, has three options for including items on your envelope:

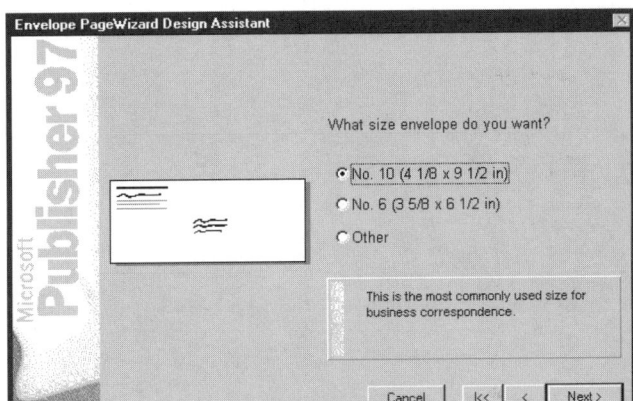

Figure 4.27

Wizard Design Assistants lead you through the process to create envelopes.

- Include a picture
- Include my company's initials
- I don't want either, thanks

5. Leave the third option button checked and click on Next.

 TIP   If you have a company logo (like the one you'll create in the last session of this book) you could choose to include a picture here and insert your logo file on the envelope.

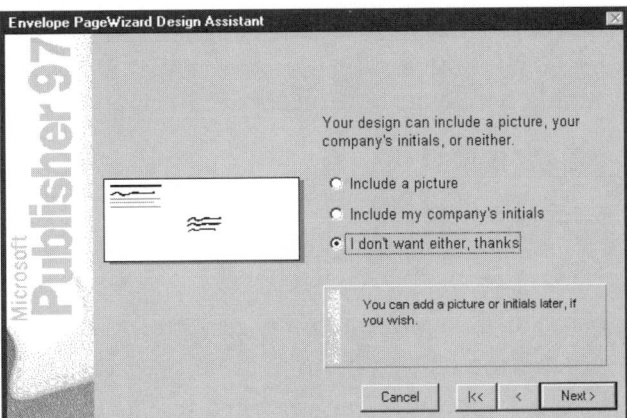

Figure 4.28

You can decide to add graphics after you finish the Wizard.

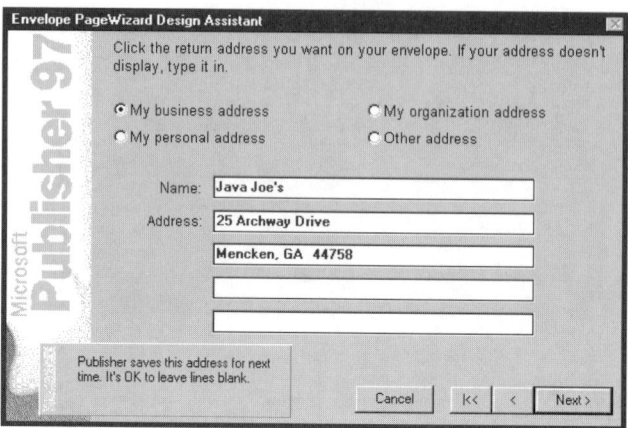

Microsoft Publisher 97

Figure 4.29

The business address you enter here may pop up in other Wizards from time to time.

6. In the next dialog box that appears (Figure 4.29) click on the My business address option button and enter the return address for the envelopes you'll use with the invitations: **Java Joe's, 25 Archway Drive, Mencken, GA 44758**.

NOTE You can enter a different address for each of these four option button items; any time you run a Wizard with your return address options, the last Wizard entries for each choice will appear, saving you the time of reentering addresses you use all of the time.

7. Click on Next to proceed. The dialog box that follows asks if you want any one of three pieces of information included:

○ Air Mail

○ Confidential

○ Urgent: Reply Requested

8. None of these options apply to your invitation, so click on the option button labeled Nothing, thanks, and click on Next. The dialog box that appears now gives you a Yes/No choice: do you want to use your default printer?

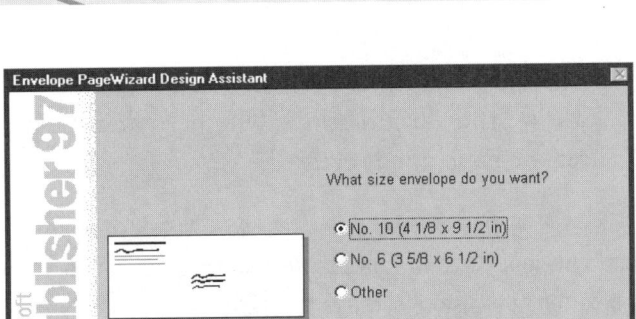

Figure 4.30

Some invitations would fit in the smaller No. 6 size envelope, but yours needs a larger one.

9. Click on Next to accept the default answer of Yes. The dialog box in Figure 4.30 appears. Here you have to select an envelope size. The two sizes listed here are common envelope sizes (No. 10 is the standard business letter envelope).

10. Click in the option button labeled Other, and then click on Next to see how you create a custom envelope size. The dialog box in Figure 4.31 appears.

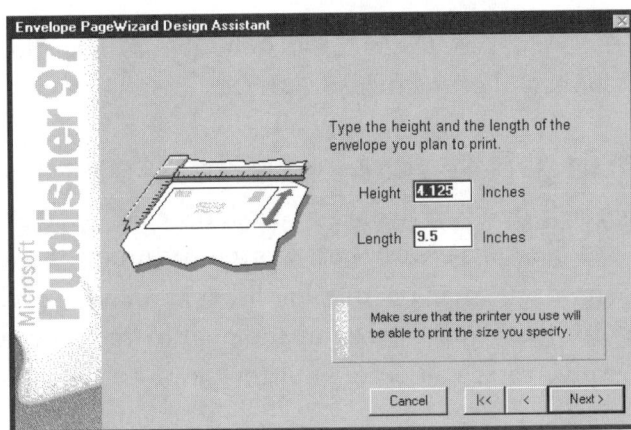

Figure 4.31

Usually the standard sizes are fine; you're making this modification here just so you know how it works.

11. Modify the Height to four inches, and then click on Next. The final question the Wizard asks is whether you'd like to set up mail merge after the envelope is created.

TIP Standard envelope sizes in Europe are slightly different, so you may need to use this dialog box to make custom settings for them.

12. Click on the Yes option button, and then on Next. (Actually, there's nothing to stop you from using mail merge when you're done, even if you select No here). A dialog box with a single button labeled Create It! appears.

13. Click on the button to create the envelope.

A message indicates that the envelope is being created. When Publisher finishes, the envelope document appears, as shown in Figure 4.32.

Now it's time to run through the mail merge procedure for your envelopes. However, this time, because you've already saved your address list, you'll open an existing data source file, rather than creating one from scratch. To get ready to insert merge fields, follow these steps:

1. Select and delete the placeholder text (THE MAILING ADDRESS GOES HERE) in the middle of your envelope. You'll replace it with merge fields shortly.

2. Resize the address text box to be about three and a half inches wide so that all of the fields will fit.

Using an Existing Data Source for Your Envelopes

Often you'll have the names and addresses of friends or clients already saved in a file. This file can be a Word for Windows table, an Excel spreadsheet, an Access database, or a Publisher address list file. Using that list of names can make quick work of the mail merge process. To use the data source you created earlier for your invitation to generate envelopes, follow these steps:

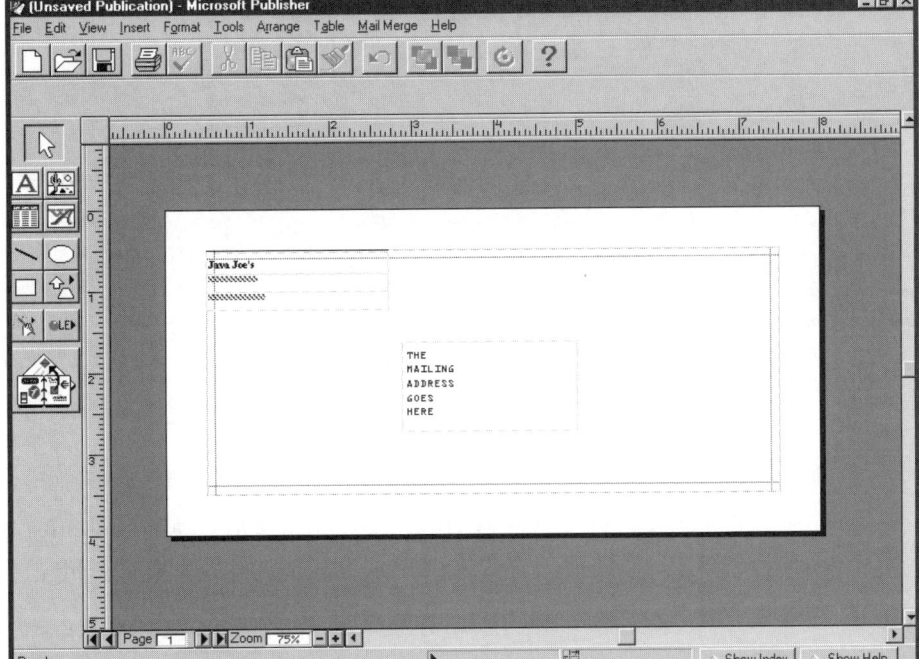

Figure 4.32

There's a placeholder for the mailing address.

1. Select <u>M</u>ail Merge, <u>O</u>pen Data Source. You'll see a message offering an overview of the process or offering to give you step-by-step instructions. (If you choose the overview, you'll get a series of seven screens telling you what I've just told you.)

2. Click on Continue. The dialog box in Figure 4.33 appears.

Figure 4.33

If you choose the Create line you'll see the New Address List dialog box you saw earlier in this session.

Open Data Source

To merge information into this publication, you'll need a data source that contains that information, such as a Word document, an Excel worksheet, or a database file. You can merge from a file you already have, or create one in Publisher.

> Merge information from a file I already have

> Create an address list in Publisher

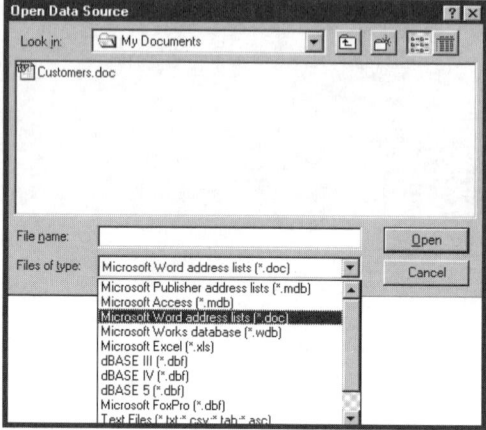

Figure 4.34

Use the Files of type drop-down list to find other types of files.

3. To use an existing file, click on <u>M</u>erge information from a file I already have. The Open Data Source dialog box in Figure 4.34 appears.

4. Use the Look in list box to locate the address file you created and saved in Publisher.

NOTE At this point you could also use this dialog box to open a data source created in other programs such as Excel, Word, or Access. You may need to modify the Files of type list box, shown open in Figure 4.34, to locate the file format you're looking for.

5. When you locate the file, click on <u>O</u>pen. The dialog box and message shown in Figure 4.35 appears.

NOTE For example, if you choose a Word file that contains a table of information as a data source, Publisher will translate the column headings from the table into field names.

6. Click on the dialog box to get rid of the message.

7. If you need to, drag the dialog box out of the way so that you can see the address text frame on the envelope and click on the text frame.

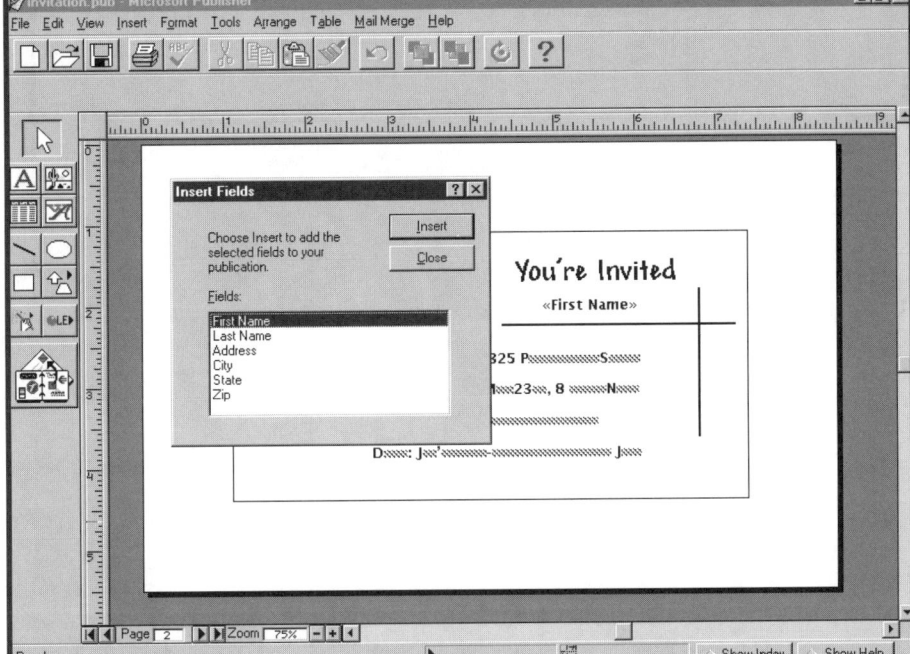

Figure 4.35

This is the same dialog box you used to place merge fields in the previous section.

8. Click on the item Title in the dialog box list, and then on the Insert button. The title field appears on the envelope.

9. Press the spacebar, and then click on and insert the First Name field.

10. Click on the spacebar, and then click on and insert the Last Name field.

11. Press Enter to move down one line.

12. Click on the Company Name item, and then on Insert to place it on the envelope.

13. Press Enter to move down one more line.

14. Repeat the steps to insert the Address Line 1 item and press Enter again to move down to the final line of the address.

15. Click on and insert the City item, and then type **a comma** and **a space**.

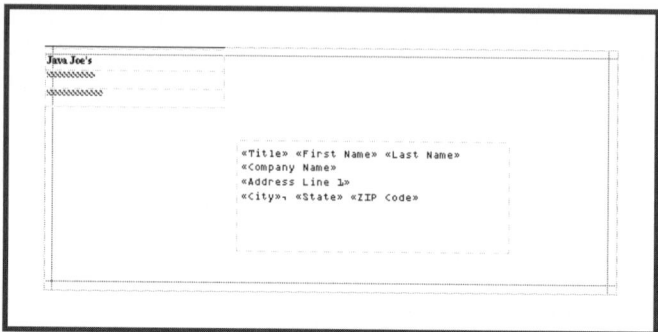

Figure 4.36

An envelope ready
to be printed as a
mail merge.

16. Click on and insert the State item, and then press the spacebar once.

17. Finally, click on and insert the Zip Code item. Your envelope should now look like the one shown in Figure 4.36.

18. Select Mail Merge, Merge. The Preview Data dialog box appears (see Figure 4.37), with your first address in the envelope document. You can use the arrow keys in the dialog box to scroll through and display the various addresses in your list, merged with the envelope.

You've now produced a personalized invitation and the envelopes in which to mail them. That's all there is to mail merge. After you have address lists that you use often saved in Publisher, mail merges can be done in a matter of a minute or two. What a time savings over typing dozens of envelopes by hand!

What's Next?

In this session, you've become acquainted with Publisher's drawing tools, including predefined custom shapes and the Design Gallery of special design elements. Hopefully you've also picked up several more pieces of advice about good design along the way. You also learned the ins and outs of performing mail merges and building your own address lists in Publisher.

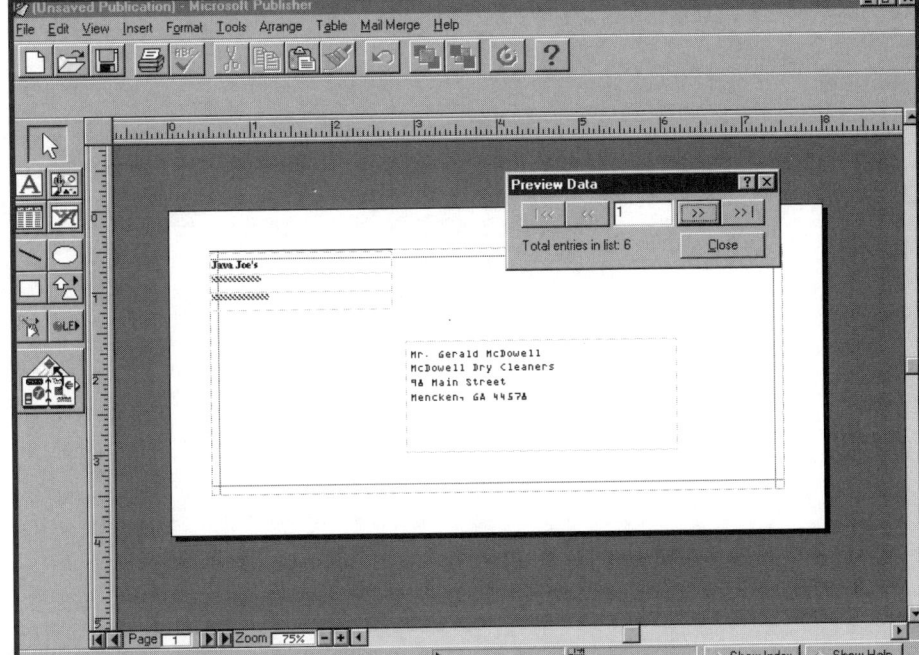

Figure 4.37

Now you can just place envelopes in your printer and print!

In the next and final session for the weekend, you get to bring all of the skills you've learned to the project of creating stationery and business cards. You'll design a company logo and meet a couple of other Wizards to help you finalize your designs.

Creating Logos, Letterhead, and Business Cards

- ✿ Matching your logo to your identity
- ✿ Grouping and sizing the logo
- ✿ Designing letterhead
- ✿ Providing balance and readability
- ✿ Running the Business Card Wizard

Just as a book is often judged by its cover, the collateral materials you design for your business can drive that all-important first impression. Whether you run a small business or an association, whether you're purely self-employed or have a business on the side, well-designed letterhead and business cards are key to your professional image.

In this final session, you'll take all the skills you've picked up over the course of the weekend and use them to create business letterhead and business cards that will dazzle your clients. You'll build a company logo and work with fancy first letters. Then you'll use both the Letterhead and Business Cards Wizards to see what Publisher's design sense and your new desktop publishing skills can do together.

Advice on Designing Logos

Your company or organization logo is like your taste in clothes: it's the symbol by which you are known. Your logo may never be as famous as the golden arches of McDonald's or the flowing white script on the red background of Coca-Cola, but it's still vital to your business image.

Huge corporations spend big bucks and agonizing months of debate designing logos. They do market research. They run possible designs by test groups. They pay legions of lawyers to make sure no one else is using that logo for a competing product.

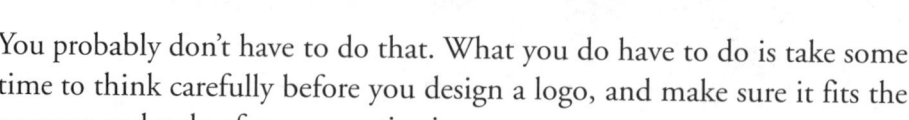

You probably don't have to do that. What you do have to do is take some time to think carefully before you design a logo, and make sure it fits the purpose and style of your organization.

Match Your Logo to Your Identity

The first thing to think about is whether the style of logo you're considering makes a statement about your company.

✿ Is there a graphic symbol in it that shows just what service you provide or what product you offer? For example, Planter's Peanuts uses a little character in the shape of a peanut for a logo (with a top hat and cane, no less). Figure 5.1 shows such a logo.

CAUTION Although clip art like that shown in Figure 5.1 is technically OK for a logo, be careful not to use an image that you see often in every community newsletter and small business brochure. If you've got a piece of clip art, so does every Tom, Dick, and Mary with Publisher. If you do use clip art, add something to it or modify it to be truly unique.

Figure 5.1

Traditional theater masks reflect this business.

Figure 5.2

An eagle suggests
vigilance.

⚙ Is there a more abstract graphic that may not tell anything about your product in itself, but suggests an attribute of the product that you wish to call to mind? For example, Jaguar automobiles have a logo with an image of a leaping jaguar. This suggests not the cars themselves, but attributes of the cars that resemble a jungle cat in motion: speed and agility. Figure 5.2 shows such a logo.

⚙ Do you prefer a logo that consists only of text? If so, the choice of font becomes of paramount importance. There are few logos as iden-tifiable as that of IBM: three simple letters in a solid, strong-looking font, for example. Figure 5.3 shows a text-only logo based on Publisher's WordArt feature.

Any of these approaches can work, as long as you think carefully about who you are, what image you want to project, and how your customers will perceive the image you set forth.

Use a Logo That's Easy to Reproduce

Another issue to think about when designing a logo is how you're going to reproduce that logo. Will you have one-color stationery that a black-and-white printer can cope with perfectly well? Do you want complicated color

Figure 5.3

A fun font fits nicely
with a comic book
publisher.

and shading effects, even though they may get lost or look muddy when copied? Or will you design a logo that looks good in both color and black and white, so you have the flexibility to produce materials of both types?

Designing a complex color logo or one with gradations and shadings can tie you into producing only color pieces and only with high-quality (expensive) printing services. Remember, no matter what your intentions about producing fancy materials, somebody, somewhere, is going to run black-and-white copies of your stationery or brochure. The simpler and cleaner your logo, the better those copies will look.

TIP If you feel strongly about having a fancy logo and using colors and shadings, try creating both a color and a black-and-white version. That way you have the flexibility and the option of creating an extra-impressive color version when the project requires it.

NOTE Publisher has a feature to help you with color printing. Select Tools, Options and select the check box titled Improve screen and printer color matching. This controls the way screen colors resemble the actual printed results.

Finally, consider that you'll probably end up reproducing your logo in various sizes. The logo on your business card can end up pretty tiny to leave room for your name, address, and so on. Will the logo you're designing lose definition when you reduce it? Will the text become unreadable? At the other end of the scale, if you blow it up to put it on a poster, will the edges of the text or graphics look jagged and unprofessional? The simpler the logo, the less you have to fiddle with it when you reduce and expand it to different sizes. Try making some copies of your logo at different percentages of the original size to see how it works.

Building a Logo

Now it's time to take a swing at building a logo. As you do, you'll use many of the skills you've already learned and get some additional tips on design.

Here's the scenario: you are buying a small business to provide billing services to the legal community and you want to create an up-to-date logo for it. Your clients are professional and typically conservative. How does this information translate into a logo? First, you could consider images that relate to the law, such as scales of justice. Your text should probably be somewhat formal and professional-looking, like your clients. Consider the legal letterhead you've seen: there's hardly ever any kind of flashy graphics. Match the mood of your business to that of your clients and you'll appeal to their sensibilities.

Choosing a Graphic Image for Your Logo

So, assuming you decide to include a graphic in your logo, how do you select that graphic? Look at Figure 5.4. Here you can see five graphic images that could relate to the legal world: a document with a seal, a set of thick reference books, a judge with a gavel on the bench, a set of scales, and an old-fashioned scroll. Which, if any of these, would make a good graphic in your logo? Take a look at them one by one:

- The document with a seal is a possibility. Even though it uses a couple of colors in addition to black for the seal, the image would probably reproduce pretty cleanly. With a piece of clip art like this,

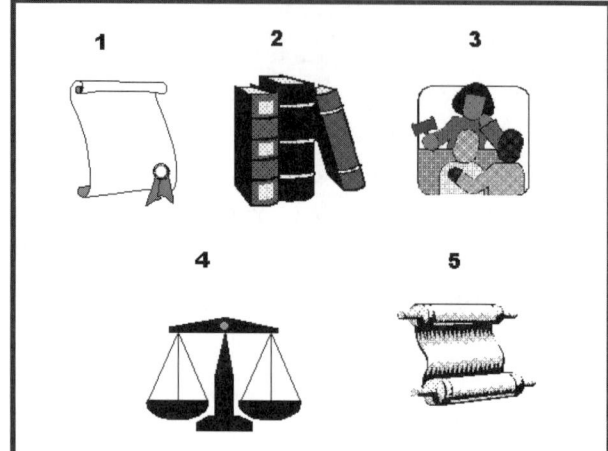

Figure 5.4

Any of these could suggest the law, but which would work well in a logo?

you could even place any logo text within the graphic image, making the logo more compact.

- The books may suggest professional scholarship, however, they are very dark and need shading and color for a reader to be able to clearly make out the shapes and differentiate between them.

- The judge addressing people at the bench is a very complex graphic, because it uses shadings, patterns, and color to make itself understood. In addition, the patterns used in the color fills would become grainy and unattractive if this image were blown up to a larger size.

- The scales image is a nice one. It seems the best one here in terms of logo design, because it is almost entirely black, providing a clean silhouette that should be easy to reproduce. However, the edges of some of the shapes are a bit jagged and might suffer with enlargement.

- The scroll graphic suggests a legal document, but its very old-fashioned look makes it somewhat dated. Also, it uses shadings that might be hard to reproduce, and it might not read well in smaller versions.

So, the best choices here are numbers 1 and 4. Because I say so (and it's my book), you're going to use number 4 for the graphic in the logo. With a blank full page document open, follow these steps to insert this piece of clip art:

1. Select Insert, Clip Art to open the Microsoft Clip Gallery 3.0 dialog box.

2. Choose the Signs category of images and use the scroll bar to locate the scales image.

3. Click on Insert to place the clip art on your page.

4. Hold down the Shift key and drag inward on a corner selection handle to reduce the picture frame to about one inch square.

Adding Text with a Design Gallery Element

Usually, you would include text in your logo, perhaps just the initials of your company or perhaps the actual company name.

TIP

Some logos even include a motto or company catchphrase, but that tends to make a logo busy and harder to read. I recommend sticking to the company name as the only text in your logo. You can always place a tag line beneath the logo itself in advertisements and brochures.

As you've seen throughout this book, there are a few different ways to add text. You can simply draw a text frame on the page. You can insert a WordArt object to take advantage of certain special effects like curved text. You can also use an element from the Design Gallery that has a WordArt object included within it.

No matter which route you choose for your real company logo, the important thing to remember about combining text with graphics is balance. You don't want the graphic element to overwhelm the company name. On the other hand, if a graphic element becomes so small as to be incidental,

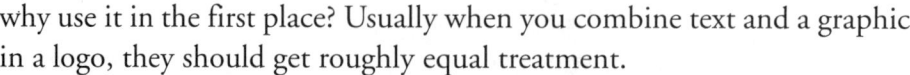

why use it in the first place? Usually when you combine text and a graphic in a logo, they should get roughly equal treatment.

You can also consider creating a design effect by the way you juxtapose text with a graphic in a logo. For example, look again at the security company logo you saw earlier in Figure 5.2. Notice how the length of the text frame and the reverse text effect give it enough substance to balance the large graphic. Also, the angle of the triangle behind the eagle's head and the angle of the eagle's neck to the text frame create a nice geometric feel to the logo.

For the logo you're building here, you'll include a Design Gallery element for your text. Follow these steps to add the object to your page:

1. Click on the Design Gallery button to open the Design Gallery dialog box.

2. Select the Attention Getters category.

3. Click on the More Designs button and select Plain Designs.

4. Scroll until you see the design called "Boxy" shown in Figure 5.5 and click on the design.

5. Click on Insert Object to place the design on your page. You many need to move the newly inserted object so it's not right on top of your clip art.

6. Double-click on the WordArt object to display the WordArt environment shown in Figure 5.6.

7. Type **AG Legal**, press Enter, and then type **Billing**.

Figure 5.5

This design is mainly text, but it has a nice woodcut feel to it.

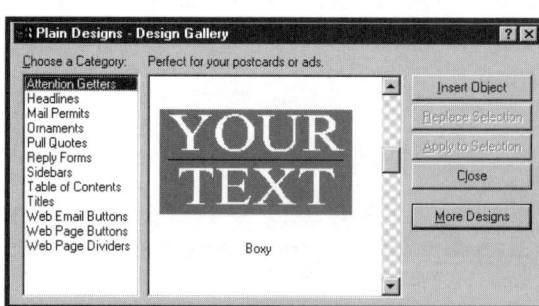

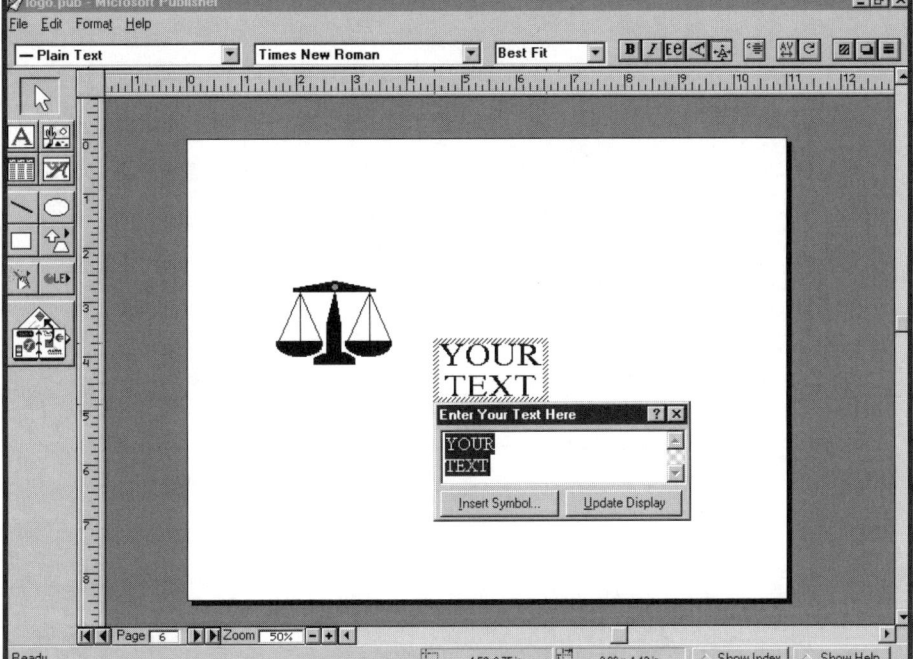

Figure 5.6

The font used here
may not be quite
right for your logo
but don't worry, you
can change that.

8. Change the font to Copperplate Gothic Light, a slightly more gen-teel and professional-looking font.

9. Click anywhere outside the WordArt object to return to the Publisher environment.

You now have two elements, a graphic symbol and a text element (Figure 5.7). Now comes the tricky part: finding the best way to fit them together.

Combining Text and Graphics

There are many ways you could combine these two objects to make a logo. Here are some things to keep in mind:

✿ Arrange the objects so that the whole logo is compact enough to fit on documents as small as business cards without having to shrink the objects to the point of illegibility.

Figure 5.7

Both elements have
a strong look; you
have to create a
balance between
the two.

- Avoid very long or very wide logos: they're not as easy to resize nor as flexible to arrange on different page sizes or orientations.

- If the objects use two different colors and you overlap them, remember that in a black-and-white version of the logo you won't have the benefit of the colors to help the reader make out the two elements. You can deal with this by choosing shades of gray in a black-and-white version of the logo.

Figure 5.8 shows four possible ways to combine these two elements into a logo. The logo in the bottom right corner is obviously not a good choice: trying to overlap these two objects this way makes the text hard to read and the graphic object hard to discern. It would be a disaster in black and white. The choice in the lower left corner isn't bad; the objects don't overlap too much but a connection between them is suggested by this placement. The logo in the upper right corner, with the two objects simply placed side by side, makes for a rather wide logo; it would be hard to size and place on a tiny business card. The balance of the logo in the upper left corner is probably the best: the two frames are balanced for equal impact and the thin black border around each element ties them together.

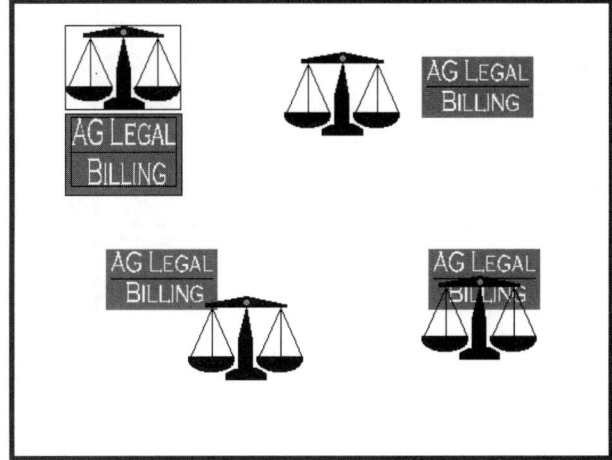

Figure 5.8

The trick here is to find unity and balance between the objects. The logo in the upper left corner does that nicely.

Arrange your objects to form this logo by following these steps:

1. Place the two objects on your page to match the placement in the sample in the upper left corner of the page, as shown in Figure 5.8.

2. Select the clip art object.

3. Click on the Border button on the picture formatting toolbar to display the drop-down list shown in Figure 5.9.

4. Click on the thinnest of the three line samples displayed on the list. This places a border around the clip art object.

5. Click on the Box tool on the Publisher toolbar.

6. Click on the upper left corner of the text object and drag to draw a box around it.

Figure 5.9

You can select a border width from this list.

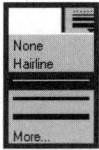

Figure 5.10

This logo should work well in the corner of either letterhead or a business card.

CAUTION Don't try using the Border tool to place a border around the Design Gallery object; it modifies the line that surrounds the text inside the orange fill color.

The logo should now look like the one in Figure 5.10.

Grouping and Sizing the Logo

Now that you have the elements of the logo placed and arranged on the page, you should group the various objects that make it up. That way, you can resize the logo and copy it as a single object.

1. Hold down the Shift key and click on each object in turn (don't forget to click on the box around the Design Gallery text as well). The three objects will be surrounded by gray handles and a Group Objects tool appears at the bottom of the group (see Figure 5.11).

2. Click on the Group Objects tool. The handles turn black, and the Group Objects tool changes to show that the separate objects are now one grouped object (see Figure 5.12).

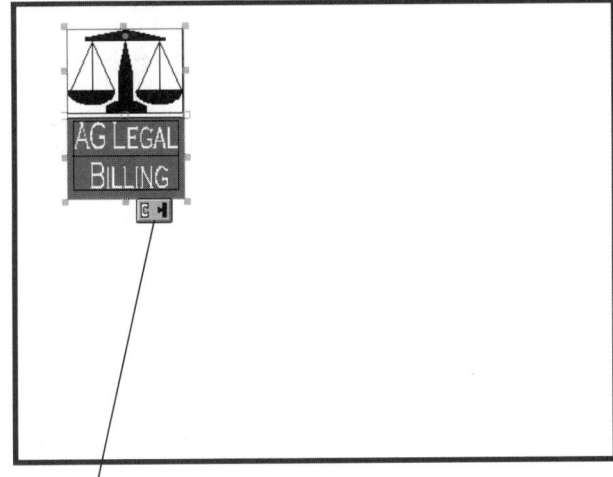

Figure 5.11

The two little figures on the Group Objects tool indicate that the objects are not currently grouped.

Group Objects tool

TIP You can also select Arrange, Group Objects to accomplish the same thing. To ungroup objects, just click on the tool at the bottom of the group again, or select Arrange, Ungroup Objects.

Figure 5.12

The two little symbols on the Group Objects tool are now locked together, indicating the objects have been grouped.

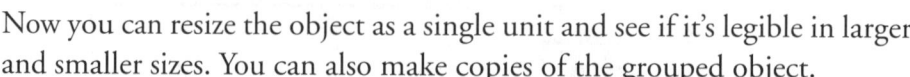

Now you can resize the object as a single unit and see if it's legible in larger and smaller sizes. You can also make copies of the grouped object.

1. Hold down the Shift key and move the mouse pointer over a corner of the logo until you see the Resize cursor (a line with an arrow at either end).

2. Click and drag the corner to make the logo smaller, about half an inch wide and an inch tall.

TIP   Graphic designers sometimes generate sheets of logos in various sizes on special graphic paper and cut out different sizes to paste onto layouts of artwork for printers. You don't have to do this: you can resize your logo anytime you like with a click and drag, and place it in any electronic version of a document using Publisher.

3. With the object still selected, click on the Copy button.

4. Click on the Paste button to paste a copy. The copy will overlap the original object.

5. Move the copy to the middle of the page and resize it to be about 2 inches wide by 3 inches tall. You now have two logos, which look something like those shown in Figure 5.13.

NOTE   This logo will work equally well printed in black and white or on a color printer because there is no shading or pattern. The orange color surrounding the reverse text will print as black on your printer and all the lines of text and the clip art should come across clearly.

Take a Break

Now that you've got a logo to play around with, you can build letterhead and business cards from it. Before you tackle that, it's time to take your last break of the book. When you come back, you'll finish the journey you started on Friday night and be an accomplished Publisher pro. Take a few jumps on the stair stepper and I'll see you in five.

Figure 5.13

Once you've grouped objects, they are easy to copy and resize; one of these will work on letterhead and the other will work on a business card.

Designing Letterhead

Letterhead comes in all kinds of designs, from simple to elaborate. Figures 5.14, 5.15, and 5.16 show letterhead created using different styles offered

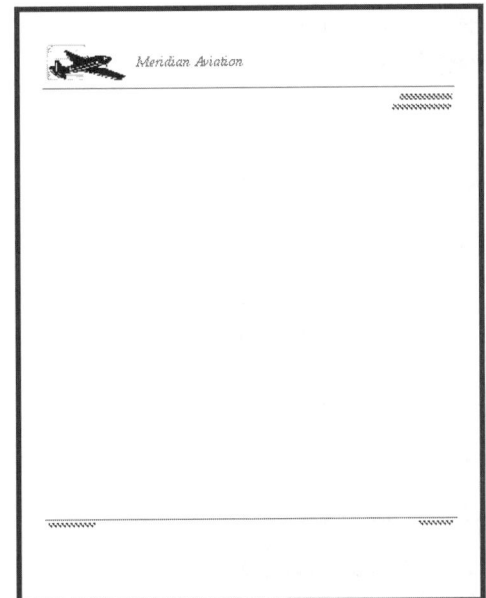

Figure 5.14

The Woodcut style gives a simple, straightforward look that works for many businesses.

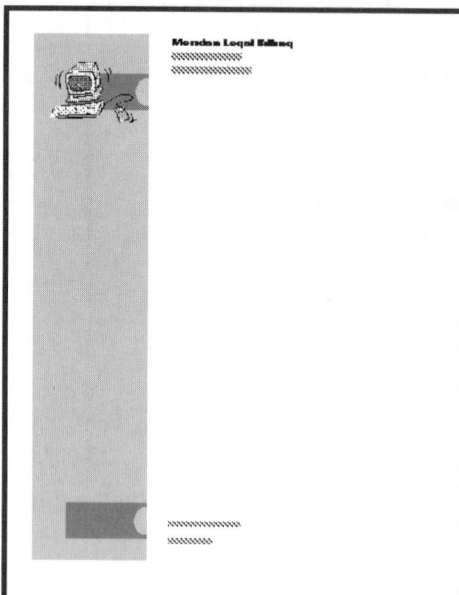

Figure 5.15

The Jazzy style is more graphic. You'll have to balance the content of your correspondence against the large shaded box on the left.

Figure 5.16

The Fun style is just that: a large, shaded graphic and casual font.

by Publisher's Letterhead Wizard. Each offers a different mood for your business correspondence.

When designing letterhead you should consider how you're going to use it. The letterhead in Figure 5.15, for example, looks best when you keep the text of your correspondence to the right of the large shaded box on the left—leaving less room for text on the page. If your typical correspondence can fit in that space, fine. If this is going to force you to use a second sheet for most letters, consider the cost of that extra piece of paper as well as the need to design and print second sheets of letterhead.

TIP   If you print forms such as invoices on letterhead, go for a simpler look. This gives you more space to fit the elements on the form and stops the lines and data that usually make up forms from fighting with graphic elements.

Make sure the contact information is easy to read on your letterhead. Typically, the company name and address are listed at the top of the letterhead, and the phone number, fax number, and e-mail address, if any, go at the bottom. This creates a balance on the page. Often, as in Figure 5.14, there's also a simple graphic element at the bottom, such as a line, to frame the contents of the correspondence.

Providing Balance and Readability

Since the objects included in letterhead often fall around the outside of the page, Layout Guides can be a great help in placing them on the page. For example, Figure 5.17 shows stationery with a logo in the upper left corner and a graphic image in the bottom right. You can use the corners of the guides to make sure these objects balance on the page. You can also use the left side guide to line up the text frames that contain contact information.

Whether you balance elements on the left and right or top and bottom of the page, remember that the final purpose for letterhead is to provide a background for your correspondence. Think carefully before creating letterhead that has a large background image, as shown in Figure 5.18. Will the text

Figure 5.17

With no text at the bottom of the page, this letterhead needs the graphic element at the bottom right for balance.

Figure 5.18

The dots that form the large graphic that fills this page can conflict with text.

have to fight to be read against this pattern? What extra printing costs will you incur from having this screened back graphic?

Running the Letterhead Wizard

So, you say you've had enough of this theory: time to create some letterhead. You're right. You'll do just that by running through the Letterhead Wizard; then you'll add the logo you built earlier and make a minor design change. Be sure to save the logo you created earlier before beginning these steps:

1. Select <u>F</u>ile, Create New Publication.

2. Select the PageWizard tab shown in Figure 5.19.

3. Click on the Letterhead Wizard and then on OK to begin the Wizard. The dialog box in Figure 5.20 appears.

NOTE If you've run other Wizards, your first step might be different: Publisher might offer to use the last style you selected. If that dialog box does appear, click on the No, I want a different look option button and then on Next to reach the dialog box in Figure 5.20.

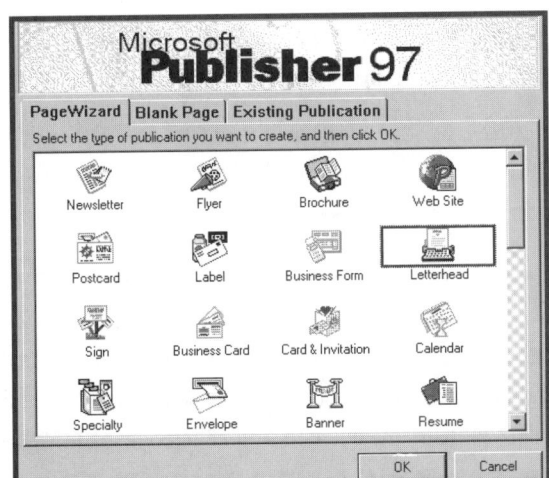

Figure 5.19

Both letterhead and business cards have their own Wizards.

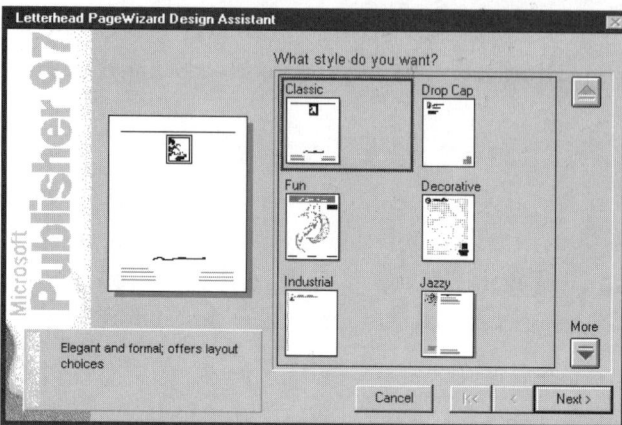

Figure 5.20

To see more styles
you can use the
More arrow key
in the bottom
right corner.

TIP

Pick a style of letterhead that matches your business style; a conservative accounting
firm should shy away from the Fun and Decorative styles and a toy store would do itself
no good by selecting the straitlaced Industrial style.

4. Click on the option button labeled No, I want a different look and
   then on Next to see more styles.

5. Click on the Modern style and then on Next to proceed. The dialog
   box in Figure 5.21 appears.

6. The Include a picture option button should be checked by default.
   You want a picture as a placeholder for your company logo, so make
   sure that the option is selected and then click on Next to proceed.

TIP

If you don't have a company logo but want to generate one quickly, select Include my
company's initials in this dialog box. Publisher will use your company's initials as a graphic
element that functions as a simple text logo. (Warning: do not use this option if your company name is Phillips Industrial Group or a similar acronym disaster just waiting to happen.)

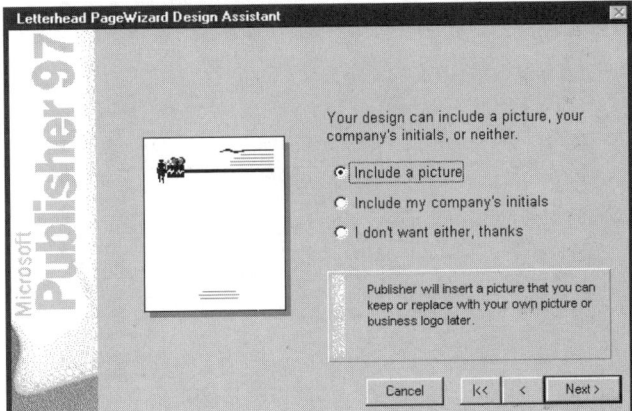

Figure 5.21

You can choose
whether to use a
picture or
your company's
initials as a
design element.

7. The next dialog box, shown in Figure 5.22, is where you enter your address information. Type: **AG Legal Billing, 32 Delancy Street, Warwick, RI 66789**.

8. Click on Next to proceed. The dialog box in Figure 5.23 is the next thing you see.

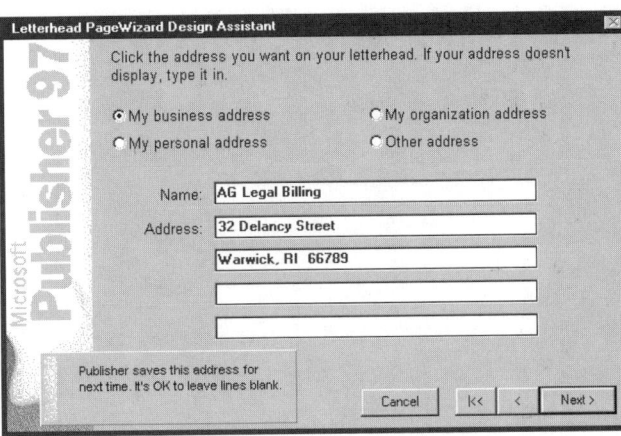

Figure 5.22

Enter the company
name in the Name
text box and
the street, city,
state, and zip
under Address.

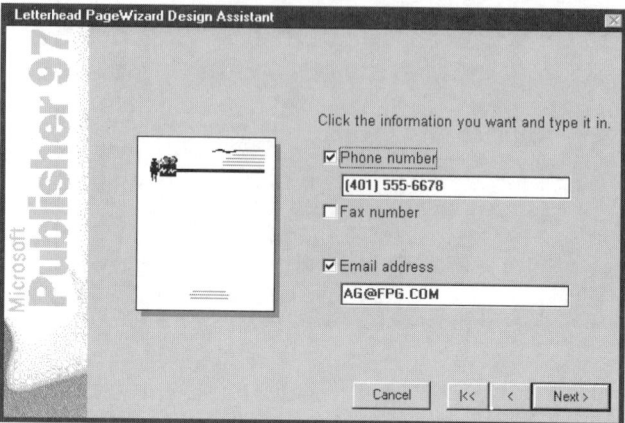

Figure 5.23

Here's where you enter your phone, fax, and e-mail information.

9. Click on the check box for Phone number. A text box appears. Type **(401) 555-6678**.

10. Click on the Email address check box. A text box appears. This time, type **AG@FPG.COM**.

11. Click on Next. The final dialog box, shown in Figure 5.24, appears.

12. Click on the Create It button to generate your letterhead.

For a moment a small dialog appears telling you Publisher is creating the letterhead. When it's done, a dialog box asks if you want any help. The

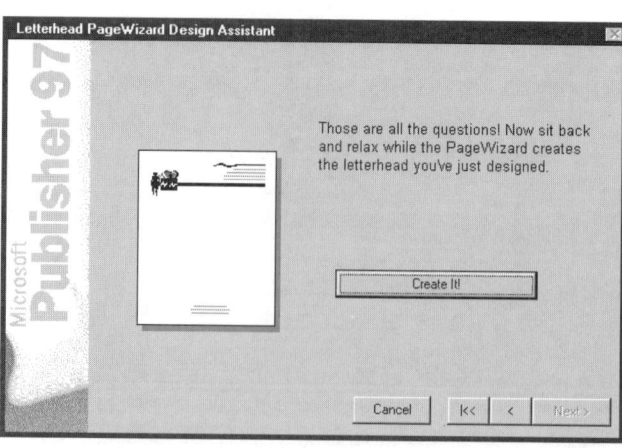

Figure 5.24

If you wanted to review any of your choices, you could use the Back arrow key before creating the letterhead.

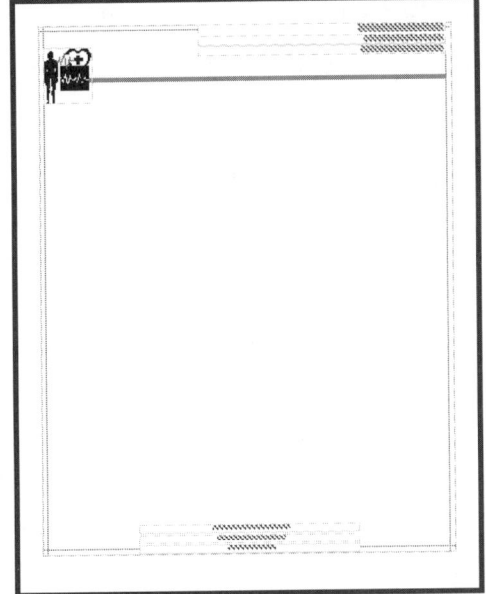

Figure 5.25

The letterhead has
a simple look that
will fit well with
your company logo.

default is not to get step-by-step help (which simply displays the Help window onscreen). Click on OK to see the letterhead displayed, as shown in Figure 5.25.

Modifying the Wizard's Work

Often when you work through a Publisher Wizard you'll want to tweak the results to make the publication truly your own. You may want to add or delete an element such as a graphic or your company logo. Perhaps you'll change the font that Publisher has selected to one more appropriate to your company image.

Now that you've generated a letterhead design, you'll fine-tune it for your needs. As luck would have it, this letterhead uses the Copperplate Gothic Bold font, so it's a nice match to your logo text. However, you'll want to replace the graphic Publisher inserted with your own logo. This will involve a few simple steps:

1. Click on the current picture to select it.

2. Press Delete to delete it from your document.

3. Save the letterhead file with any name you like.

4. Open the file containing the company logo you created earlier.

5. Click on the smaller version of the logo and select Edit, Copy Group.

6. Open the letterhead file.

7. Select Edit, Paste Object(s). The logo appears.

8. Move the logo to line up with the blue guidelines that form the upper left corner of the page.

9. Click on the thick line that runs across the heading of the page and drag to resize it so that it ends just short of the logo, rather than running into it. Your letterhead should look like the image in Figure 5.26 (I've hidden the guides so you can see it more clearly).

I'm going to suggest one more thing to help the text on the bottom balance with the masthead of the stationery. Making the text at the bottom of the

Figure 5.26

The letterhead looks fine, though a little plain.

page into reverse text will give a little more emphasis to it, and make the whole thing feel less top heavy. Follow these steps to make reverse text:

1. Press F9 to zoom in on the document, and scroll to the bottom of the page. You'll see that there are actually two text frames: one for the phone number and one for the e-mail address.

2. Select the first frame and holding down the Shift key, click on the second frame so that they're both selected.

3. Click on the Fill Color button on the Formatting toolbar.

4. From the palette shown in Figure 5.27, click on the black color choice.

5. Click to the left of the text in one text frame and drag to the right to select it.

6. Click on the Text Color button. Select white for the text color.

7. Repeat steps 5 and 6 for the second text frame. If you press F9, you'll see the overall impact on the balance of your page from making these lines reverse text (see Figure 5.28).

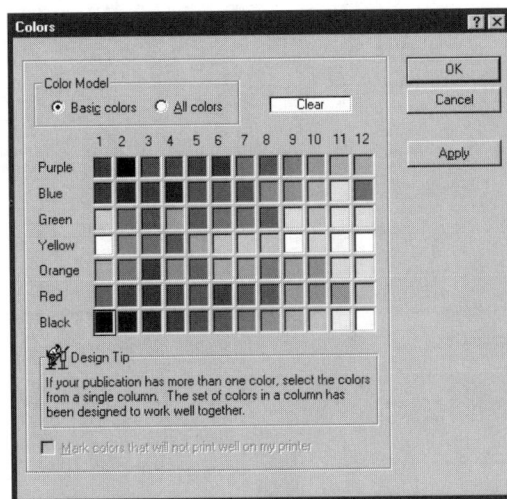

Figure 5.27

This palette is arranged by colors of the spectrum. Choose the black square on the far left.

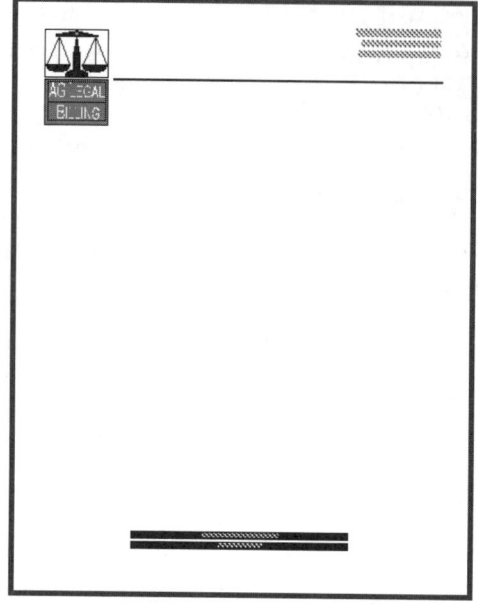

Figure 5.28

You could also choose to make these text frames a little shorter or place all the text in a single text frame running across the page.

Designing Business Cards

Now that you have letterhead, make sure your business cards convey the same general impression. Since Publisher uses the same styles when it produces documents with Wizards, running the Business Card Wizard and selecting the Modern style should give you the same look. But before you do that, a word about business card design.

 **NOTE** You can also use the Envelope Wizard and choose the same style to create envelopes that match your letterhead and business cards. You used this Wizard in the Sunday Morning session, if you'd like a review.

Keeping Text Readable

Since business cards are such Lilliputian publications, there is naturally a concern about keeping text readable. To be able to keep text as large as

Figure 5.29

This card manages to include a lot of information, yet retains plenty of white space for a clean look.

possible, you have to include only the information that's important. Do you need to show all your company's branches, or just the main office? Do you need a slogan, list of products, or product logos in addition to a company logo? Business cards that crowd too much information on them don't serve their purpose very well.

Figure 5.29 shows a business card that uses one of the optional logo designs you saw earlier. Notice how I've kept this from looking too busy by shifting text from one side of the card to the other.

TIP

To save money, especially with business cards that use more than one color, consider printing sheets of business cards in quantity, leaving out only the individual's name, title, and phone number. This quantity printing saves you a lot of money over smaller print runs, since the setup of the presses with ink colors is a large part of the printing cost. Printers can then print an employee's specific information in black ink on card masters as needed.

Choosing Orientation

For years business cards came one way: the top of the card ran along the long edge of the card. But in recent years clever graphic designers have

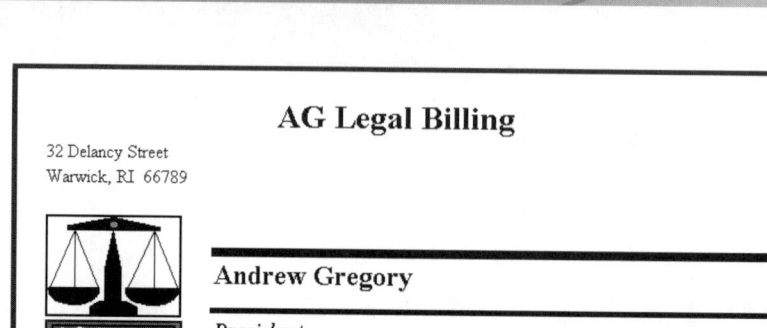

Figure 5.30

Most business
cards come in this
orientation.

turned things around and designed business cards that have the top on the
side. Figure 5.30 shows a more traditional business card with a landscape
orientation. Figure 5.31 shows a business card with a portrait orientation.

Figure 5.31

The portrait
orientation can
differentiate your
card from others.

Which way should you go with your business card? Here are two reasons for using landscape orientation:

✿ Rolodex files that hold business cards orient them as landscape, so people have to crane their necks to read information on a portrait-oriented card.

✿ Most business-card holders that sit on a desktop are better suited for displaying landscape cards. In addition, presentation folders that have business card slits cut in them usually accommodate landscape cards.

On the other hand, here are two reasons for using portrait orientation:

✿ Landscape-oriented cards are much more common. If you want your card to stand out from all the others, portrait orientation can help get attention.

✿ If you're in a creative business such as advertising or landscape design, the more unusual portrait orientation can reflect that creativity.

In short, although there are a few practical considerations, it's entirely up to you. There are no hard-and-fast rules, and in the end, it's probably a matter of taste.

Running the Business Card Wizard

Now it's time to see what the Publisher Business Card Wizard can do for you. Several dialog boxes it offers you will be familiar from the Letterhead Wizard. Before you begin, save any file you have open, and then follow these steps:

1. Select File, Create New Publication to open the New Publication dialog box.

2. Click on the PageWizard tab.

3. Click on the Business Card icon and then on OK to begin the Wizard. The dialog box in Figure 5.32 appears.

4. If this dialog box offers Modern as the style to use (the style you used for your letterhead), click on Next to proceed. If it suggests some other style, click on the No, I want a different look option

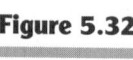

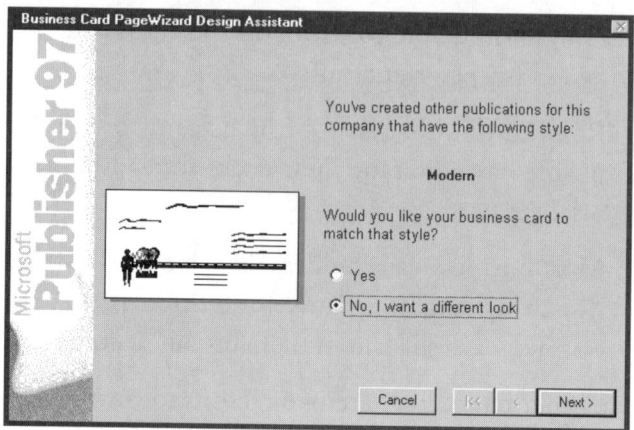

Figure 5.32

Publisher suggests
that you use the
last style you
selected when you
ran a Wizard; the
last one you used
was probably
Modern.

button and click on Next. Choose Modern from the dialog box in
Figure 5.33, and then click on Next. The next dialog box that appears is one you saw in the Letterhead Wizard: it simply wants to
know if you'd like to include a picture or company initials.

5. Click on Next to accept the default choice of including a picture.
The dialog box shown in Figure 5.34 appears. It should still contain
the business address you entered for your letterhead, so you don't
need to type anything else now.

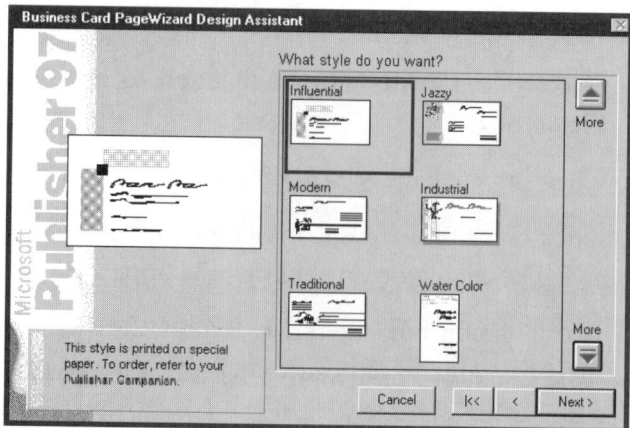

Figure 5.33

There's only one
style with a portrait
orientation built in.

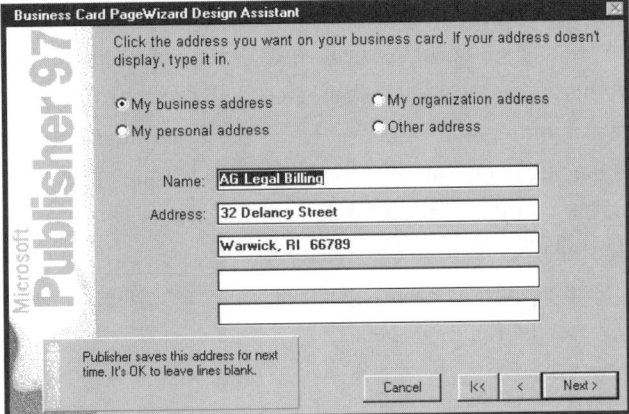

Figure 5.34

Publisher saves
four different
addresses so you
can move through
Wizards quickly.

6. Click on Next to proceed. You'll see the dialog box shown in Figure 5.35. Make sure each check box is selected and type the fax number **(401) 555-5676**.

7. Click on Next. The dialog box that appears asks you how you'd like business cards set up on the page: one card or multiple cards.

8. Make sure the selection is Lots on the page and then click on Next. The last dialog box sports the single Create It! button.

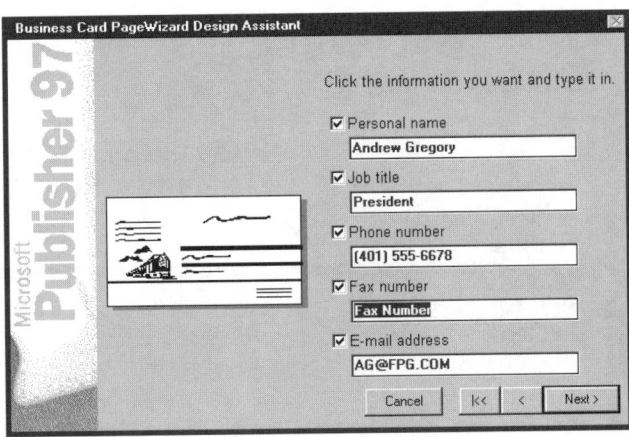

Figure 5.35

This is a lot of
information, but
Publisher's Wizard
will help organize it
neatly on the card.

> **NOTE**
> If you're printing your own business cards, setting up multiple cards on a page will allow you to print on sheets of blank card stock you can purchase at any office supply store. Professional printers sometimes prefer to get cards *one up* on a page, which means one card on the page only. The printer will then lay out the appropriate number of copies of the card on a page to take advantage of the size of card stock he's using to print the cards. This allows the printer to avoid wasting card stock, and thus saves you money. If you're not printing these cards yourself, ask your printer how many card images you should put on the Publisher page.

9. Click on the Create It! button.

10. When you see the dialog box that asks if you want step-by-step help, select No and click on OK.

Figure 5.36 shows the resulting business card (I've hidden the guides so you can see it more clearly).

Now you'll need to replace the Wizard's choice of graphic with the logo you created, just as you did with the Wizard-generated letterhead. Here's the gist of what you have to do, but you know the routine well enough to do it on your own by now:

Figure 5.36

The use of the same Modern style gives you the consistency of the Copperplate font that matches your logo.

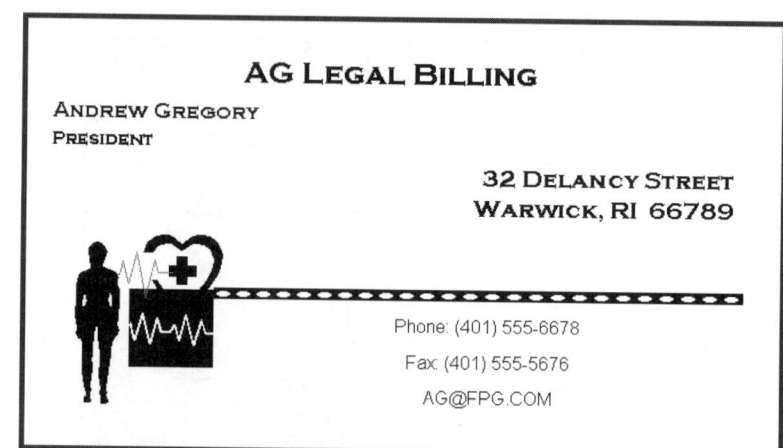

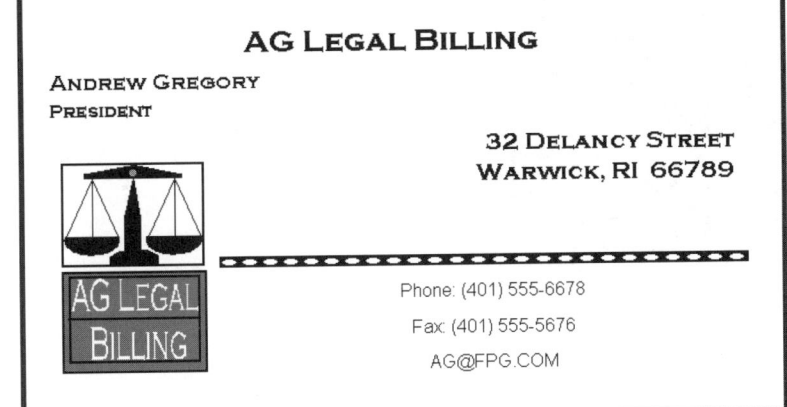

AG LEGAL BILLING

ANDREW GREGORY
PRESIDENT

32 DELANCY STREET
WARWICK, RI 66789

AG LEGAL
BILLING

Phone: (401) 555-6678

Fax: (401) 555-5676

AG@FPG.COM

Figure 5.37

This card should
complement the
letterhead almost
perfectly.

1. Save the new business card.

2. Open the logo file and copy the logo.

3. Open the business card file and replace the picture the Wizard put
   there with your logo (which you'll probably have to resize), so that it
   looks like Figure 5.37.

The Final Touch

Yes, you're almost done, but I can't help myself: I have to suggest a couple
of small changes to make the card just right. The first thing has to do with
the line that the Wizard has placed on the card. This line has a border style
applied to it that I find busy and old-fashioned. Take just a moment to
modify it and see if you don't agree.

1. Select the line and right-click to display the shortcut menu shown in
   Figure 5.38.

2. Select the Border command from the menu. The BorderArt dialog
   box shown in Figure 5.39 appears.

3. Use the scroll bar to locate the border called "Circles and Rectangles"
   and select it.

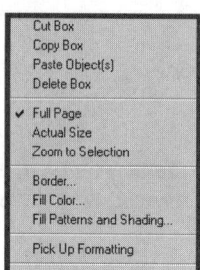

Figure 5.38

This shortcut menu gives you access to several formatting options for the selected line.

4. Now, select the text frame with the company name AG Legal Billing in it.

5. Select Edit, Delete Text Frame. Since the name of the company is so clearly called out in the logo, you don't really need this extra text cluttering up the card.

The resulting card is shown in Figure 5.40. See how a little tweaking can make a good design even better?

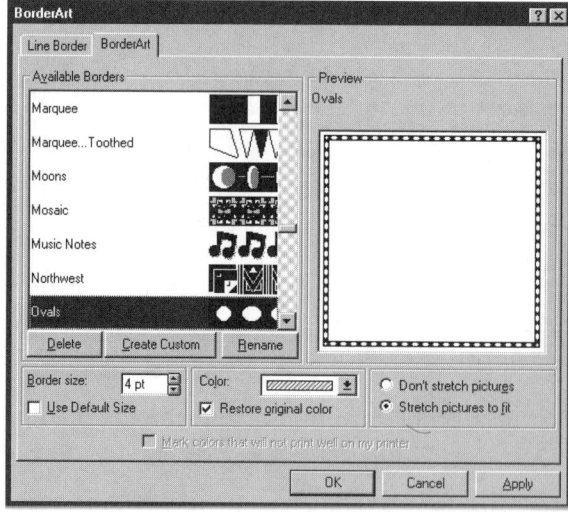

Figure 5.39

The current choice, Ovals, is a bit busy.

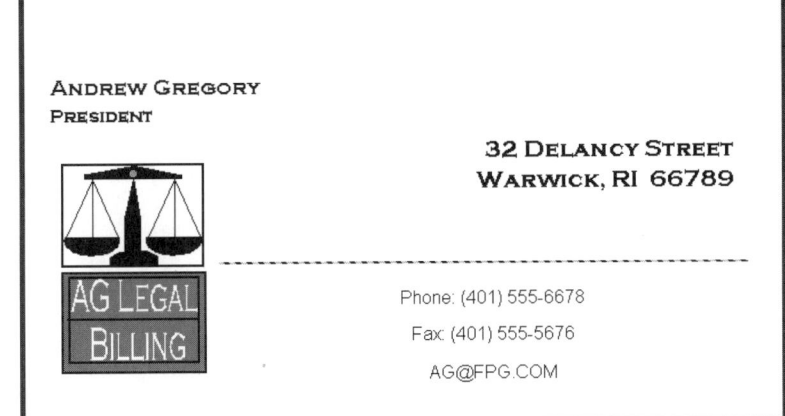

Figure 5.40

Small changes, but they can make your design look much more professional.

What's Next?

You've done it. You've made it through the weekend, and mastered all the major features of Publisher. You've learned how to work with text, columns, and WordArt. You played around with Publisher's table feature. You've placed graphics and poked around in the Design Gallery. You've merged, saved, and printed documents. And along the way, you've picked up a lot of design rules of thumb that will help you down the road.

So, what's next? Well, as your piano teacher told you when you were 10: practice, practice, practice! The best way to get to be a better desktop publisher is to publish. It's especially important that you use Publisher for a few projects over the next couple of weeks to help you remember all you've learned (you'd be surprised how much more of this you'll retain by just practicing a couple of hours a week).

Use some of the design ideas throughout this book and in the appendixes that follow to keep you going. Now that you have the tools to design publications, the only limitation on your creativity is you. (And I know that means the sky's the limit.) Above all, have fun!

Wizard Gallery

Publisher Wizards are great shortcuts. However, it's helpful to have an idea of what sort of document each one produces without having to run through all their steps.

In this appendix, I've included the results of each of the 18 Wizards: what you'll see here is what you'll get if you make all the default choices from the Wizard dialog boxes. (OK, so in a few cases I added a bit of text so you could see how to use something like the mailing label, but basically, this is what you'll get). Remember, by choosing different styles or other options during the Wizard process, you can get several variations on these publications.

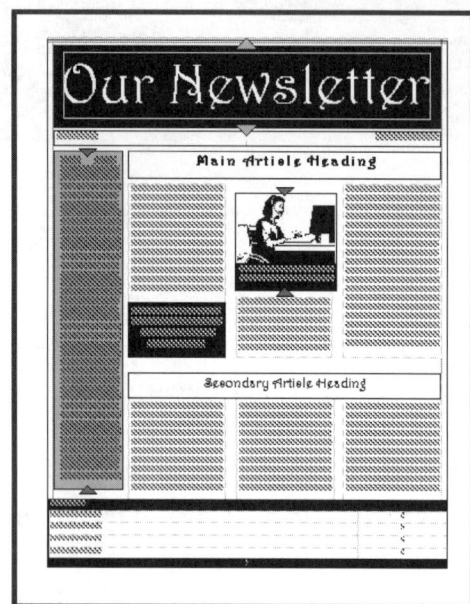

Figure A.1

The Newsletter Wizard

Figure A.2

The Flyer Wizard

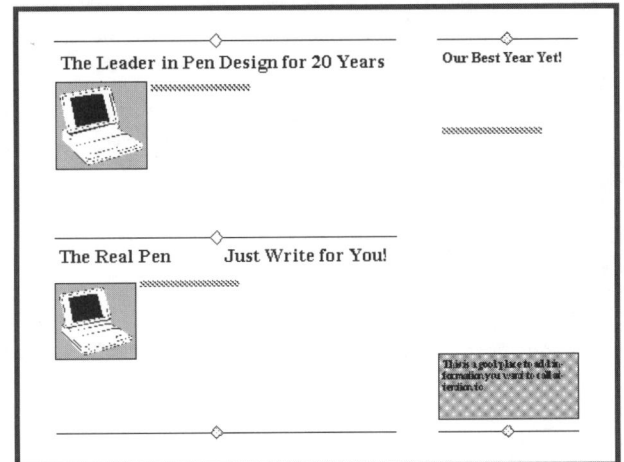

Figure A.3

The Brochure
Wizard

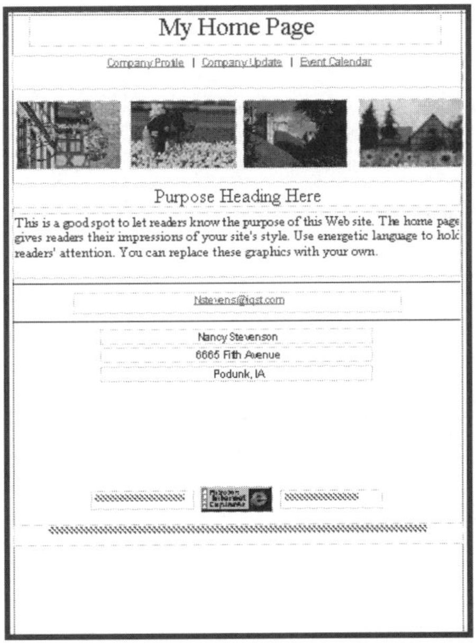

Figure A.4

The Web Site
Wizard

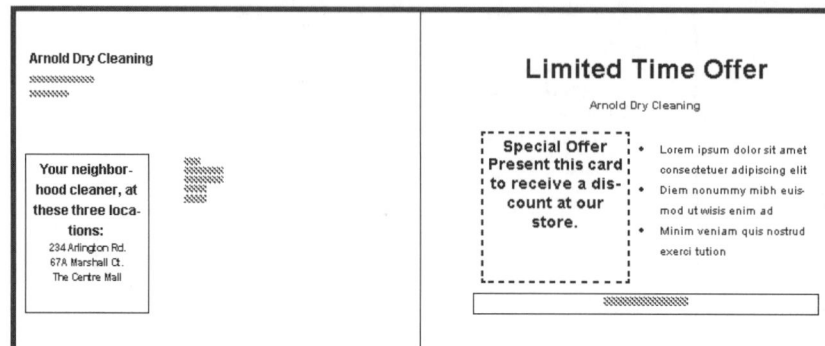

Figure A.5

The Postcard Wizard

Harry Marshall
Marshall Markets
222 West Indiana Street
Irvington, MA   22356

Figure A.6

The Label Wizard

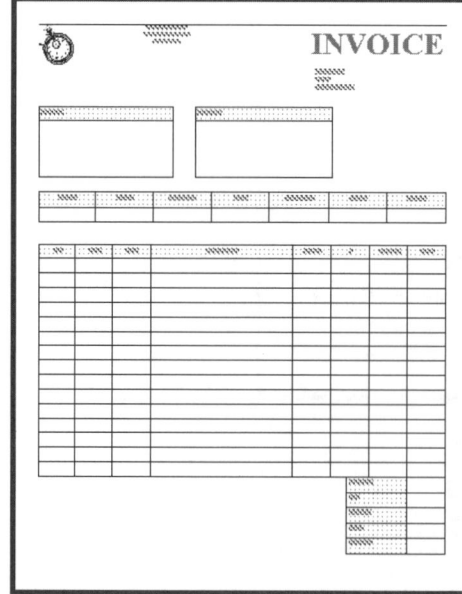

Figure A.7

The Business Form Wizard (this is the invoice form choice, which is the default).

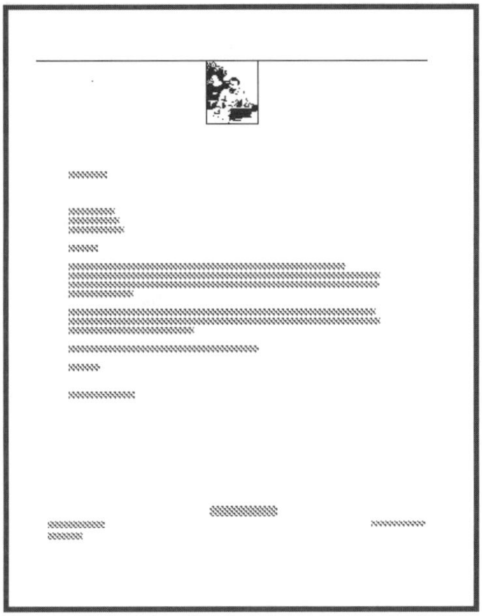

Figure A.8

The Letterhead
Wizard

Figure A.9

The Sign Wizard

Nancy Stevenson

665 Fifth Avenue
Podunk, IA 67889

Nstevens@iqst.com

Figure A.10

The Business Card
Wizard

Figure A.11

The Card/Invitation
Wizard

Figure A.12

The Calendar
Wizard

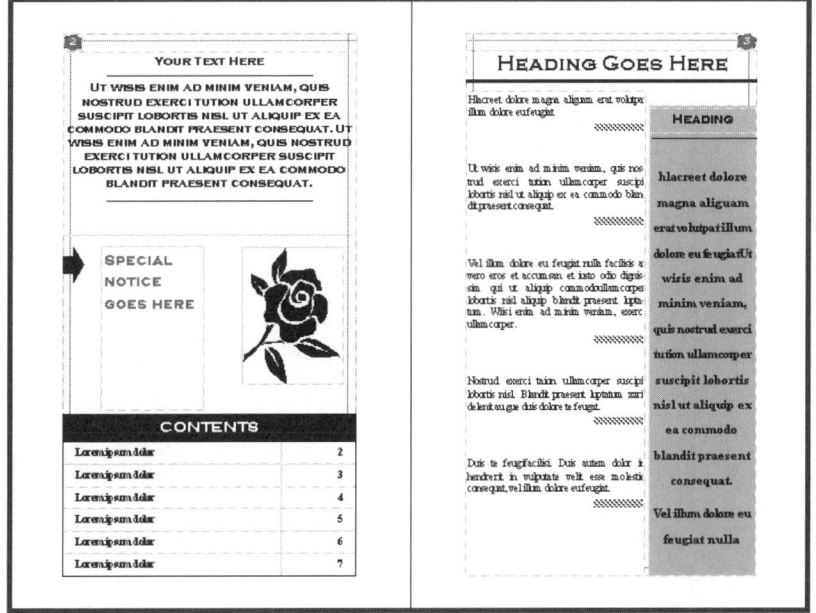

Figure A.13

The Specialty
Wizard (catalog)

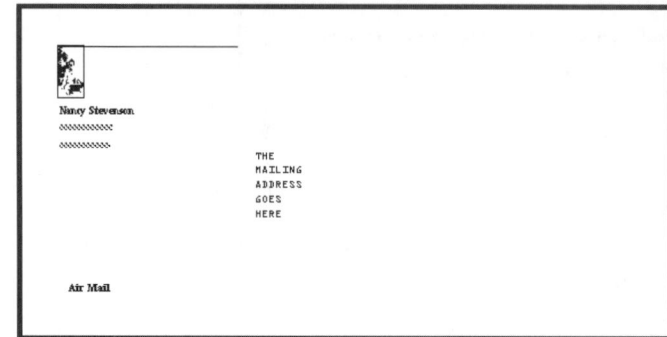

Figure A.14

The Envelope
Wizard

Figure A.15

The Banner Wizard

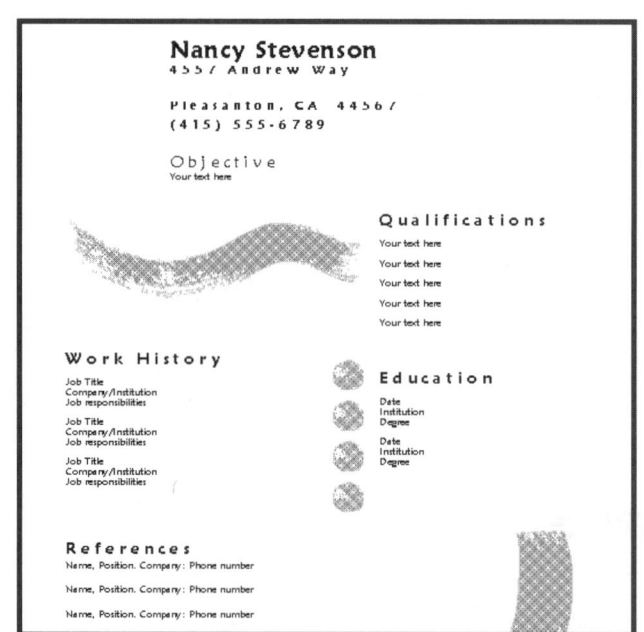

Figure A.16

The Resume Wizard

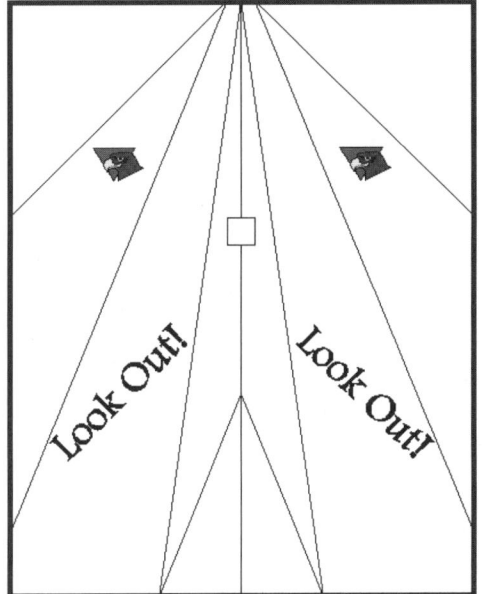

Figure A.17

The Airplane Wizard

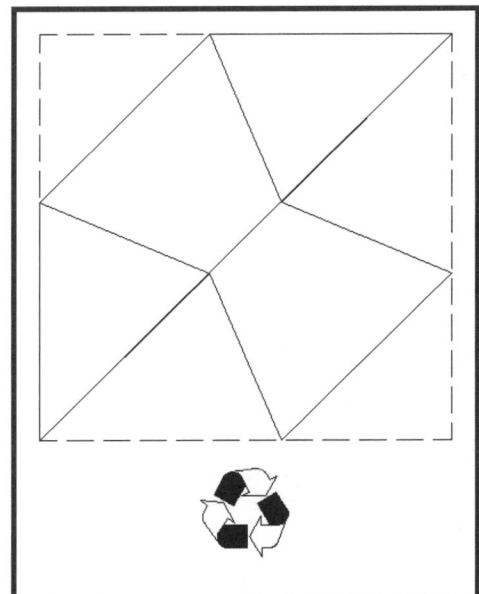

Figure A.18

The Origami
Wizard (cup)

Design Gallery
Ideas

This appendix shows you some of the design elements that are in the Publisher Design Gallery. You can browse through here for ideas for your own publication. At the end of this appendix, I've used several of Publisher's design elements, including some from the Design Gallery and Clip Gallery, to give you a few ideas of how these can be used in actual publications.

The Design Gallery lets you pick and choose from among 11 categories of elements in one of four styles. For example, you might insert a Headline element in the Jazzy style. The first four figures show an element from five of the categories, Attention Getters, Headlines, Ornaments, Titles, and Web Page Buttons, shown in each of the four style types, Plain, Classic, Jazzy, and Modern. You can compare the looks of these four styles to see which appeals to you.

Design Gallery Sampling

The Design Gallery is chock-full of design elements like title designs, pull quotes, and attention getters that you can use to snaz up your documents. Use this sampling to get ideas about which style and type of element might fit your need.

Figure B.1

Here's an assortment of elements in the Plain style. When you've placed one on your page, simply double-click on the placeholder—Your Text—to enter your own text.

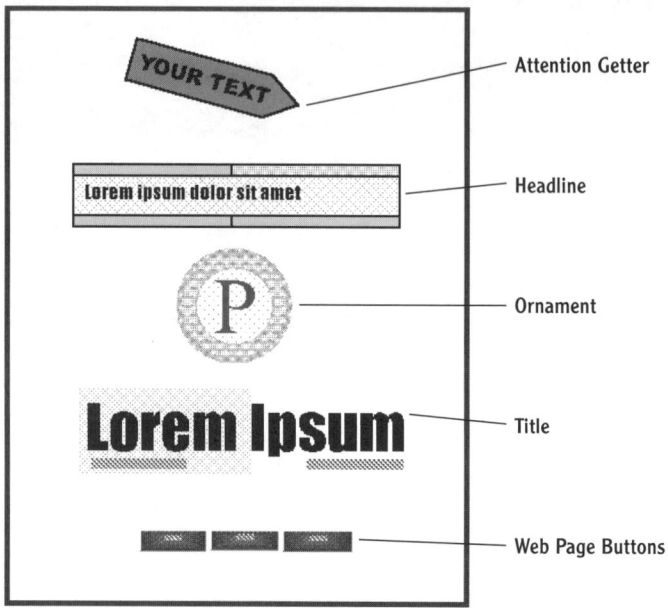

Attention Getter

Headline

Ornament

Title

Web Page Buttons

Figure B.2

The Classic style relies on ornamentation that pulls on Greek, Art Deco, and other traditional design types. Use it for an old-fashioned or more staid look. Since many of these elements are in black and white, they're great for one-color printing.

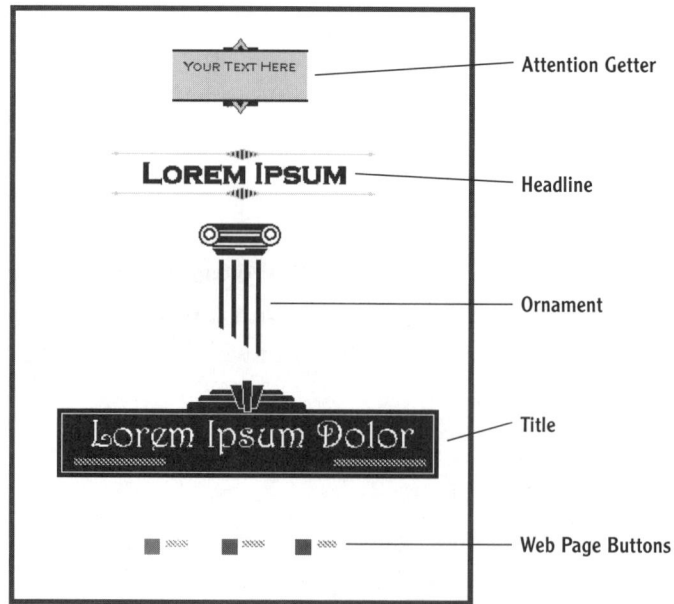

Attention Getter

Headline

Ornament

Title

Web Page Buttons

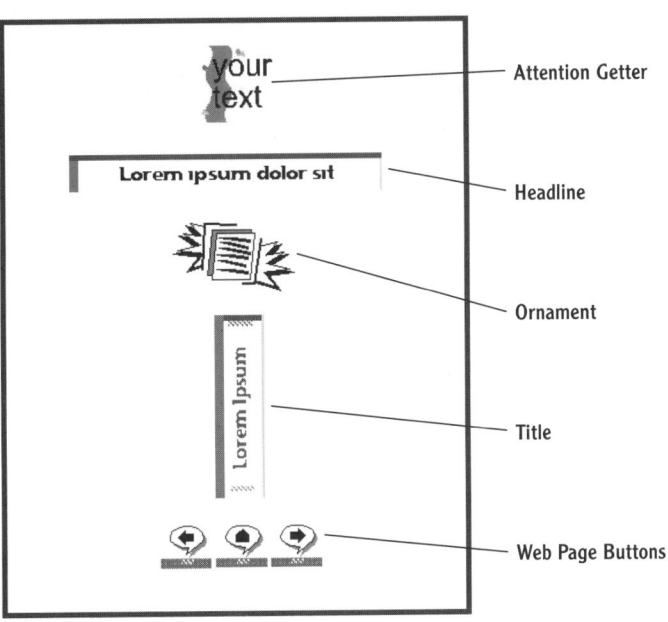

Figure B.3

Use any of these Jazzy style elements to provide a distinctive fun look for your publications. The Jazzy style makes great use of color, so if you're printing in color, check it out.

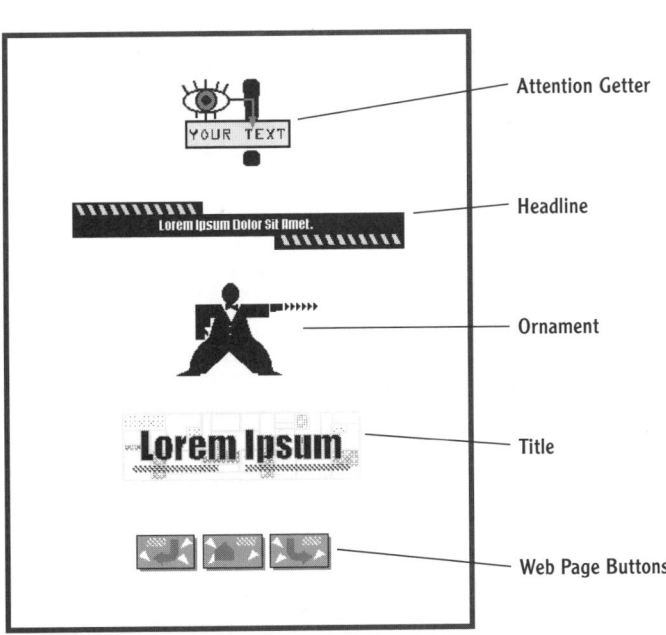

Figure B.4

If the Museum of Modern Art is your idea of heaven, you'll probably lean toward the Modern style of Design Gallery elements. Images are clean and graphic, with the occasional eyeball staring back at you.

Design Ideas

Now it's time to see how you might use some of these elements in real publications. Here are five examples to spark your imagination.

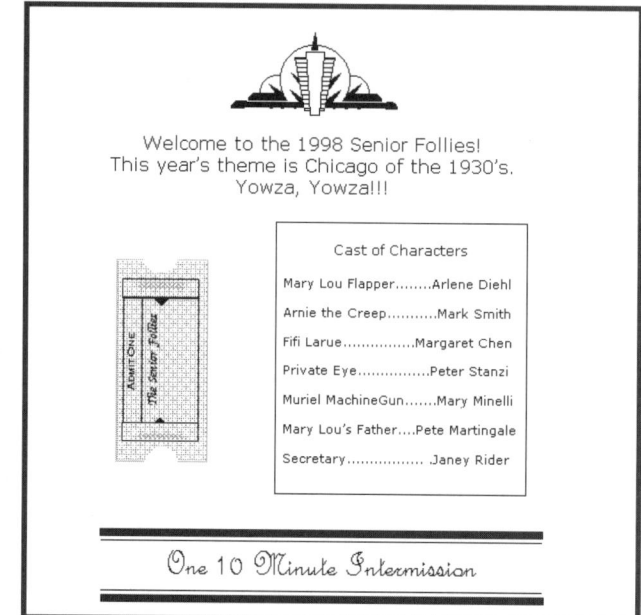

Figure B.5

This program uses three Ornament elements (at the top, the side—the ticket, and along the bottom). Notice how the ticket element has been rotated to fit the design better.

Figure B.6

This business card uses a Classic style pull quote element for its company logo. Note the use of reversed type to make the all-important phone number stand out.

Figure B.7

This classy-looking invitation uses a coffee pot clip art object and a Modern style Attention Getter for the Coffee Clatch text. The white space is used to good effect as well.

Figure B.8

Using the basic Jazzy style Reply Form, build a mailing list form by adding some clip art at the top and your own motto or message in a text box at the bottom.

Figure B.9

This sample Web page design uses three Design Gallery Web Page Buttons, a Design Gallery Title at the top, and a very feline piece of clip art.

10 Steps to a Publisher Web Site

I f you are interested in creating your very own Web site, whether for your small business or community organization or just to introduce yourself to the online world, you'll be glad to know that Publisher has a simple-to-use Web Site Wizard. This appendix takes you through the basic steps of using this Wizard to create your own Web site.

Web Site Design Tips

Before you follow the steps in the next section to create your own Web site, here are some basic Web page design rules of thumb to keep in mind:

✿ Be careful as you use different fonts: some Web browsers can't read certain fonts. Those fonts will appear to the visitor in some neutral but boring font like Courier. To test this, get a few of the most common browsers (many are available for free download) and view your page yourself. To be safe, stick with the fonts the Publisher Web Site Wizard uses.

 TIP You can use the Publisher Web Site Preview feature to see how the site will look when viewed with your own browser. This tool is available from the Standard toolbar when you have a Web page displayed.

✿ Make sure the way you navigate from page to page on your Web site is clear to the visitor: use the Web buttons in the Publisher Design

Gallery or those provided by the Web Site Wizard to add these hyperlinks to your page.

✿ Keep your page up-to-date by frequently adding new, fresh information and graphics. This will keep your visitors coming back for more.

✿ Use text, buttons, and graphics to get your message across, but don't clutter up the page with too much information. Remember, you can always create more pages on your site to contain detailed information on subtopics.

✿ The look of the site should quickly become familiar to the visitor, with common graphic elements, color, and designs on its various pages to create a single environment. Give a Web site the same consistency of design that you give the rooms in your home.

✿ Provide a way for your visitors to send you feedback on your page through an e-mail hyperlink. The Web Site Wizard puts one on the page for you.

✿ Use color and media like graphics, photographs, and sound for extra excitement.

Making Your Own Web Site

Using the Web Site Wizard is as easy as using any of the other Wizards you've encountered in this book. I've provided a step-by-step guide to the Wizard, with some tips along the way to help you make your choices.

Launch the Web Site Wizard from the New Publication dialog box (File, Create New Publication), and then use the following 10 simple steps to produce a professional-looking Web site.

Step 1: Who Does Your Web Site Represent?

The first step of the Wizard displays the dialog box shown in Figure C.1; the Business option will be selected by default. This offers a simple choice: Is your Web site being created for a business, a community organization, or you, personally?

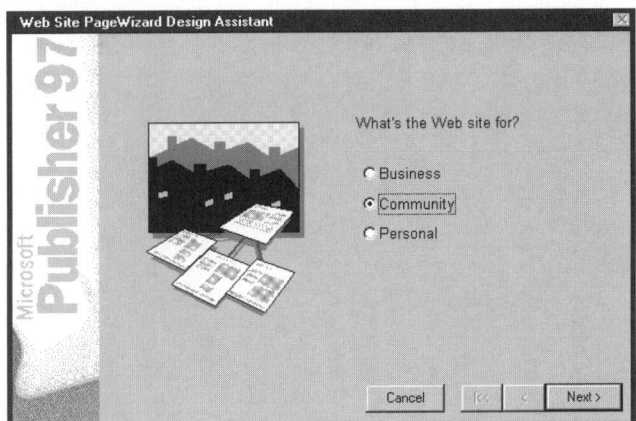

Figure C.1

This step helps you define the purpose of your Web site.

You can make only one selection here by clicking on one of the three option buttons. The choice you make here will affect the types of pages the Wizard will suggest for your site. For this walk-through, click on the Community selection. Click on Next to proceed.

Step 2: A Single or Multiple Page Web Site?

The next step in the Wizard is shown in Figure C.2. This step involves choosing whether you should create a Web site made up of a single Web page or Web site with multiple pages. With the second choice, the multiple pages of the Web site are linked together, and a visitor can move easily among the pages. If you think you'll have more than a page worth of information to convey, you should probably choose the site option. This will keep you from crowding too much information on a single page and give you more flexibility down the road. Select the Multiple-page site, and click on Next.

 TIP   You can add pages to a single page later on to make it a Web site. However, selecting the Multiple-page site option now lets Publisher set up all the links for you.

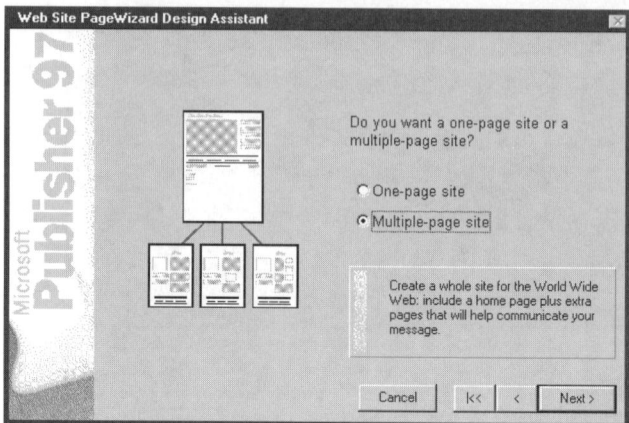

Figure C.2

Will a single page get your point across, or are you the more verbose type?

Step 3: Define Your Pages

The next Web Site Wizard dialog box allows you to define the pages on your site (see Figure C.3). Note that if you had chosen the One-page site option on the previous screen, this dialog box would not appear. Also, the choices here vary depending on whether you chose a personal, community, or business-oriented site during the first step.

Figure C.3

Choose as many of these pages as you think you'll need—but remember, don't leave stray blank pages on your site to confuse visitors.

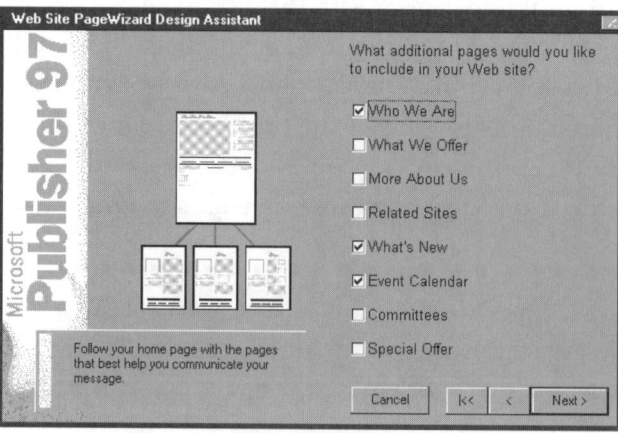

You can always change the headings on these pages later. If none of these titles is right for you but you know you'll want three pages, just check any three and change the headings once the site has been created. For now, click on Next to accept the default pages.

NOTE   It's a good idea, particularly if you're promoting a product or service, to include contact information for your organization on a Who We Are page. Provide a contact name, phone number, and e-mail and street addresses.

Step 4: What's Your Style?

You've seen different styles offered by Publisher before. Remember the variety of design styles used in the Design Gallery? The next step of the Web Site Wizard asks you to define a look for your site (see Figure C.4). There are five style choices: Basic, Bold, Classic, Jazzy, and Modern.

The best way to get an idea of which style is right for you is to click on each one and look at the preview that appears in the dialog box. However, use your knowledge of your organization and its typical customer or user as a guide. If you're creating a Web site for a bank, a Classic design might be

Figure C.4

Remember, the style you choose makes a statement about your business, organization, or personality!

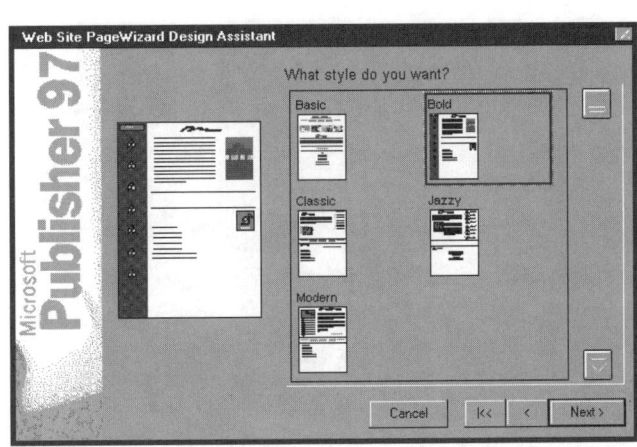

appropriate. If your site is for a Jazz Club, try Jazzy or Modern to appeal to your sophisticated clientele. And remember, you can always reorganize and add to or delete elements from these pages once you've created them to provide your own look. For this exercise, click on Bold, and then on Next to proceed.

Step 5: Define Your Background

A page's background can be as important a design element as any picture or block of text. Plain backgrounds make text easy to read, and, on a more crowded page, might be the best choice. Solid backgrounds provide a similar ease to reading text, but also add color to your page. A textured background is a little busier, but if you make good use of empty space around objects on your page, a textured background can create the most sophisticated look of all. Take a look at them, and then choose Plain from the dialog box shown in Figure C.5. Click on Next to proceed to the next Wizard step.

Step 6: How Will Your Visitors Get Around?

This step involves making a choice of how to help your reader move around your Web site (see Figure C.6). Visitors move from page to page by clicking on elements such as colored text, buttons, or pictorial icons to initiate a hyperlink.

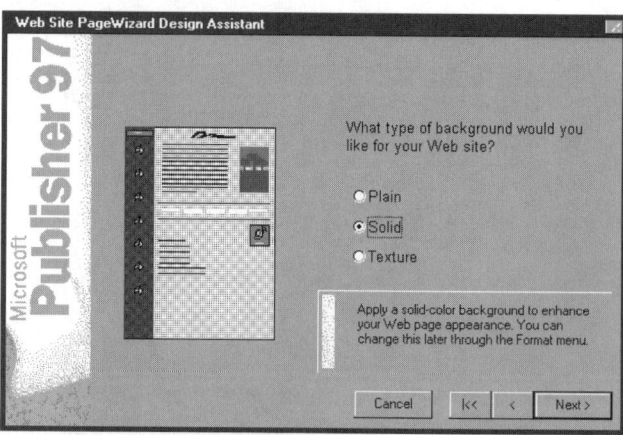

Figure C.5

Test the backgrounds out by clicking on each one to get a preview.

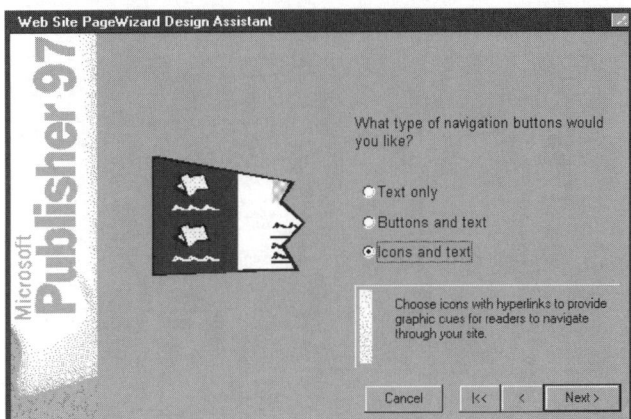

Microsoft **Publisher 97**

Figure C.6

You will need to decide what people will click on to move around your Web site.

✿ *Text only* is just that: a word or phrase describing the link that appears in color on the page.

✿ *Buttons* add a visual element; they resemble a 3-D button for the visitor to click on, which is a comfortable visual metaphor for some. Buttons come with clear text labels to tell the visitor where he or she is going.

✿ *Icons,* on the other hand, are mechanisms to make the leap to another page that provide visual clues as to the nature of what's at the other end of the hyperlink. For example, an icon for a Who We Are page could display an image of your company logo.

Your choice here depends somewhat on how sophisticated you think your visitors are about using Web pages. Most Web visitors recognize all three ways of moving around, but if your Web site will attract those new to the Web, a choice with text clearly explaining where they're going might be best. For now select the Icons and text option, and then click on Next.

Step 7: What's Your Home Page Heading?

The next step is simple: you have to type a heading for your home page (see Figure C.7). The home page is like the main hub for your Web site; it's the

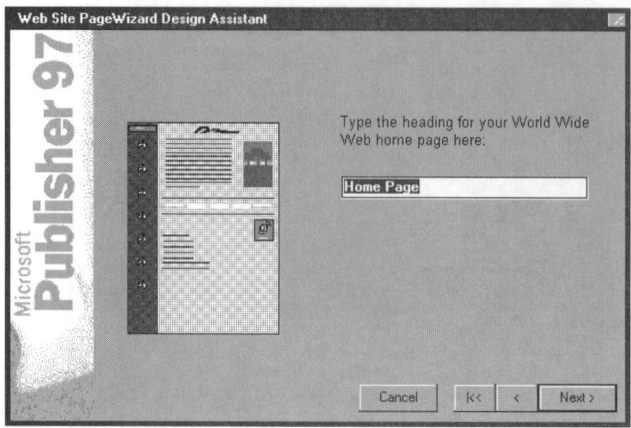

Figure C.7

Type a heading that reflects your site's contents.

way people enter your Web site, and often provides an overview of who you are as well as hyperlinks to the other pages.

Your heading might be as simple as your organization name: for example, The Springfield Wine Club. Or, it could be specific to your Web site: Springfield Wine Club on the Web! Whatever your heading, it is the first thing people see when they enter your site: make it clear where they are and what they'll find here. For our purposes, type the name of your organization (or simply the words "My Club") and click on Next.

Step 8: How Will They Contact You?

The next Wizard step, shown in Figure C.8, is another simple choice: do you want to add a street address to your Web Site? If you prefer that people not know your street address, you would say no here. If, however, you're publicizing a business or organization, including an address might be a good idea. It's up to you. For now, leave the default choice of Yes, please! and click on Next to move ahead.

Step 9: Where Will They Contact You?

In the dialog box that follows, shown in Figure C.9, you can enter your address. Check which type of address you're entering: Personal, Business,

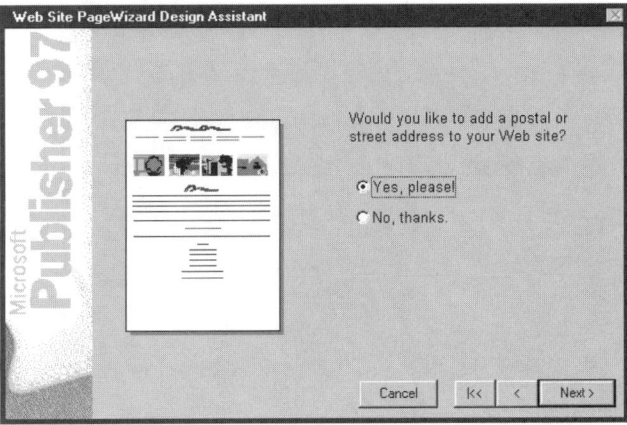

Figure C.8

If you want to keep your contact with visitors strictly online, choose No, thanks in this dialog box. You can always add e-mail contact information later.

Organization, or Other. Click on the Organization option button, and then type in your name and an address. When you finish, click on Next.

TIP Publisher will save the address you enter here. (In fact, you can enter four different addresses by checking each option button in turn.) Next time you run the Wizard, they'll already be filled in.

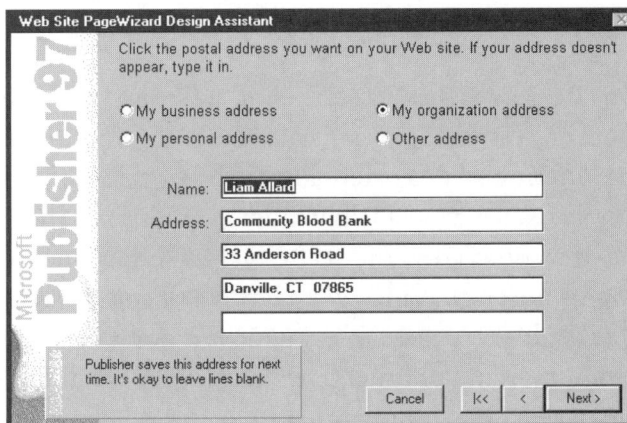

Figure C.9

If you'd rather not put your own name, just list your organization.

Figure C.10

When you click to place a check mark in each of these check boxes, a text box opens for you to enter the contact information.

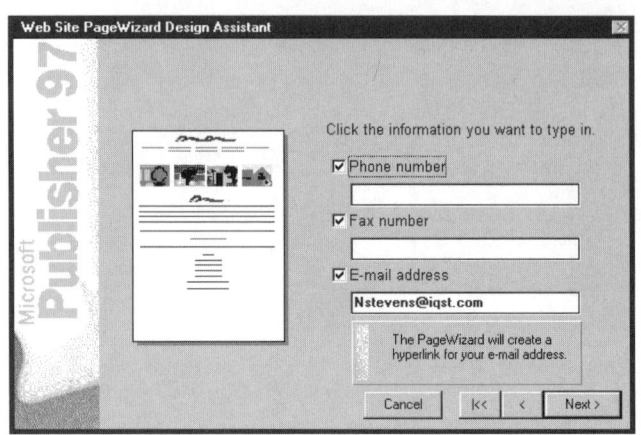

Step 10: You're Almost There!

The last pieces of information Publisher needs are your phone and fax numbers and your e-mail address (Figure C.10). It offers you these options whether or not you chose to enter your street address earlier.

When you enter e-mail information during this step, the Wizard will automatically create a hyperlink to your e-mail address and place it on your page. Click on E-mail address and enter your e-mail address in the text box that opens. Click on Next to complete the Wizard.

What Now?

The final Wizard screen has one choice: Create It! When you click on this, Publisher creates your pages (it may take a few moments). You'll see a dialog box offering step-by-step advice for working on your Web site. This will simply display your Help window with information about Web pages. Select No to proceed without the Help window and your first Web page will appear onscreen. Since you chose to create a Web site, you have produced several Web pages. You can move among these pages using the page navigation tools in Publisher. Each page will have different items; the Who We Are page is shown in Figure C.11.

Figure C.11

The plain background makes the text easy to read; icons suggest where a hyperlink will take the reader.

Some placeholder text on these pages suggests how you could customize the page. You'll also probably want to replace pictures or graphics with ones relevant to your organization. Just use the skills you've learned in this book to replace and format text and work with graphics.

TIP   You can add new pages to your site at any time by simply selecting Insert, Page.

NOTE   When you have a Web page displayed, a tool called Picture Hot Spot is added at the bottom of the Publisher toolbar. Use this to place hyperlinks to other sites; when your visitors click on these pictures they will be taken to the Web location you designate.

For more help with Web pages, open the Help Index and type the keyword **Web**. There's also a helpful demo called "Creating a Web Site." Run this demo by clicking on Help, Quick Demos and selecting it from the list of demos that appears.

 **NOTE** You can take any publication you create in Publisher and create a Web site from it. Select File, Create Web Site from Current Publication to do so. To publish a Web page to the Web, select File, Publish to Web and follow Publisher's Web Publishing Wizard steps.

Remember, the key to an exciting Web site is to keep it fresh, place things on it that appeal to your visitors, and explore your own creativity to modify Publisher's basic design. Have fun!

Online Design Resources

There are many sources on the World Wide Web for information and products that enhance your desktop publishing experience with Publisher. Here are a few to check out.

Downloadable Images

In this category are sites that offer downloadable photographs and illustrations for you to use in your publications. However, always be sure to check the fine print to find out whether you have the right to unlimited use, or if you have to give credit to or pay a fee to the creator. Most of these services do charge a fee per image use.

ArtToday
http://www.arttoday.com/free-trial/

Go to this Web site to download a 30-day trial of their graphics service. They have over 579,000 images and several fonts. These folks charge a monthly fee, rather than a per-image fee, so if you use a lot of images, this may be the way to go.

The Art Center
http://clip-art.com/index.html-ssi

This site touts its product as illustration art rather than clip art. It offers more sophisticated images than many clip art companies. They have free sample images available.

desktopPublishing

http://www.desktoppublishing.com/cliplist.html

If you're looking for photos visit this site, which also offers clip art collections.

The John Stewart Company

http://www.westworld.com/~jonart/products.html

If you need an old-fashioned look to your publications, visit this spot. They have categories such as Antiquities Clip Art and Illuminations (old manuscript ornamentation).

Microsoft Clip Gallery Live

http://www.microsoft.com/publisher/clipdwn.htm

This site has free clip art you can download and use with Publisher as you wish.

NewsArt on the Net

http://www.newsart.com/

This site specializes in clip art suited for newspapers and newsletters. You can download samples or get electronic files by e-mailing orders with credit card information directly to **boz@crosslink.net**.

People in Business Clip Art

http://choicemall.com/dc/dc108-01/index.html

If you use Publisher for your small business publications you might find the images here useful. Try this clip art to add interest to proposals or reports.

Three D Graphics

http://www.threedgraphics.com/compadre

If you'd like textures to use as publication backgrounds or additional Web buttons for Web page design, try this site.

Whelan's Church & School Clip Art

http://www.datasys.net/edpak/whelan2.html

This fee clip art service specializes in images useful for schools and churches, divided into categories like Holidays, Family, Sports, and Evangelism.

Microsoft and Microsoft Partner Sites

Microsoft has a few sites that you might want to visit on a regular basis for information and updates on Publisher.

Microsoft Publisher Home Page

http://www.microsoft.com/publisher/

From here you can get articles about Publisher, technical support, and more. You can also reach this through Publisher's Microsoft on the Web item on the Help menu.

Online Publisher Demo

http://www.microsoft.com/publisher/html/demo1.htm

You can also download this demo rather than running it online (it's very image intensive). Downloading it takes about 1.2MB of memory and approximately 15 minutes.

Printovation

http://www.microsoft.com/publisher/97/printovat.htm

This company has partnered with Microsoft to offer professional printing services for Publisher users. You can send your Publisher file to them online and they'll provide full-color printing.

Avery Dennison

http://www.microsoft.com/publisher/97/averyd.htm

Another Microsoft partner, Avery, the label king, can help you out with stock for labels, cards, and report covers.

Paper Direct

http://www.microsoft.com/publisher/97/paperdir.htm

If you want paper stock for your Publisher documents you can get it here, and receive a 15 percent discount.

Templates

A couple of areas on Microsoft's Web site offer templates to use with Publisher.

Jumpstarts by Roger C. Parker

http://www.microsoft.com/publisher/html/jumpstrt.htm

A well-known author on desktop publishing topics, Parker has put together several templates such as an overhead transparency presentation and an event program designed to work with Publisher.

Do It With Publisher

http://www.microsoft.com/publisher/html/doit.htm

This site offers articles on techniques as well as templates for kids' stationery, pop-up promotion pieces, and cut-out invitations.

Font Collections

Adobe Systems, Inc.

http://www.adobe.com

If you need additional fonts, Adobe is one of the undisputed leaders. Adobe Type On Call CD-ROM allows you to download typefaces as you need them.

Jerry's World

74431.225@compuserve.com

You can buy several kinds of graphics here, including fonts, photos, and clip art.

Publications

If you really get into using Publisher on a regular basis, you might want to subscribe to a monthly newsletter offering tips and techniques to explore.

The Page from The Cobb Group

http://www.cobb.com/tpg/free1001.htm

The Cobb Group is well known for its regular newsletters on a variety of software topics. Their subscriptions run about $40 a year, but you can order a free copy at their Web site to get an idea of what you'll get for your money. This publication offers useful general information on desktop publishing for both Mac and Windows software users.

Other Resources

Books

Arth, Marvin; Ashmore, Helen; and Floyd, Elaine. *The Newsletter Editor's Desk Book,* 4th edition. St. Louis: Newsletter Resources, 1995.

Ayto, John. *QPB Dictionary of Difficult Words.* New York: Quality Paperback Book Club, 1996.

Beach, Mark. *Editing Your Newsletter,* 3rd edition. Portland: Coast to Coast Books, 1988.

Biggs, John R. *Basic Typography.* New York: Watson-Guptill, 1968 (out of print).

Black, Roger. *Desktop Design Power.* New York: Bantam Books, 1991.

Brown, Alex. *In Print: Text and Type in the Age of Desktop Publishing.* New York: Watson-Guptill, 1989.

Bruno, Michael H., ed. *Pocket Pal: A Graphic Arts Production Handbook,* 14th edition. Memphis: International Paper Company, 1989.

Burchfield, R. W., ed. *The New Fowler's Modern English Usage,* 3rd edition. New York: Oxford, 1996.

Burke, Clifford. *Type from the Desktop: Designing with Type and Your Computer.* Chapel Hill: Ventana Press, 1990.

Cosman, Madeleine Pelner. *Medieval Wordbook.* New York: Facts on File Inc., 1996.

Craig, James. *Designing with Type: A Basic Course in Typography,* revised edition. New York: Watson-Guptill, 1980.

Crane, Mark W.; Pierce, Joseph R.; and Holzgang, David A. *Laserjet Companion.* Redmond, WA: Microsoft Press, 1991.

———. *Word for Windows Companion.* Redmond, WA: Microsoft Press, 1990.

De Grandis, Luigina. *Theory and Use of Color.* New York: Harry N. Abrams, 1986.

Dorn, Raymond. *How to Design & Improve Magazine Layouts,* 2nd edition. Chicago: Nelson-Hall, 1986.

Dover Publications, Inc. 180 Varick St., New York, NY 10014. Publishers of an extensive variety of clip art. Write for a free catalog or call (516) 294-7000.

Edwards, Paul and Sarah, and Douglas, Laura Clampitt. *Getting Business to Come to You.* New York: G. P. Putnam's Sons, 1991.

Evans, Poppy. *The Graphic Designer's Guide to Faster, Better, Easier Design and Production.* Cincinnati: Northlight Books, 1993.

Feiring, Roy A. *"The Neoclassic Printing Movement, 1890-1940."* Master's thesis, University of Oregon, 1976.

Fiske, Robert Hartwell. *Writer's Digest Dictionary of Concise Writing.* Cincinnati: Writer's Digest Books, 1990.

Frenza, J. P. and Szabo, Michelle. *Web and New Media Pricing Guide.* New York: Hayden Books, 1997.

Fry, Andrew and Paul, David. *How to Publish on the Internet.* New York: Warner Books, 1995.

Gordon, Karen Elizabeth. *The Deluxe Transitive Vampire.* New York: Pantheon Books, 1984, 1993.

Gosney, Michael and Dayton, Linnea. *The Desktop Color Book.* New York: MIS:Press, 1995.

———. *The Gray Book.* Chapel Hill: Ventana Press, 1990.

Green, Chuck. *Clip Art Crazy.* Berkeley: Peachpit Press, Inc., 1995.

———. *The Desktop Publisher's Idea Book.* New York: Random House Electronic Publishing, 1993.

Grossman, Joe and Doty, David. *Newsletters from the Desktop,* 3rd edition. Chapel Hill: Ventana Press, 1994.

Hurlburt, Allen. *Layout: The Design of the Printed Page.* New York: Watson-Guptill, 1977 (out of print).

———. *Publication Design.* New York: Watson-Guptill, 1971 (out of print).

Kieran, Michael. *Understanding Desktop Color.* Berkeley: Peachpit Press, Inc., 1994.

Lamott, Anne. *Bird by Bird: Some Instructions on Writing and Life.* New York: Anchor Books, Doubleday, 1995.

Levinson, Jay Conrad and Rubin, Charles. *Guerilla Marketing Online: The Entrepreneur's Guide to Earning Profits on the Internet.* New York: Houghton Mifflin Company, 1995.

Lichty, Thomas W. *Design Principles for Desktop Publishers.* Glenview, IL: Scott Foresman, 1988.

Microsoft Small Business Council. *Smart Marketing for Small Business: Strategies for Developing Effective Marketing Materials from the Microsoft Small Business Council.* New York, NY.

Morris, Bruce. *HTML in Action.* Redmond, WA: Microsoft Press, 1996.

Neff, Glenda T. and Biederman, Roseann S., editors. *The Writer's Essential Desk Reference,* 2nd edition. Cincinnati: Writer's Digest Books, 1996.

Nelson, Roy Paul. *Publication Design,* 5th edition. Dubuque, IA: William C. Brown, 1991.

Niederst, Jennifer and Freedman, Edie. *Designing for the Web: Getting Started in a New Medium.* Sebastopol, CA: O'Reilly & Associates, 1996.

Parker, Roger C. *Looking Good in Print,* 3rd edition. Chapel Hill: Ventana Press, 1993.

———. *The Makeover Book: 101 Design Solutions for Desktop Publishing.* Chapel Hill: Ventana Press, 1989.

Plotnik, Arthur. *The Elements of Expression: Putting Thoughts into Words.* New York: Henry Holt and Company, 1996.

Rawson, Hugh. *Wicked Words.* New York: Crown Trade Paperbacks, 1989.

Sabin, William A. *The Gregg Reference Manual,* 7th edition. New York: GLENCOE, 1992.

Seldes, George. *The Great Thoughts.* New York: Ballantine Books, 1985, 1996.

Simone, Luisa. *Publisher by Design,* 4th edition. Redmond, WA: Microsoft Press, 1996.

Skillin, Marjorie E.; Gay, Robert M.; and other authorities. *Words in Type,* 3rd edition. Englewood Cliffs, NJ: Prentice-Hall, Inc., 1974.

Southworth, Miles; McIlroy, Thad; and Southworth, Donna. *The Color Resource Complete Color Glossary.* San Francisco: The Color Resource, 1992.

Spickermann, Erik and Ginger, E. M. *Stop Stealing Sheep.* Mountain View, CA: Adobe Press, 1993.

Stone, Sumner. *On Stone: The Art and Use of Typography on the Personal Computer.* San Francisco: Chronicle Books, 1991.

Strunk, William, Jr. and White, E. B. *Elements of Style,* 3rd edition. New York: Macmillan, 1979.

United States Postal Service. *Designing Business Letter Mail,* Publication 25. USPS, August 1995.

United States Postal Service, *Designing Flat Mail,* Publication 63. USPS, May 1995.

United States Postal Service. *Designing Reply Mail,* Publication 353. USPS, July 1995.

United States Postal Service. *Postal Addressing Standards,* Publication 28. USPS, August 1995.

United States Postal Service and Braddock Communications. *Postal Business Companion.* Reston, VA: Braddock Communications, Inc., 1995.

White, Jan V. *Color for the Electronic Age.* New York: Watson-Guptill Publications, 1990.

White, Jan V. *Designing for Magazines,* 2nd edition. New York: R. R. Bowker, 1982.

———. *Editing by Design,* 2nd edition. New York: R. R. Bowker, 1982.

——. *Mastering Graphics.* New York: R. R. Bowker, 1983.

Wilde, Richard and Wilde, Judith. *Visual Literacy: A Conceptual Approach to Solving Graphic Problems.* New York: Watson-Guptill, 1991.

Williams, Robin. *The Non-Designer's Design Book.* Berkeley: Peachpit Press, Inc., 1994.

——. *The PC Is Not a Typewriter.* Berkeley: Peachpit Press, Inc., 1992.

Zinsser, William K. *On Writing Well,* 5th edition. New York: Harper's Perennial, 1994.

The Chicago Manual of Style, 14th edition. Chicago: University of Chicago Press, 1993.

The Merriam-Webster Dictionary of English Usage, 1st edition. Springfield: Merriam-Webster, Inc., 1989.

The Oxford Dictionary of Quotations, 3rd edition. New York: Oxford, 1979.

Periodicals

Aldus Magazine. Aldus Corporation., 411 First Avenue South, Seattle, WA 98104. Bimonthly.

Before & After: How to Design Cool Stuff. 1830 Sierra Gardens Drive, Suite 30, Roseville, CA 95661. Bimonthly.

Communication Arts. Coyne and Blanchard, 410 Sherman Oaks, Palo Alto, CA 94303. Eight issues a year.

Corel Magazine. Omray, Inc., 9801 Anderson Mill Road, Suite 207, Austin, TX 78730.

Desktop Communications. 2 Hammarskjold Plaza, New York, NY 10017. Bimonthly.

Do It with Microsoft Publisher. 77 Franklin Street, Suite 310, Boston, MA 02110. Monthly.

Font & Function, The Adobe Type Catalog. Adobe Systems, P. O. Box 7900, Mountain View, CA 94039-7900. Three issues a year.

Font Minder. Ares Software. 565 Pilgrim Drive, Suite A, Foster City, CA 94404.

HOW, the Bottomline Design Magazine. F&W Publications, Inc. 1507 Dana Avenue, Cincinnati, OH 45207.

Letter Arts Review. 1624 24th Avenue, SW, Norman, OK 73072.

Print: America's Graphic Design Magazine. RC Publications, 6400 Goldsboro Road, Bethesda, MD 20817. Bimonthly.

Publish. PCW Communications, 501 Second Street, San Francisco, CA 94107. Monthly.

U&lc (Upper and Lower Case). International Typographic Corporation, 2 Hammarskjold Plaza, New York, NY 10017. Bimonthly.

Working Solo Newsletter. P.O. Box 190, New Paltz, NY 12561. Quarterly.

Writer's Digest. 1507 Dana Avenue, Cincinnati, OH 45207. Monthly.

x-height. Fonthaus. 1375 Kings Highway East, Fairfield, CT 06430. Three issues a year.

Paper Suppliers

Idea Art. P.O. Box 291505, Nashville, TN 37229.

On Paper: The Paper Source. 3342 Melrose Avenue NW, Roanoke, VA 24017.

Paper Access. 23 West 18th Street, New York, NY 10011.

PaperDirect. P.O. Box 1514, Secaucus, NJ 07096.

Pocket Pal. New York: International Paper Company, 1963-1983.

Queblo. P.O. Box 1393, Hagerstown, MD 21741.

Clip Art, Photographs, and Utilities

3-G Services. 23632 Highway 99, #F-407, Edmonds, WA 98026.

A Bit Better Corporation. 127 Second Street, Suite 2, Los Altos, CA 94022.

Corel Corporation. 1600 Carling Avenue, Ottawa, Ontario. K1Z 8R7 Canada.

Dover Publications. 31 East Second Street, Mineola, NY 11501.

Image Club. 10545 West Donges Court, Milwaukee, WI 53224-9985.

Library of Congress. National Reference Service, Washington, DC 20540-5570, (202) 707-6394.

Monotype Typography, Inc. 150 South Wacker Drive, Suite 2630, Chicago, IL 60606-4202.

National Archives and Records Administration. Washington DC 20408, (202) 501-5400.

New Vision Technologies, Inc. 38 Auriga Drive, Unit 13, Nepean, Ontario, Canada, K2E 8A5.

PhotoDisc. 2013 Fourth Avenue, Suite 402, Seattle, WA 98121.

GLOSSARY

A

Ascender. The portion of a lowercase letter rising above the main character body. Lowercase b, f, h, and t all have ascenders, for example.

Audience. The readers of your publication, who will receive its message and identity. Also see *Identity* and *Message*.

Autofill. The ability to automatically copy and fill the cells of a table.

B

Banner. See *Masthead*.

Baseline. An imaginary line at the bottom (base) of a line of text. A stronger baseline, such as occurs with serif fonts, makes body text easier to read.

Baseline alignment. Placement of text in adjoining columns to keep their respective baselines in line, thereby avoiding distracting shifts. Baseline alignment is also vital across gutters in facing pages.

Bezier curve. A complex line segment whose result resembles a French curve. A Bezier curve is made up of the line itself and up to four separate points: a starting point, an ending point, and one or two control points that can be used to manipulate the curve. Bezier curves are stored as multiple line segments in Windows metafiles, while the PostScript metafile format preserves them. Also see *Metafile* and *PostScript*.

Bit. The elementary unit of digital information, a bit can have only one of two values: on or off. Bit is a contraction of *BInary digiT*.

Bitmaps. Images created by a pattern of individual dots, or *bits*. Photographs are typically stored in a bitmap format for use in Windows. Bitmapped is the same as *raster* in this context. Also see *Vector* and *Object*.

Blackletter type. An old-style type characterized by heavy lines and accents. Also known as Old English.

Bleed. A printing image placed to extend past the trim edge to the page edge. In the finished publication, the bleeds from successive pages form guides that can assist the reader in locating sections.

Blurb. A terse assessment of the subject discussed by a document or publication, typically placed beneath the initial heading.

Body text. Text that comprises the actual content of a publication, as opposed to text used in headings or decorative elements. Typically, body text is 12 points or smaller. Also see *Text* and *Display text*.

Bold or boldface. A darker, wider style of a regular typeface or font. Boldface is typically used for emphasis or to distinguish special segments of text.

Border. A graphical element defining the boundaries of another element. A border can be anything from a simple line to a running block of clip art.

Break. In publishing, interrupting the flow of text to begin a new page or column. Beginning or ending a column or page with a widow is considered a bad break. Also see *Widow*.

Byte. A unit of digital information, comprised of eight bits. In general terms, a byte is the amount of RAM or disk storage it takes to store a single character.

C

Camera-ready. A copy of a publication that is suitable to be photographed with a graphic arts camera for reproduction.

Color separation. In publishing, the process of printing a separate page for each color to be produced in the final publication. Typical resolutions are one, two, and four color separations.

Condensed. A compressed or slender style of a particular typeface. Condensed type is not used as much as other styles because it is usually more difficult to read and can produce a cramped, unattractive effect.

Consistency. The practice of using similar formatting and design patterns for elements that are similar. Proper consistency should extend to the text and terminology used within body text. Also see *Theme*.

Continuous tone. Graduated intensities of black, made by concentrations of individual dots. Computers use a *halftone* or *dithering* process to simulate gray. Photographic images are continuous-tone. Also see *Halftone* and *Dithering*.

Cropping. Trimming or hiding a part of a photograph or image that is extraneous or unwanted.

Crossline. A small flourishing line that completes the stroke of a letter in a Serif type. Also see *Serif* and *Serif type*.

D

Dateline. A line placed at the beginning of an article describing the date and location of the piece.

Descender. The portion of a lowercase letter sinking below the main character body. Lowercase g, p, q, and y all have descenders, for example.

Display text. Text used for all elements other than body text, including headlines, subheads, blurbs, and pull quotes. Display text is typically any text set larger than 12 points. Also see *Body text*.

Dithering. The process of representing continuous-tone images using clusters of printer dots or screen pixels. Also see *Halftone* and *Continuous tone*.

Drop cap. A first letter of an article or section that sinks one or more lines beneath the baseline of the first line of body text. Typically, text is wrapped around the drop cap. Also see *Initial cap*.

Dummy. A test layout using placeholder text and illustrations to demonstrate the effectiveness of a publication design.

E

Em. In publishing, a unit of measurement exactly equal to the width of an uppercase M in the current font.

Embedded object. In the Windows operating system, an object that stores a reference to the application that created it. In Publisher 97, you can double-click on an embedded object to launch the original application and modify the object. See *Linked object*.

En. In publishing, a unit of measurement exactly one half the width of an em. It is typically used to define the width of a space. Also see *Em*.

Expanded type. A type style designed to be wider than regular type.

F

Family. In typography, a group of fonts that are stylistically similar. Typically, a type family includes regular or roman, italic, bold, and bold-italic fonts.

Flush-left. Text aligned at the left edge of a column is said to be flush-left. Justified text is flush both right and left. Also see *Flush-right* and *Justify*.

Flush paragraph. A non-indented paragraph, fully aligned with the column.

Flush-right. Text aligned at the right edge of a column is said to be flush-right. Justified text is flush both right and left. Also see *Flush-left* and *Justify*.

Folio. Information that appears at the top, bottom, or side of a page, including date, time, chapter, title, and page number. The folio may run several lines and can include rules, borders, and graphics.

Font. A complete character set in a particular type size and style, including letters, numbers, and punctuation.

Font class. An assortment of fonts grouped by their characteristics and uses. There are six general classes: Blackletter, Sans serif, Script, Serif, Specialty, and Typewriter. Also see *Blackletter, Sans serif, Script, Serif, Specialty*, and *Typewriter*.

Footer. In publishing, a text element placed at the bottom of a page, typically including page numbers.

Frame. In Publisher 97, a control element placed in a publication to contain text or graphics. Once selected, a frame has handles you can use to resize it. Also see *Handle*.

G

GIF. Graphic Interchange Format, a commonly used graphic format on the World Wide Web.

Gutter. White space that appears between adjoining columns in a layout, between a printed region and the end of a page, or between two facing pages.

H

Halftone. A method used to reproduce continuous-tone elements, such as photographs. Halftoning converts the image into dots of varying sizes. Halftoning can be simulated through software by dithering. Also see *Continuous tone* and *Dithering*.

Handle. One of the eight small black squares appearing on the edges of an object selected in Publisher 97. You can drag a handle to resize or crop an object.

HTML. The Hypertext Markup Language that formats Web documents and enables them to be read by Web browsers.

http. A term that identifies a link on the World Wide Web and precedes all Web site addresses.

Hyperlink. An element that contains an address to another page or site on the Internet. Clicking on the hyperlink takes the reader to that address. Also see *URL*.

Hypertext. An online document that can include text, graphic images, audio files, and video clips. The World Wide Web is a hypertext environment.

I

Identity. The essence that defines your publication in the minds of its audience. Also see *Audience* and *Message*.

Initial cap. The first letter of an article or section, enhanced either by typographical or graphical methods. Also see *Drop cap*.

Italic. A slanting type style, as compared to roman or regular styles. Italics are most often separate fonts derived from their roman brethren and are commonly used for emphasis within body text. Also see *Oblique*.

J

Jump. A text element that starts on one page and continues on a different page. References indicating the jump destination are typically placed at the end of the origin column, whereas references for the jump origin are used at the top of the destination column.

Justify. Alignment of text with both the left and right sides of a column. Justifying text produces smooth left and right margins but can also create annoying gaps within the justified element. Also see *Flush-left* and *Flush-right*.

K

Kerning. Reducing the space between character pairs, causing them to appear closer together. Also see *Letter spacing* and *Spacing*.

Kiss. Reducing the space between characters until they softly touch, or kiss. Also see *Kerning* and *TNT*.

L

Leader. Characters such as dots or dashes used to guide the reader's eye across a page. Leaders are typically used to make tables more readable.

Leading. Pronounced "ledding," the distance between the tops of two lines of text. It is usually expressed in points.

Letter spacing. Increasing the space between character pairs to make them appear farther apart; the opposite of kerning. Also see *Kerning* and *Spacing*.

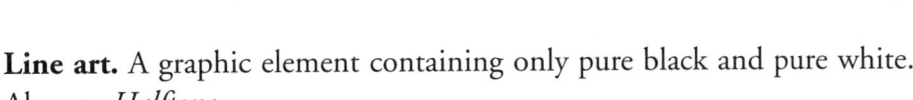

Line art. A graphic element containing only pure black and pure white. Also see *Halftone*.

Line spacing. See Leading.

Linked object. In the Windows operating system, an object that stores a reference to a data file on disk. The linked object is updated whenever the data file is modified. Also see *Embedded object*.

Lowercase. The small, non-capital letters in a font. Also see *Uppercase*.

M

M. An abbreviation for 1,000 sheets of paper, not to be confused with em, which is a measurement of space.

Masthead. The title of a publication, appearing on the front or editorial page, or a printed notice displaying the staff, ownership, and circulation details of a publication.

Message. The aggregate information that your publication delivers to its audience. Also see *Audience* and *Identity*.

Metafile. A graphic format capable of storing raster and vector information, as well as text. The most popular Windows metafile formats are .WMF and .EMF files.

Moire. An uneven and unattractive pattern generated when halftones are overprinted with incorrect screen angles. Changing the size or shape of a bitmapped or raster image can also produce moire patterns.

Monospace type. A font in which each character is as wide as all other characters. Also called Typewriter type.

O

Object. A term used to describe complex graphic elements containing arcs, ellipses, lines, and rectangles. Also see *Bitmaps*, *Raster*, and *Vector*.

Oblique. A form of italic, in which the regular or roman character style is slanted to one side. Many sans serif families use oblique as a substitute for italic. Also see *Italic*.

Orphan. The last word of a paragraph that appears by itself on a line. Also see *Widow*.

P

Pica. A unit of measurement used in typesetting. A pica equals 12 points, or $\frac{1}{6}$ inch.

Picture hot spot. A special type of hyperlink that enables you to jump to different destinations depending on where you click a particular picture. Picture hot spots are also referred to as image maps.

Point. A unit of measurement used in typesetting to express type sizes and leading. The modern point is equal to $\frac{1}{72}$ inch.

PostScript. A metafile graphics format, proprietary to the Adobe Corporation. PostScript is a full-featured page-description language entirely supported in the Windows operating system. Also see *Bezier* and *Metafile*.

Pull quote. A quotation taken directly from body text and enhanced in some way to draw the reader's attention.

R

Race. A collection of type families joined by common characteristics. Also see *Family*.

Ragged margin. Text aligned with an even margin on one side and an uneven margin on the other. The most common use of ragged margin is flush-left with ragged right. Also see *Flush-left*, *Flush-right*, and *Justify*.

Raster. An image created with a pattern of individual dots on the printer or pixels on the screen. Raster is the same as bitmapped in this usage. Also see *Object* and *Vector*.

Roman. A type race characterized with serifs and distinct differences between thin and thick strokes. Roman is also used to describe the regular font within a family. Also see *Bold*, *Italic*, *Family*, and *Race*.

Rotatable. In publishing, a rotatable font can be accurately portrayed at any angle. TrueType fonts are rotatable. Also see *Scalable* and *TrueType font*.

Rule. Any line that prints. Also see *Border*.

Running header. A heading or headline placed at the top of consecutive pages in a publication. See also *Footer*.

Runaround. See *Wrapped text*.

S

Sans serif type. A typeface drawn without serifs, the ornamental crosslines placed on the ends of characters. Also see *Serif* and *Serif type*.

Scalable. In publishing, a font that can be enlarged to any size without distortion or loss of detail. TrueType fonts are scalable. Also see *Rotatable* and *TrueType font*.

Scaling. Changing the size of an image or font to suit a particular space.

Scanner. A device that processes images and documents and transforms them into electrical signals understood by a computer. Also see *Bitmaps* and *Raster*.

Script type. A font designed to imitate handwriting or calligraphy.

Serif. The ornamental crosslines placed at the end of characters in a font. Also see *Sans serif* and *Serif type*.

Serif type. A font whose characters are decorated with small crosslines or serifs. Also see *Sans serif type* and *Serif*.

Sidebar. Text related to but not directly associated with body text. Typically, sidebar text is information that is additional to or background for the main discussion. Sidebars are enhanced to separate them from the main body text.

Small caps. Capital letters smaller than normal uppercase characters, typically by 20 percent.

Specialty type. A font designed for a particular purpose. For example, to depict symbols or icons, or even entire words. Sometimes called Picture type.

T

Text style. In Publisher 97, a software construct that stores the various settings needed to re-create a particular formatting pattern.

Theme. The use of consistent and related design elements and terminology to establish a mood or setting for a publication. Also see *Consistency*.

Tombstone. In publishing, vertically aligning elements of equal strength or identical type in adjacent columns. The effect is unattractive and difficult to read.

Tone. A measure of how a publication relates to its audience. A publication can have either a friendly or formal tone, a mixture of the two, or an extreme. Also see *Voice*.

TrueType font. First introduced in Windows 3.1, a TrueType font is a combination of raster and vector technology. TrueType fonts are scalable and rotatable. Also see *Rotatable* and *Scalable*.

U

Uppercase. The large, capital letters in a given font. Also see *Lowercase*.

URL. Universal or Uniform Resource Locator. The address of a resource on the Internet. Typically, the first part of the URL specifies the protocol used to access it.

V

Vector. A vector graphic is one described in multiple primitive elements, such as arcs, ellipses, lines, and rectangles. More advanced vector formats may also include curves and fills. Typically, vector graphics can be resized without any loss of quality. Also see *Object* and *Raster*.

Voice. The property describing the verbs used in your publication. Text in the active voice is generally more effective than text written in passive voice. Also see *Tone*.

W

Watermark. A faint design or image placed "under" elements in the foreground of a publication. Watermarks can also be imprinted by the manufacturer at the time the paper is made.

Web browser. A program such as Microsoft Internet Explorer or Netscape Navigator that lets you view Web pages.

White space. Space within a page or column that is not occupied by a printing element. Also see *Gutter*.

Widow. A single line of a paragraph that appears alone at the top or bottom of a page or column. Also see *Break* and *Orphan*.

Wrapped text. Text placed to surround a design element.

X

X-height. The height of all lowercase characters in a font, without ascenders and descenders being considered. X-height is derived from the body of the lowercase x in a given font and size. Also see *Ascender*, *Baseline*, and *Descender*.

INDEX

A

actions, undoing last, 19, 60

Actual Size (F9) key, 30

address, listing on Web site, 256–257

address lists

mail merge field entries, 172

mail merges, 171–173

applets

accessing from Insert Object dialog box, 114

described, 112

WordArt, 112–117

Arrange menu, 24

Arrange, Bring Closer command, 129

Arrange, Group Objects command, 91, 159, 203

Arrange, Line Up Objects command, 89

Arrange, Nudge Objects command, 90

Arrange, Rotate/Flip command, 86

Arrange, Send Farther command, 129

Arrange, Send to Back command, 128

Arrange, Ungroup Objects command, 91, 203

arrow keys, document navigation, 33

AutoFormat dialog box, 137–139

B

backgrounds

defining for Web site, 254

described, 143–144

newsletter modifications, 143–145

Backspace key, deleting text, 60

blank document

opening, 55–57

page styles, 55–56

bleed, described, 101

BorderArt dialog box, 75–76

borders, 73–77

applying to one side of text frame only, 76

logos, 201

styles, 76–77

boundaries, described, 20

D

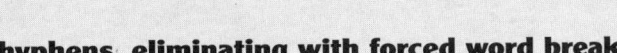

Prima's Visual Learning Guides

fast & easy

Relax, learning new software is now a breeze. You are looking at a series of books dedicated to one idea: To help you learn to use software as quickly and easily as possible. No need to wade through boring pages of endless text. With Prima's Visual Learning Guides, you simply look and learn.

WordPerfect® 8
Diane Koers
0-7615-1083-4
368 pgs.
$16.99 (Can. $23.95)

Word 97
Nancy Stevenson
0-7615-1007-9
384 pgs.
$16.99 (Can. $23.95)

Excel 97
Nancy Stevenson
0-7615-1008-7
352 pgs.
$16.99 (Can. $23.95)

Office 97
Elaine Marmel
0-7615-1162-8
432 pgs.
$16.99 (Can. $23.95)

Windows® 95
Grace Joely Beatty, Ph.D.
David C. Gardner, Ph.D.
1-55958-738-5
288 pgs.
$19.95 (Can. $29.95)

WordPerfect® 6.1 for Windows
Grace Joely Beatty, Ph.D.
David C. Gardner, Ph.D.
0-7615-0091-X
288 pgs.
$19.95 (Can. $29.95)

Excel 5 for Windows®
Grace Joely Beatty, Ph.D.
David C. Gardner, Ph.D.
1-55958-736-9
288 pgs.
$19.95 (Can. $29.95)

PRIMA

http://www.primapublishing.com

OTHER BOOKS FROM PRIMA PUBLISHING, COMPUTER PRODUCTS DIVISION

ISBN	Title	Price
0-7615-1175-X	ACT! 3.0 Visual Learning Guide	$16.99
0-7615-0680-2	America Online Complete Handbook and Membership Kit	$24.99
0-7615-0417-6	CompuServe Complete Handbook and Membership Kit	$24.95
0-7615-0692-6	Create Your First Web Page In a Weekend	$24.99
0-7615-0743-4	Create FrontPage Web Pages In a Weekend	$29.99
0-7615-0428-1	The Essential Excel 97 Book	$27.99
0-7615-0733-7	The Essential Netscape Communicator Book	$24.99
0-7615-0969-0	The Essential Office 97 Book	$27.99
0-7615-0695-0	The Essential Photoshop Book	$35.00
0-7615-1182-2	The Essential PowerPoint 97 Book	$24.99
0-7615-1136-9	The Essential Publisher 97 Book	$24.99
0-7615-0752-3	The Essential Windows NT 4 Book	$27.99
0-7615-0427-3	The Essential Word 97 Book	$27.99
0-7615-0425-7	The Essential WordPerfect 8 Book	$24.99
0-7615-1008-7	Excel 97 Visual Learning Guide	$16.99
0-7615-1194-6	Increase Your Web Traffic In a Weekend	$19.99
0-7615-1137-7	Jazz Up Your Web Site In a Weekend	$24.99
0-7615-1193-8	Lotus 1-2-3 Visual Learning Guide	$16.99
0-7615-0852-X	Netscape Navigator 3 Complete Handbook	$24.99
0-7615-1162-8	Office 97 Visual Learning Guide	$16.99
0-7615-0759-0	Professional Web Design	$40.00
0-7615-0063-4	Researching on the Internet	$29.95
0-7615-0686-1	Researching on the World Wide Web	$24.99
0-7615-1192-X	SmartSuite 97 Visual Learning Guide	$16.99
0-7615-1007-9	Word 97 Visual Learning Guide	$16.99
0-7615-1083-4	WordPerfect 8 Visual Learning Guide	$16.99
0-7615-1188-1	WordPerfect Suite 8 Visual Learning Guide	$16.99

YOUR COMMENTS

Send Us

Dear Reader:

Thank you for buying this book. In order to offer you more quality books on the topics *you* would like to see, we need your input. At Prima Publishing, we pride ourselves on timely responsiveness to our readers' needs. If you'll complete and return this brief questionnaire, *we will listen!*

Name: (first) _____ (M.I.) _____ (last) _____

Company: _____ Type of business: _____

Address: _____ City: _____ State: ____ Zip: _____

Phone _____ Fax: _____ E-mail address: _____

May we contact you for research purposes? ❑ Yes ❑ No

(If you participate in a research project, we will supply you with your choice of a book from Prima CPD)

❶ How would you rate this book, overall?
❑ Excellent ❑ Fair
❑ Very Good ❑ Below Average
❑ Good ❑ Poor

❷ Why did you buy this book?
❑ Price of book ❑ Content
❑ Author's reputation ❑ Prima's reputation
❑ CD-ROM/disk included with book
❑ Information highlighted on cover
❑ Other (Please specify):

❸ How did you discover this book?
❑ Found it on bookstore shelf
❑ Saw it in Prima Publishing catalog
❑ Recommended by store personnel
❑ Recommended by friend or colleague
❑ Saw an advertisement in: _____
❑ Read book review in: _____
❑ Saw it on Web site: _____
❑ Other (Please specify): _____

❹ Where did you buy this book?
❑ Bookstore (name) _____
❑ Computer Store (name) _____
❑ Electronics Store (name) _____
❑ Wholesale Club (name) _____
❑ Mail Order (name) _____
❑ Direct from Prima Publishing _____
❑ Other (please specify): _____

❺ Which computer periodicals do you read regularly? _____
_____
_____
_____

❻ Would you like to see your name in print?
May we use your name and quote you in future Prima Publishing books or promotional materials?

❑ Yes ❑ No

❼ Comments & Suggestions: _____
_____
_____
_____

PRIMA PUBLISHING
Computer Products Division
3875 Atherton Rd.
Rocklin, CA 95765

PLEASE
PLACE
STAMP
HERE

---

⑧ Where do you use your computer?

Work	❏ 100%	❏ 75%	❏ 50%	❏ 25%
Home	❏ 100%	❏ 75%	❏ 50%	❏ 25%
School	❏ 100%	❏ 75%	❏ 50%	❏ 25%

Other _____

⑨ How do you rate your level of computer skills?

❏ Beginner
❏ Advanced
❏ Intermediate

⑩ What is your age?

❏ Under 18
❏ 18-24   ❏ 40-49
❏ 25-29   ❏ 50-59
❏ 30-39   ❏ 60-over

⑪ I would be interested in computer books on these topics

❏ Word Processing   ❏ Database
❏ Networking   ❏ Spreadsheets
❏ Desktop Publishing ❏ Web site design
❏ Other _____

SAVE A STAMP

Visit our Web Site at: **http://www.primapublishing.com**

and simply fill in one of our online Response Forms

Prima's In a Weekend™ Series

**Create Your First Web Page
In a Weekend**
Steven E. Callihan
416 pp. • 0-7615-0692-6 • CD-ROM
$24.99 (Can. $34.95)

Jazz Up Your Web Site In a Weekend
Paul E. Robichaux
456 pages • 0-7615-1137-7 • CD-ROM
$24.99 (Can. $34.95)

**Increase Your Web Traffic
In a Weekend**
William R. Stanek
480 pages • 0-7615-1194-6
$19.99 (Can. $27.95)

GOOD NEWS! You can master the skills you need to achieve your goals in just a weekend! Prima Publishing's unique *In a Weekend* series offers practical fast-track guides dedicated to showing you how to complete your projects in a weekend or less!

Also Available

Upgrade Your PC In a Weekend
Russel Jacobs
400 pages • 0-7615-1138-5
$19.99 (Can. $27.95)

Learn Word 97 In a Weekend
Faithe Wempen
432 pages • 0-7615-1251-9
$19.99 (Can. $27.95)

Learn HTML In a Weekend
Steven E. Callihan
400 pp. • 0-7615-1293-4 • CD-ROM
$24.99 (Can. $34.95)

**Create FrontPage Web Pages
In a Weekend**
David Karlins
364 pp. • 0-7615-0743-4 • CD-ROM
$29.99 (Can. $41.95)

**Organize Your Finances with
Quicken In a Weekend**
Gail Perry • 400 pages
0-7615-1186-5
$19.99 (Can. $27.95)

Learn the Internet In a Weekend
William R. Stanek
400 pages • 0-7615-1295-0
$19.99 (Can. $27.95)

**Create PowerPoint
Presentations In a Weekend**
Brian Reilly
400 pages • 0-7615-1294-2
$19.99 (Can. $27.95)

**Learn Windows 98
In a Weekend**
Michael O'Mara
400 pages • 0-7615-1296-9
$19.99 (Can. $27.95)

www.primapublishing.com

Prima Publishing and In a Weekend are trademarks of Prima Communications, Inc. All other product and company names are trademarks of their respective companies.

To Order Books

Please send me the following items:

Quantity	Title	Unit Price	Total
_____	_____	$ _____	$ _____
_____	_____	$ _____	$ _____
_____	_____	$ _____	$ _____
_____	_____	$ _____	$ _____
_____	_____	$ _____	$ _____
_____	_____	$ _____	$ _____

Shipping and Handling depend on Subtotal

Subtotal	Shipping and Handling
$0.00–$14.99	$3.00
$15.00–$29.99	$4.00
$30.00–$49.99	$6.00
$50.00–$99.99	$10.00
$100.00–$199.99	$13.50
$200.00+	Call for Quote

Foreign and all Priority Request orders:
Call Order Entry department
for price quote at 916-632-4400

This chart represents the total retail price of books only
(before applicable discounts are taken).

Subtotal $ _____

Deduct 10% when ordering 3–5 $ _____

7.25% Sales Tax (CA only) $ _____

8.25% Sales Tax (TN only) $ _____

5.0% Sales Tax (MD and IN only) $ _____

Shipping and Handling* $ _____

Total Order $ _____

By Telephone: With MC or Visa, call 800-632-8676, 916-632-4400. Mon–Fri, 8:30–4:30

Orders Placed via E-mail: sales@primapub.com

By Mail: Just fill out the information below and send with your remittance to:

**Prima Publishing
P.O. Box 1260BK
Rocklin, CA 95677–1260
www.primapublishing.com**

My name is _____

I live at _____

City _____ State _____ Zip _____

MC/Visa # _____ Exp. _____

Check/Money Order enclosed for $ _____ Payable to Prima Publishing

Daytime Telephone _____

Signature _____